The Number One Real Estate Investment No One Talks About

Sanford W. Hornwood

and

I. Lucretia Hollingsworth

Prentice-Hall, Inc.
Englewood Cliffs, New Jersey

Prentice-Hall International, Inc., *London*
Prentice-Hall of Australia, Pty. Ltd., *Sydney*
Prentice-Hall Canada, Inc., *Toronto*
Prentice-Hall of India Private Ltd., *New Delhi*
Prentice-Hall of Japan, Inc., *Tokyo*
Prentice-Hall of Southeast Asia Pte. Ltd., *Singapore*
Editora Prentice-Hall do Brasil Ltda., *Rio de Janeiro*
Prentice-Hall Hispanoamericana, S.A., *Mexico*

© 1987 *by*

PRENTICE-HALL, INC.
Englewood Cliffs, N.J.

This publication is designed to provide accurate and authoritative
information in regard to the subject matter covered. It is sold with the
understanding that the publisher is not engaged in rendering legal,
accounting, or other professional service. If legal advice or other
expert assistance is required, the services of a competent professional
person should be sought.
. . . *From the Declaration of Principles jointly adopted by a Committee*
of the American Bar Association and a Committee of Publishers and
Associations.

Likewise, the authors cannot make any representation with
respect to the contents of this book and specifically disclaim any
implied or express warranties of merchantability or fitness for any
particular usage, application, or purpose. We have done our best to
provide the reader with useful and accurate information relating to
investments in discounted mortgages. You should be aware that legal
references are to California law; the laws in other jurisdictions may
be different, and laws in *any* jurisdiction are subject to change and
differing interpretation. You are charged with the responsibility of
verifying all material read here before relying upon it.
Neither the authors nor the publisher makes any guarantees
relative to the uses to which the information in this book may be put.

Library of Congress Cataloging-in-Publication Data

Hornwood, Sanford W.
    The number one real estate investment no one talks about.

    Includes index.
    1. Mortgages. I. Hollingsworth, I. Lucretia.
II. Title. III. Title: Number one real estate investment no one talks
about.
HG4655.H67   1987   332.63′244   86-25482

ISBN 0-13-626482-4

Printed in the United States of America

for *Rita*

*　*　*　*　*

to *Jeff* and *Erich*
Owners in fee of the
province of my heart

Acknowledgments

I am indebted to several individuals and organizations for their assistance and contributions to this volume. In particular, I want to thank Steven H. Hornwood, attorney and broker, of Steven Hornwood Realty in Sylmar, California, and Roberta Hornwood of the Westmark Commercial Group in Las Vegas, Nevada, for their support and encouragement of this project from its inception.

The charts and graphs found in the material on yields were contributed by the late Francis Lebus. These materials have proven their utility time and again, and I gratefully acknowledge here the authorship of these useful tools.

Special recognition and thanks must go to Rita Hornwood for her excellent critical analysis of this work, which contributed immeasurably to its scope and substance, and whose judgment has stood us in good stead from the first word to the last.

Sanford W. Hornwood

I want to express my gratitude for the cooperation of all of those individuals who have assisted us in the compilation of these materials. In particular, Andrea L. Kobliner—Los Angeles broker, realtor, and teacher—graciously read the manuscript and provided practical advice on many fine points. The staff of Mid-Columbia Title Company and Don Nunamaker, Ann Watt, and Chris Burgess of Don Nunamaker Inc., Realtors, all of Hood River, Oregon, patiently gathered charts, tables, and forms for our research purposes.

Any volume of this scope must by necessity involve many others whose contributions may be indirect in terms of substantive content but nonetheless direct in terms of positive support. Included in this number are Susanne Parker and Carla Vossler of Manhattan Beach, California, who provided unlimited hospitality during the first draft of this volume, and Jeff and Erich Simon who generously surrendered coveted computer time to a project that did not even faintly resemble a video game.

I. Lucretia Hollingsworth

A Word from the Authors

If you have built castles in the air, your work need not be lost: that is where they should be. Now put the foundations under them.

—Henry David Thoreau

An All-American Dream

The purpose of this book is to show you *in no uncertain terms* how you can join the ranks of self-made millionaires. Fortunes have been made based upon the experiences and methods outlined within these pages. We earnestly feel that if you share this particular all-American dream, then you will have the incentive to read on.

Whether you're a doctor, musician, retailer, hairdresser, repairperson or if you're already retired, *this book was written for you.* Regardless of occupation, most people share the same dream: They want to make money; they want to own property; and they want to accomplish this as quickly as possible while investing as little of their own money as possible.

Impossible Dream?

Is this an impossible dream? It doesn't have to be. There are thousands of organizations and private investors who have made this dream come true. And it wasn't difficult! It was done by acquiring some easy, basic knowledge that provided the tools to make that dream possible. Savings and loan associations, commercial banks, insurance companies, unions (through their pension funds), and many others are making huge profits every year. There's no reason why you can't do it as well; all you have to do is learn how. And this book is specifically designed to teach you everything you need to know. It is specially written in a unique self-study format for the layperson without special training in any field.

By buying this book, you have just taken the first step toward structuring a solid foundation beneath your own dreams. It is going to be done by learning how to buy, sell, and trade discounted mortgages that are secured by real property. This book will teach you the *ABC's* of investing in real estate using the exclusive vehicle of discounted mortgages. This book is a step-by-step guide on how to get started, what to look for, what to avoid, what to do, and how to do it. The secrets of leveraging (using other people's money instead of your own), compounding, pyramiding, utilizing tax shelters, appraising, making computations, calculating yields, and servicing your investments will all be explained in easy-to-understand language.

Getting Started: Sandy's Story

Fifty years ago, in the midst of the Depression, I was a struggling young attorney just beginning my own family. I developed a law practice over the years that specialized in the area of personal injury. Although I worked very, very hard during those early years to support my family, the truth was that I was not getting *ahead* financially. We were paying our bills every month, but frankly I wanted more than that—much more. I dreamed of the financial independence that is the reward of self-made millions. The only problem was that I really had no idea of how to go about it!

A Quirk of Fate

Then one day one of those unexplainable quirks of fate came my way in the form of a simple real estate transaction. What I was to learn from that "simple" transaction, however, was destined to change the course of my entire life; through it, I saw the means whereby I might be able to put the foundations under my own "castles in the air."

The answer was really quite simple, although at the time—even as an experienced attorney—it seemed more complicated than it actually was. What that initial transaction showed me were the profits that could be made by buying, selling, and trading discounted mortgages.

I began my education in discounted mortgages by reading everything available on the subject. Then gradually and ever so cautiously I started to invest. Through many years of trial and error my portfolio of investments and knowledge grew until the day came that I realized I had built a firm foundation beneath my own dreams—I was, in fact, a millionaire.

How You Can Be a Millionaire

You can be, too. Anyone can. We believe it's a simple function of knowledge, self-confidence, and desire. The purpose in writing this book was to provide you with the first variable in this equation. Self-confidence will grow correspondingly with your knowledge and experience. *You* must provide the final ingredient—the desire to build the foundation to support your dreams.

But Why Discounted Mortgages?

It is appropriate to ask yourself, "Why discounted mortgages?" Why not learn instead about municipal bonds or blue chip stocks or the antique market? Well, it was Andrew Carnegie who is credited with this important observation: "Ninety percent of all millionaires became so through owning real estate. *More money has been made in real estate than in all industrial investments combined.*"

And if this is not enough to convince you, then consider these interesting facts reported in a recent real estate journal:

1. Seven out of every ten American millionaires made their money in real estate.

2. Shelter is one of the necessities of life.

3. Real estate enjoys the most favorable legislation of all other investments. The tax benefits are enormous.

These facts certainly attest to the value of investing in real property, but why should you specialize in just one particular area of real estate? The response to that question is really very simple: Because experience shows that discounted mortgages are the single most unexplored area of real estate investing *and* the single most secure form of real estate investing.

A Deep, Dark Secret

The methods for successful discounting have been a deep, dark secret for a long time. Now, they're available to you. The opportunities that are available for you are infinite as more and more opportunities spin off from one another.

Now Let's Talk About You

Ask yourself these questions: Did you work hard today? How much money did you earn? Did you earn enough to pay your bills, take care of your family's needs, and still have something left over for savings? Are you getting anywhere financially, or are you struggling twice as hard to stay in the same place? Where will you be three years from now? Five years? Twenty?

Don't Sell Yourself Short

Right now you may be thinking, "What am I getting myself into?" You might even be wondering if you can sell this book to someone else—at a loss! Basically that's the very premise of discounting. If you were to sell it now at a lesser price than what you paid for it, you would receive a certain amount of cash immediately. The buyer, on the other hand, would get the full value (reading) at a discount price plus all the benefits (profits) the information would bring at a later date. Stop worrying and forget about selling this book; it may be your last realistic chance to attain wealth and independence.

Everything You Need Is Here

The beauty of it—the excitement of it—is the fact that you don't need any previous knowledge in order to enter this lucrative profession. This material is designed to be read and understood by the person with no experience in accounting, financing, economics, or even real estate. All you have to do is to read it, and you will have access to all of the information you will need, as well as complete and simple directions on how to apply it. Everything described here has been tried, tested, and proven successful over many years. Hundreds of investments have been handled, both for ourselves and, as practicing attorneys, for hundreds of clients. All of this knowledge and experience is incorporated within these pages. What an opportunity for you to avoid the risks and losses suffered by so many others who didn't have a book like this to guide them!

A Word to the Wise

One word of caution: You won't find gimmicks, schemes, or magical panaceas by which you can supposedly "get rich quick" without working for it. This book is intended for the serious-minded individual who is ready and willing to devote several hours of work every week to the pursuit of success. You won't have to take time away from your regular occupation; your spare time, both after work and during weekends, will suffice. If you can accept this minimal commitment, you will learn quickly, you will succeed, you will meet some very interesting, knowledgeable people, and you will have a lot of fun—all while becoming very wealthy.

A Word by Way of Introduction

Before we turn to the task at hand, we wanted to let you know who the "we" are that you will find reference to throughout this work. Sandy is an attorney and investor with two-score years of experience in the field of discount mortgages. Lucretia is also an attorney who practiced business law for seven years before taking on a second career in writing.

It's Time to Start

Now you know what to expect from this book. It's time to start making you rich. It's time to start putting a foundation under *your* "castles in the air."

Sanford W. Hornwood
Los Angeles, California

I. Lucretia Hollingsworth
Los Angeles, California
Hood River, Oregon

Table of Contents

7   Uncovering the Role of Escrow in the Transfer of Real
     Property Interests • 95

     The Function of an Escrow • 95
     The Legal Requirements of a Valid Escrow • 97
     Understanding Escrow Instructions • 97
     The Tasks Performed By an Escrow Holder • 98
     How to Close an Escrow • 104

8   How to Size Up and Limit Your Investment Risk in Discount
     Mortgages • 107

     How to Determine if Fraud Occurs in the Discount Mortgage
     Field • 107
     The Common Law Elements of Fraud and Deceit • 108
     How to Use Case Law to Define the Parameters of Fraud • 108
     The Difference Between Civil and Criminal Fraud • 109
     Eight Deceptive Mortgage Practices • 109
     A Hypothetical Case of Fraud • 110
     Twelve Safeguards Against Fraud • 111

9   How to Manage Mortgage Investments • 115

     The Primary Goal of Mortgage Management • 115
     The Part That Personal Style Plays in Mortgage
     Management • 115
     Alternative Ways of Managing Investments • 117
     Preliminary Steps to Be Taken by All Mortgage
     Managers • 118

10   How to Cure Delinquencies and Turn Foreclosures to Your
     Advantage • 121

     How to Minimize Investment Risks by Good Mortgage
     Management • 121
     How to Determine When a Delinquency Occurs • 121

1. The First Step: Understanding How Mortgage Financing Is Utilized in Real Property Transfers

UNDERSTANDING WHY REAL ESTATE PRINCIPLES ARE IMPORTANT TO MORTGAGE FINANCING

A decision to invest in real estate by trading in discounted mortgages calls for a consideration of several basic real property concepts: What is real property, why is it desirable, and how is it acquired? A thorough understanding of this conceptual groundwork will make it easier to appreciate and use the tools that come later. Even if you feel you are too knowledgeable for these simple basics, you are strongly urged to review this material. It might serve to clear up some popular misconceptions you may have that could easily cost you many thousands of dollars. Rest assured, it will be well worth the few extra minutes of reading time.

Distinguish Real Property from Personal Property

Property may be divided into two classes: Real (or immovable) property and personal (or movable) property. Real property consists of the following:

1. Land;

2. Anything permanently attached to land (whether by nature,

such as trees and vegetation, or by humans, such as buildings and structures); and

3. Anything incidental to the use of land (such as easements and rights-of-way).

Everything else comprises personal property. The emphasis here is on real property, otherwise known as real estate.

Why Is Real Estate So Desirable?

Perhaps the best answer to this question was given by Will Rogers, the American humorist, who wasn't trying to be funny when he observed, "Land is the best investment, as no more is being made." The economic law of supply and demand never changes. If the demand exceeds the supply, the value goes up. If the supply exceeds the demand, the value goes down. And if "no more is being made," everyone wants a piece of what already exists, thereby constantly increasing its value.

Real estate was always the ultimate security, even before inflation. Now, because of that inflation, it's an even better security. Our accelerated monetary expansion has resulted in an economic climate making today's and tomorrow's real estate investments the only way to protect the future for ourselves and our families. It's a fixed asset, comparatively easy to convert into cash. It's a hedge against inflation, maintaining good purchasing power because its value not only keeps up with inflation's annual percentage rise, but generally exceeds it. Possibly the best example of this phenomenon occurred back in the early 1980s when the national inflation rate rose as much as 15 percent while the value of residential real estate rose at the rate of 25 to 30 percent.

What other investments can you think of that have done as well? When properly structured, real estate investments can provide profit from cash flow, tax benefits, appreciation, exchanges, and trades. There is no doubt that when you own an interest in real estate, you have significantly increased your present and future net worth.

HOW REAL PROPERTY TRANSFERS ARE TYPICALLY FINANCED

There are many ways by which an interest in real estate can be acquired. For now, you're concerned with the purchase of that interest, and a purchase is usually based upon various instruments used in financing.

Buying real estate is no different from buying anything else. You give something of value, and you receive something of value in return. What you give is money (or the equivalent of money, or the promise to pay money, or any combination thereof) the value of which is equal to the value (purchase price) of the interest in real property you're getting in return.

Let's say you decide to buy a $100,000 home. You have the following options:

1. Give the seller all cash (if you have it);

2. Give the seller some cash and the balance in something you own (cars, diamonds, *etc.*) that has enough of a cash value to make up the difference; or

3. Finance whatever portion you don't have in cash by promising to pay that amount over a period of time, either to the seller or to someone else.

The lender of any borrowed funds (seller, savings and loan association, commercial bank, or whatever) will now have a lien on the subject property until the obligation is paid off. Naturally, this lender needs security to assure that, in case of a default, it can look to the property for the recovery of its money. As a simple note usually won't suffice to provide adequate protection, the instrument used for this purpose will be either a mortgage or a deed of trust (also referred to as a trust deed, depending upon which part of the country you live in). A sample of a mortgage and trust deed as well as their supporting notes may be found in Appendix A.

Three Ways Mortgages and Trust Deeds Differ

A mortgage is a lien against a borrower's real property that serves to secure the payment of a debt. A mortgage loan consists of two parts, a note (or bond) and the securing instrument. While the note provides legal evidence of the debt, the securing instrument is a separate document that is recorded with the appropriate local official. This security document serves to give notice of the lender's interest in the real property. Thus, if the lender could be assured that the borrower would never default, no mortgage would be necessary—the note alone would suffice to prove that the obligation exists.

A trust deed is very similar to a mortgage. It, too, consists of a securing instrument and is accompanied by a note as evidence of the debt. Its purpose is identical to that of a mortgage, inasmuch as it places a lien on an interest in real property to protect the lender in case of borrower default. However, there are certain differences between the two, as we shall now discover.

1. *Number of Parties.* In a mortgage, only two parties are involved: the borrower (called the mortgagor) and the lender (called the mortgagee). If the mortgagor defaults, either in the payments or in any of the other provisions of the mortgage, the mortgagee may start foreclosure proceedings at its option.

In a trust deed three parties are involved: the borrower (called the trustor), the lender (called the beneficiary), and a neutral third party (called the trustee) who, in case of a default, starts the foreclosure proceedings. The trustee can be any responsible, disinterested person or entity, although generally it is a bank trust officer or attorney.

2. *Foreclosure Procedure.* A foreclosure is the forced sale of real property to satisfy a debt. Property that is secured by a mortgage can be foreclosed only by the mortgagee's instituting a foreclosure action in court. When the court establishes the fact of the default, the mortgagor has a fixed period of time within which to bring the account current before the court will order a sale of the property. After the sale, which is held by the sheriff or the court commissioner, the mortgagor has one year within which to redeem the property by paying off the entire debt, plus interest and all charges. If the mortgagor is able to accomplish this, the foreclosure sale is nullified; if not, the property goes to the successful bidder at the foreclosure sale. This time duration is known as the "period of redemption," and during this period the mortgagor can continue to reside on the property.

Property secured by a trust deed, on the other hand, can be foreclosed either as if it were a mortgage following the same procedure as above, or by a trustee's sale, by virtue of the power-of-sale clause in the trust deed. In the latter case, no court action is required. If a default takes place and the beneficiary exercises the right to foreclose, the beneficiary informs the trustee of the default and requests that the trustee start foreclosure proceedings.

In some jurisdictions the trust deed is used almost exclusively in preference to the mortgage. This is because the authority granted by the power-of-sale clause allows the property to be sold more quickly, with no court action and no one-year redemption period, and the sale is final.

3. *Title.* The question of who has possession of the title during the period of the loan can be confusing, especially to the neophyte. In a mortgage, the mortgagor not only has the title to the property recorded in his or her name but also has physical possession of the deed that

conveyed the title. This means the legal title is conveyed to the mortgagor immediately and the mortgagee has nothing further to do with the title unless a foreclosure action has actually taken place.

A trust deed works differently. The title to the property is still recorded in the borrower's name, but the borrower doesn't receive physical possession of the deed until the loan has been paid. Until then, the borrower has what is called *equitable title* to the property. When the trust deed has been executed (formalized), the trustor conveys the legal title to the trustee, to be held in trust during the term of the loan. Upon satisfaction of the debt, the beneficiary instructs the trustee to reconvey legal title to the trustor. (It's no different from buying a car on time. You own the car, but the lender keeps the pink slip. When you pay off the debt, you receive the pink slip to the car.) As already noted above, in case of a default, the beneficiary instructs the trustee to commence the foreclosure action.

Bear in mind that in both the mortgage and the trust deed, legal title is recorded in the name of the borrower. The only difference between the two is in who has physical possession of the deed during the term of the loan.

Note: From this point on, it will no longer be necessary to refer to both mortgages and trust deeds as such. You've now learned that the only differences between the two are those listed above. Otherwise, they are identical in purpose and usage. Therefore, for the sake of expediency, we'll hereafter use the term "mortgage" to represent both forms and will differentiate between the two only if the need arises.

HOW SECONDARY FINANCING DIFFERS FROM PRIMARY FINANCING

Not all mortgages are first liens on the property. There can be (and usually are) second, third, fourth, and fifth liens on the same property. These subsequent liens are called junior mortgages because they are behind the first mortgage in priority of repayment in the event of a default. Because many of the mortgages you'll be working with will be junior liens, now is a good time to discuss them.

How Junior Mortgages Provide Secondary Financing

Junior mortgages are used to provide secondary financing for the purchase of property when cash plus primary financing cannot cover the full amount of the purchase price. Remember that $100,000 home we talked about at the start of this chapter? Normally you could purchase it by making a down payment of $20,000 and getting a lender to loan you the remaining $80,000. That $80,000 loan would be considered primary financing and would be recorded by the lender as a first mortgage on the property. So far, that's simple with no problems to contend with.

But what if you only had $10,000 for the down payment, instead of $20,000? Unless the lender would agree to give you a $90,000 loan, you would have to come up with an additional $10,000 in order to buy the home. That's where secondary financing comes in.

A lot of home sellers would be willing to "loan" you the additional funds (so that they can complete a sale), but that doesn't mean the seller would actually give you $10,000 in cash. Instead, the seller would take back a second mortgage for that amount, and this second mortgage would be recorded in the name of the seller. You would make payments on the first mortgage to the primary lender *and* payments on the second mortgage directly to the seller.

Let's take it one step further. Suppose the seller were willing to take back a second mortgage, but only for $5,000 rather than $10,000. You would then have to look for someone who would be willing to loan you the needed $5,000. This lender, then, would record a third mortgage against the property.

The above example was based on your obtaining a new first mortgage for $80,000 from a lender and adding a second and a third mortgage, together with your cash to make up the $100,000 purchase price. The complete breakdown would be:

$10,000 - down payment
80,000 - first mortgage
5,000 - second mortgage
5,000 - third mortgage
$100,000 - total purchase price

How about a home that has a legally assumable loan on it that you would like to take advantage of because of its low interest rate? Let's take the same $100,000 home. Assume now that it has an existing, assumable loan of $60,000 with an interest rate of only 9½ percent, but you still have only $20,000 in cash. The financing here would work the same way as in the first example. The existing first mortgage stays on the property and you assume it. That takes care of $60,000. You use your $20,000 cash as a down payment. The remaining $20,000 would be obtained from another lender or from the seller's taking back a second mortgage.

Why One Mortgage Has Priority over Others

Mortgages are numbered in the order in which they are recorded. A mortgage that is recorded first automatically becomes a first mortgage, and all subsequent mortgages will be numbered in the order in which each one is recorded. Calling a mortgage a "first" doesn't make it so, unless no other mortgage has been recorded ahead of it.

This, however, doesn't mean that mortgages can't change their positions. If a first mortgage is paid off while a second mortgage still exists, the second mortgage becomes a first, and any other existing mortgage automatically moves up one step.

How Subordination of a Mortgage Affects Its Priority

To subordinate means to place something secondary in rank to something else. Any mortgage can be subordinated to a subsequent mortgage as long as the mortgagee holding the earlier lien agrees to it.

Surprisingly enough, there are times a lien holder will be quite willing to drop down in priority. One such example might involve the purchase of vacant land for the purpose of building. Let's say a buyer purchases a lot for $200,000 with the intention of building a condominium project on it. The buyer pays $100,000 down, and the seller agrees to carry the balance in a first mortgage. When the buyer is ready to build, she finds that a construction loan can be obtained only upon the condition that the construction lender's mortgage takes precedence over the seller's mortgage, which is usually the case. In this example the borrower's equity is strong due to the large down payment, and the seller's mortgage is well secured. Therefore, the holder of that mortgage won't be taking too great a risk by allowing it to become secondary to, *i.e.*, to be subordinated to, the construction loan. In reality, when a buyer knows that a construction loan will be required, a subordination clause would most likely be included in the original contract.

As an investor in mortgages, make certain you know whether or not a subordination clause exists before purchasing the mortgage; it might save you problems later. You'll go into this more completely in Chapter 5, when you take your initial mortgage shopping trip.

**Uncover the Risk Factor
in Junior Mortgage Investing**

Is there a risk in buying junior mortgages? An honest answer has to be, "Yes, there is a risk." In spite of that risk, junior mortgages may be extremely attractive to knowledgeable investors, not only because of the high interest they pay, but especially because of the discounted price at which they can be purchased. Chapter 2 will discuss how discounts work, and Chapter 11 will show how such discounts greatly increase the investor's yield. Once you know what you're doing and how to be selective (both of which you'll know by the time you finish this book), those risks will have been reduced to a bare minimum.

Keep in mind that this isn't a horse race. There, you bet on one horse, and because all the other horses are trying to beat yours, the odds are against you. In the discounted mortgage field the odds are with you for the simple reason that most borrowers have every intention of paying off their debt, and the great majority of them succeed in doing so. However, we do have to accept the fact that sometimes there is a default making a foreclosure action necessary. We'll examine foreclosures thoroughly in Chapter 10.

CONCLUSION

You've just completed a basic review of real estate and the instruments used to finance its purchase. You've seen what real estate really is and why it's so desirable. And you've also learned that it's the safest security in the world because its value keeps rising at a faster pace than inflation. You now know what mortgages and trust deeds are and how they differ in parties, foreclosures, and possession of legal title. Finally, you have discovered the differences between senior and junior mortgages and explored their purposes, recordation priorities, risk factors, and subordination clauses.

Real property and its financing, two practically inseparable subjects, will provide the course you'll be traveling as you journey toward financial independence. You can see, therefore, why a complete understanding of these fundamentals is a prerequisite to making them work for you.

2. Understanding Why Real Property Mortgages Are Discounted and Traded

HOW DISCOUNTING WORKS

In Chapter 1, you learned the meaning and value of real estate and were introduced to mortgages, the security instruments by which the purchase of real estate is financed. Additionally, we discussed the differences between senior and junior mortgages. If you were not already familiar with these terms, you should now have a good, basic understanding of them.

This chapter is devoted to an explanation of the discounting of these mortgages. Usually, as you have previously seen, these mortgages will be junior rather than senior liens on the property. You'll see an actual situation demonstrating the need to create a mortgage, solely for the purpose of selling it at a discount. The resulting advantages to both the seller and the investor-buyer will be pointed out. You'll also learn how a mortgage on one property, purchased at a discounted price, can be used *at its full face value,* toward the purchase of another property.

A Discount Is a Price Reduction

Let's say that about three weeks ago you went into a clothing store hoping to find a sport shirt to give as a gift to a friend. While searching through the various styles and colors available in your friend's size, you found one that was absolutely perfect. However, you felt that the $37 ticket price was too high for this particular shirt. As much as you wanted it, you couldn't convince yourself to pay more than what you felt it was really worth. So you left without buying it.

Four days later the store advertised an inventory clearance sale. You rushed down and began looking through the stacks of shirts. You guessed it. There it was—your shirt—discounted to $25, a 32 percent reduction! Needless to say, you didn't hesitate, but bought it on the spot, thrilled to get the shirt you wanted at a price you considered fair.

So far you've learned nothing you didn't already know. A discount is nothing more than the amount, or percentage, of reduction in the price of any item available for sale.

How a Discounted Mortgage Is Different from Discounted Merchandise

Now, what is a discounted mortgage? Actually, it's not much different from the discounted shirt in the story above. A discounted mortgage is simply a mortgage that the owner (for whatever reason) wants to sell and, in order to do so, is willing to take less than its full value. In other words, if a lender takes a mortgage for $20,000 and then sells it for $15,000, the mortgage has been discounted $5,000 or 25 percent.

You were able to purchase the sport shirt at a discount because the store needed the space. A mortgage is sold at a discount because the seller wants or needs the cash. But there are other similarities between these two situations, and later on in this chapter, you'll see what they are.

The Mechanics of Discounting: A Hypothetical Example

Turn now to a hypothetical situation that will illustrate more concretely the way that discounting works in real estate financing. Ten years ago Harry bought a home for $40,000. He paid 20 percent down ($8,000) and obtained a 30-year loan for the balance ($32,000) at an interest rate of 7½ percent. Five years went by during which the home appreciated in value approximately $25,000, making it worth $65,000. During the same period, Harry's existing mortgage debt decreased to $30,200.

Harry decided that it was time to add a family room and update the kitchen for a total cost of $13,000. Instead of taking the money from his savings, he preferred to borrow on his equity that had increased to $34,800. With the home's present value of $65,000, combined with Harry's good credit, his lender was willing to refinance the home with a new loan of $52,000, raising the interest to the then prevailing rate of 9 percent.

Harry added the family room, updated the kitchen, bought a business for $25,000, and banked the rest.

Now, a startling change in real estate values began taking place. During the first five years Harry owned his home, it appreciated $25,000. But during the next five years, because of the economy, the inflation, the baby boom of the post-war years, and the prevalence of the American dream of becoming a home owner, people were suddenly buying houses as they never had before. Property values shot skyward at an unprecedented pace. *Harry's home was now worth $160,000!* His outstanding mortgage debt was only $50,000. And to add to his good fortune, his business had done exceptionally well.

One day his wife suggested it was time they started looking for a larger home in a new area. Because Harry's wife wasn't one you could easily say "no" to, Harry placed a "For Sale" sign on his front lawn.

Everything was looking up for Harry. Businesswise, he was a success. He had a huge equity in his home (around $110,000), and he was ready to move up in the world. Harry seemingly had it made.

Or had he? Let's see. Shortly after Harry's home was placed on the market, he got an offer from Bob who realized that the home was perfect for him and his family. A purchase price of $160,000 was agreed upon, but then they ran into trouble. Bob had $40,000 in cash to use as a down payment, which—although a good, solid amount —was far less than Harry's $110,000 equity.

Under normal market conditions Bob could have gone to a lender with his $40,000 and obtained a 30-year loan for the $120,000 balance. If interest rates were 10 to 11 percent, his monthly payments of principal and interest would have only cost him around $1,100, which he could easily afford.

But in real estate as in other fields, what was normal for so many yesterdays does not necessarily bear a relationship to what is normal today or tomorrow. In the past, for example, interest rates have gone as high as 17 percent. At that level, Bob's loan would have cost him around $1,700 per month. Even if he were able to afford it and were willing to pay, he probably couldn't qualify for it.

So now, Harry had a real problem. An equity of $110,000 isn't bad for a guy who bought the home for $40,000, lived in it for ten years, and most likely put a maximum of $15,000 into it. But how could he get his equity out of it? The average buyers are just like Bob; they either can't—or won't—put $110,000 down on a $160,000 home.

HOW OWNER FINANCING OPERATES IN MORTGAGE DISCOUNTING

In order for Harry to be able to sell his home, and in order for Bob to be able to buy it, Harry and Bob had to find an alternative method of financing. After much discussion and negotiation, they were finally successful in structuring a transaction both could live with. Here's how it worked.

Bob put $40,000 down and assumed the existing first mortgage of $50,000, which still had that old 9 percent interest rate. Harry took back *two* separate mortgages—a second for $50,000 at 12 percent interest, and a third for $20,000 at 14 percent interest. Each had payments amortized over thirty years, with the second due and payable in three years and the third due in five. Bob's total monthly payments on all three mortgages (principal and interest) came to only $1,150, much less than the $1,700 he would have had to pay had he gone to a lender for a new loan.

"But," you ask, "how did this arrangement get Harry his equity since he took $70,000 in paper?" Another thing—Harry took back *two* mortgages, each for different amounts and different terms. Why? Couldn't he have just taken back a second mortgage for the full $70,000? These are good questions; the answers are what this book is all about.

Before we get into the explanation, we want you to be aware of the following important fact: *Any agreement between parties to a contract is legally acceptable provided that no law (moral or otherwise) is broken. Therefore, as long as a contract isn't contrary to the law, the specific terms and provisions can be structured in whatever way will fulfill the individual needs of the parties.*

Now, how did Harry get his equity out of the property, and why structure two mortgages, each with different terms?

How Financing Can Be Structured to Meet Individual Needs, Abilities, and Goals

Harry had two needs, a present as well as a future one. The immediate need was to realize enough equity to have $75,000 in cash—$50,000 for the down payment on his new home and $25,000 for the sailboat he'd always dreamed of owning. Bob's $40,000 down payment, plus the $50,000 second mortgage, *which could be sold at a discount to an investor,* assured Harry of having more than enough to fill that present need. (Bear in mind that Harry wouldn't actually be losing his own money by selling the mortgage at a discount. When we consider what he originally paid for the home and what he had subsequently put into it, the discount would represent only a small portion of his profit.)

His future need was to provide for his daughter's college education. This need was filled by the creation of the third mortgage, which he would hold for the five-year period. Bob's monthly payment to Harry on the third mortgage amounted to $237, most of which was interest on the loan. When the note became due and payable, Harry would receive a lump sum of over $19,000, just in time to pay the college tuition.

So much for Harry. How about Bob? The setting up of two mortgages also worked perfectly for *his* needs. As the beneficiary of a large trust fund coming due in two and one-half years, he'd be able to pay off the second mortgage, while having five full years to save up enough to pay off the third.

With the needs of both parties satisfied, the transaction was consummated, and Bob bought Harry's home.

In this hypothetical story a second mortgage was created with the specific intent of selling it to an investor—very possibly *you.* The details of this transaction were specifically tailored to fit the desires, needs, abilities, and goals of the involved parties.

Investments Should Be in Accord with Needs and Goals of Individual Investors

Likewise, when you as an investor are considering buying, selling, or trading any mortgage, make absolutely certain that you're familiar with *your* needs. To do this, you must have a well thought-out plan, which should take both your present and future needs, as well as your short- and long-range goals, into account. Before investing in any mortgage, carefully check all the details of that mortgage in order to see if the terms coincide with your needs and goals. If not, investing in that particular mortgage may not be to your advantage.

Never forget: If your investments aren't in accordance with your plan, you could be working against your own interests!

By analyzing your present situation and your future goals, and by making use of the general advice and specific suggestions throughout this book, you'll find that all the excitement will be there but most of the hit-or-miss gamble will be eliminated. (By the way, before you spend a sleepless night wondering if Harry got his sailboat, you'll be happy to know that he sold his $50,000 note at 20 percent discount, receiving $40,000 in cash. This, plus Bob's $40,000 down payment gave him $5,000 more than the funds he actually needed.)

Now let's look at the hypothetical transaction from the outside investor's point of view. She paid $40,000 for a note worth $50,000. For three years, she'll be getting monthly payments of almost $515. By the end of the third year, she will have received over $18,000 and will still have more than $49,000 coming in one lump sum. That's a net gain of close to $28,000. *Do you realize this is a 70 percent return on the investment?*

By now you realize that the mortgages between Harry and Bob were designed to fit *their* situations. Because all situations are different, junior mortgages can be created to fit *any* variables, depending upon the situation at hand and the needs of the parties, merely by structuring the terms in such a way as to be mutually acceptable. First mortgage holders are usually institutional lenders, such as savings and loan associations or commercial banks, with the result that there is less opportunity for the mortgagor to negotiate the terms. But the point we want to clarify here is that you might run into just about anything.

Five Possible Variations in Structuring Mortgages

Consider the following possible variations:

1. Because the property being sold was a home, the mortgages were on that home. But the mortgages could have been on an office building, a shopping center, a tract of unimproved land, an apartment building, an industrial property, or just about any other piece of real estate. As you progress and continue to build your investment portfolio, you will become involved in any or all of these.

2. It won't always be a second mortgage that is offered for sale; it could be a third, fourth, or even a fifth. (You already know from Chapter 1 that the order in which a mortgage is recorded establishes its number. The lower the number, the higher the priority, and vice versa.) Don't scoff at the idea of a low priority mortgage. Many investors prefer them as they have a better chance of ending up with

the property in the event of a default. However, you'll see in Chapter 4 that we are suggesting you start off with nothing lower in priority than a second mortgage.

3. The duration of the loan can be for any period of time mutually agreed upon. It can be short term, less than a year, or long term, ten years or more.

4. The interest rate on the loan is also negotiable. Usually a lower priority mortgage, such as a third, fourth, or fifth, will carry a higher interest rate than a first or second. If the prospective mortgagor requests a longer term in which to pay the loan, the lender will almost always demand a higher interest rate.

5. The payback schedule can be anything the imagination, or need, can come up with. For example, the payments may be amortized over a term of a few or many years. *Amortization* is a payback method that is based upon equal (usually monthly) installments to be made over the entire term of the loan. (If you are not already familiar with the payback methodology of amortized payments, you may want to review the sample amortization schedule in Appendix B.)

In our hypothetical example, Harry's original mortgage was on a $32,000 loan at 7½ percent for thirty years. His monthly payments were $223.75, which included interest and principal. He would have paid this same amount each month for thirty years. In other words, Harry's last monthly payment would have been the same, theoretically, as his first.

Another payback method is the balloon payment, which entails one payment (at least) on an installment loan that is larger than any other payment. Although the "balloon" payment is usually the first or the last, it can be any of the payments the parties agree upon.

In our hypothetical example, the second and third mortgages Harry gave to Bob both involved balloon payments. The second mortgage, for example, was on a loan of $50,000 at 12 percent interest due in three years. The parties agreed that Bob's monthly installment payments on the second mortgage would be amortized over a thirty-year period, but the entire amount of the loan that still remained unpaid at the end of the three years became due and payable at that time.

There are countless other ways in which the payback schedule can be structured. The following are only a few:

1. No payments at all until the entire note is due, at which time the amount of the loan, plus all accrued interest, becomes payable. This is known as a *straight note.*

2. Monthly payments can be a certain percentage of the loan. For example, payments of 1 percent per month on a $35,000 loan would come to $350. If the interest on the loan were 12 percent, this payment would only take care of the interest. If the interest rate were 12½ percent, that 1 percent payment wouldn't even take care of the interest. (From an investor's point of view, this can be quite important as we'll find out in Chapter 7.)

3. The schedule may call for periodic payments on the principal in addition to the regular monthly payments. A five-year note for $20,000, with monthly payments of $250, might also provide for a $3,000 payment at the end of the second year, and a $5,000 payment at the end of the fourth.

There's absolutely no limit to the terms, conditions, and provisions that can be included in a mortgage. The flexibility is total, subject only to the mutual agreement of the contracting parties.

THE REASONS FOR TRADING DISCOUNTED MORTGAGES

Remember the sport shirt you bought at a discounted price? We said that there were similarities between it and a mortgage, which is also being offered at a discount. Now, let's see what those similarities are.

You were a buyer with a very specific goal in mind; you needed a shirt to give as a gift. Just any sport shirt wouldn't do. It had to be the right size, style, and color.

As an investor in discounted mortgages, you are exactly the same type of buyer. Just as there are millions of sport shirts on the market, there are also millions of available mortgages. Even if you could afford to invest in all of them, only certain ones would serve your needs of the moment. As you continue to build your portfolio, you will find that at different times alternative types of properties, with mortgages containing different terms, will be more advantageous for you.

That's why we caution you again. Have a well thought-out plan, so that you'll always know where you're going. Then, each acquisition you make will be one more step in getting you there.

You didn't want to pay the original price for the shirt because you didn't feel it was worth that much. And yet you wanted it, if you could buy it at a fair price.

When an investor offers less than the full amount of the mortgage, it means that although he or she wants to buy it, it's not worth the full price. That's because the investor has to wait until the end of the term to get paid. Even if the note calls for monthly payments (and most of them do, except for the already explained "straight note"), those payments usually do little more than cover the interest, and sometimes they don't even do that.

The principal, which represents the big lump sum, won't be paid until the end of the term of the note. How long the investor will have to wait until receiving that lump sum is one of the prime factors in determining the discount rate.

Another similarity between discounted merchandise and a discounted mortgage is in the viewpoint of the seller. The manager of the clothing store had a shirt that had obviously proven difficult to sell at the original price. Many shirts were sold prior to the sale. The fact that this one wasn't proved that you were not the only one who felt the price was excessive. A store's sole purpose is to sell merchandise—not to keep it on the shelves. Sometimes, the store may have to sell at a lower profit than originally expected or even at a loss. But this is preferable to not selling the item at all.

A mortgagee who wants to sell a note also has a purpose—to raise money for one reason or another, either personal or business. If the funds weren't needed, the investor would keep the note, finally ending up with the entire face amount plus all the interest. But, for whatever reason, the investor can't afford to wait that long.

In order to make the purchase more attractive to the investor, the lender has to sweeten the pot by reducing the price to an amount that is less than the face amount of the note. The investor now becomes interested because this reduction provides an opportunity for making an additional profit. The investor not only receives interest on the entire balance still owed, but also makes a profit on the discounted portion of the note. You could say that the amount of the discount represents the investor's fee charged for the willingness to be paid at a later date.

The total amount of investor profit realized after cost is known as the *yield* on the investment. A complete understanding of this concept is so vital to your success that we've devoted Chapter 11 exclusively to this subject. There, you'll find tables and easy directions on how to use them to enable you to know how discounts are calculated.

How Mortgages Can Be Traded at a Loss
Yet Increase Profits

In the Introduction to this book we promised to unlock all those secrets that the "big guys" of mortgage investing don't particularly want you to know. Here is one of them: It's easy (and legal) to engineer a deliberate loss in order to make a profit, as long as you know what you're looking for. This is done by selling one note for less than you paid for it and using the capital to purchase another note that will bring you a greater return than the one you just sold.

Let's assume you paid $30,000 for a $35,000 note bearing interest at 12 percent, all due in two years. The interest pays you an annual income of $4,200. Later, you have an opportunity to purchase a $43,100 note on a small apartment building, worth around $250,000. Because it has a five-year due date the interest is 17 percent and the mortgage can be acquired for $28,000, a 35 percent discount.

If you sell your present note for $2,000 less than what you paid for it, you'll be able to buy the new note. Because the 17 percent interest will pay you an annual income of $7,237, instead of the $4,200 you were getting before, you'll make up that $2,000 loss in under eight months. For the remaining sixteen months of the original two-year term, you'll receive $260 *more* each month than what the first note was paying you. During the same period of time, your profit from interest alone comes to $4,160!

Don't forget: Interest is paid on the entire unpaid balance of the note—not on the discounted price you paid for it. In addition to the profit from the interest, you also own a security worth *$8,100 more* than the one you sold, and most likely, an interest in a much more valuable property.

Here's another way in which the surface appearance of a loss may really be a profit. We often wonder how many mortgagees have bothered to figure out if their income from interest is adversely affecting their tax obligation. This income is taxable in most cases, and if it's large enough, that mortgagee could be ending up in a higher bracket. Discounting and selling the note would not only eliminate the tax attributable to that income, but it might even lower the bracket. Unless the income, or future worth of the security, is enough to compensate for higher tax payments, it could actually be costing the investor money out of pocket just to hold on to the mortgage. Remember this and use it when you're trying to negotiate a higher discount than a seller is willing to give.

How Mortgages Can Be Purchased at Wholesale and Traded at Retail

You've already seen how an investor benefits from the purchase of a discounted mortgage by buying it at a "wholesale" price and then collecting interest on the part of the loan that was discounted. But there's another even more exciting benefit to be gleaned from a discounted purchase price—as long as the investor knows what to look for and seizes the opportunity when it arrives. What is this benefit? *A mortgage can often be traded at its full face value even though it was purchased at a discount.* How does this work? It's easy!

Let's go back to that $43,100 mortgage you bought for the discounted price of $28,000. You've now held it two years, and the borrower (the person who owes you the money) has been sending in the payments right on time, month after month. This, then, would be called a *seasoned* note as it has a good payment history.

In your constant search for good investments, you come across a small shopping center for sale in a growing community. The asking price is $450,000, and the seller is willing to take 10 percent down and to carry the balance on a long-term note.

As part of that down payment, you offer the seller your note at its full value of $43,100. The chances are that after verifying the present and future value of the apartment building, the amount of the equity securing it, and the good payment history of your note, the seller will be willing to accept your note at its full face amount of $43,100—even though you only paid $28,000 for it. All you have to come up with is another $1,900 to make up the balance of the 10 percent down payment, and you now own an interest in a property worth $450,000!

Take a moment to consider what's been accomplished in this transaction. You've just purchased an expensive, income-producing property using only 7 percent of your own money. This is an excellent example of the phenomenon known in the real estate business as *leverage*, a concept that is discussed in greater detail in the following chapter.

CONCLUSION

A discount is a price reduction on an item offered for sale, usually made in order to make the item more attractive to potential buyers. When the item is a mortgage, the discount acts as a fee charged by the investor as compensation for the willingness to wait to be paid.

Owner financing is one of the methods by which funds are raised for the purchase of real property. This is especially true in tight money markets when interest rates are very high. In those situations, especially, about the only way for most sellers of real estate to get their equity out of their property is to create mortgages between themselves and their buyers. Because the selling price is so much greater than that which was originally paid by the seller, the seller can afford to discount the mortgage and still end up with a huge profit.

The terms and conditions of any mortgage are completely negotiable between the involved parties. The duration of the note, interest rate, payback schedule, and many other clauses are not set by law, but by mutual agreement. Therefore, these clauses can be structured in any way that will meet the needs, goals, and abilities—both present and future—of the mortgagor and mortgagee.

As an investor, you must have a plan for the future. You have to check to see that these terms and conditions satisfy *your* needs and goals before deciding to invest in any particular mortgage. Establishing both a short- and long-range blueprint is the only way to assure success in building your investment portfolio.

Every time you buy a discounted mortgage, you're making two separate profits: first, the difference between the existing balance on the loan and what you actually paid for it; and second, the interest on that entire existing balance, rather than on the discounted price.

Sometimes it pays to sell a note at a discount or even at a loss. This is true in the case where you wish to purchase another note that will result in a higher net yield.

And finally, you can purchase a mortgage at a huge discount and then trade it at its full face value toward the purchase of another property. This operates to greatly increase your net worth while using little, if any, of your own personal funds.

3. Borrow Your Way To Wealth: Leveraging to Increase Investment Yield

EVERYDAY USES OF LEVERAGING

As promised, this chapter will expose those secrets about borrowing for profit that savings and loan associations, banks, insurance companies, and union pension plan administrators, as well as thousands of private investors, have all been capitalizing on for many years.

The simple truth is that when investing in discounted mortgages, it's through judicious borrowing that the biggest percentage of profit can be made.

Think back through the last three years. In your everyday personal living, have you purchased anything using the principle of leverage in order to buy it? You don't think so? We'll bet you're wrong.

If you're like the great majority of Americans, sometime during the past three years you've bought either a car, a television set, a refrigerator, a home, or something else *on the installment plan*. You paid a certain amount down, and someone else trusted you for the balance, which you paid off over a period of time. If so, you were using leverage.

Even though at first you owed the major portion of the purchase price, you were receiving the full benefits of the item, and those benefits were worth more to you than the finance charges you were paying.

Now, go back and read the last fourteen words again: ". . . those benefits were worth more to you than the finance charges you were paying." Because profit is certainly a benefit, we can translate this into terms that are applicable to mortgage investments:

Leverage is the use of borrowed capital for the purpose of increasing the profitability of the amount invested. The *percentage of leverage* is the mathematical relationship of the buyer's own funds to the total price.

The use of borrowed capital can be profitable as long as the asset financed by that borrowed capital brings a return that is greater (in either money or other benefits) than the borrower's overall cost of the capital. The smaller the amount of the borrower's own funds used, the higher the leverage, and naturally, the opposite also holds true. What might surprise you is the fact that the most sophisticated and successful investors always strive for as high a leverage position as they can possibly get. This chapter will explain why it works this way and how you can make it work for you.

Understanding Why So Many People Fear Debt

It's interesting how things have changed since our parents' or our grandparents' time, especially when it comes to using leverage. In those days the very thought of borrowing money in order to buy something was considered embarrassing. Going into debt was something that, if it became necessary, was done secretly and with the hope that friends wouldn't find out.

When they bought property subject to a mortgage, all their efforts were concentrated on paying off the mortgage as quickly as possible. They were obsessed with owning their property free and clear. This was prompted by the constant fear that, if hard times came along, they'd lose the property and everything they had put into it. It was so important to them that it wasn't unusual to hold gala celebrations during which they burned the mortgage on the day it was finally paid off.

Unless they were sophisticated investors or speculators (and most of them weren't), they possessed no knowledge of the advantages of continued financing, or borrowing on their equity, to increase the return on their investment. And, if some of them *were* aware of the profitability, they didn't make use of it as they were much too afraid of going deeper into debt.

How Large Institutions Put Debt to Work

For many years, banks, insurance companies, and unions have been making enormous fortunes. Everywhere you look, you see huge buildings being constructed. Who do you think owns most of them?

That's right—banks, insurance companies, and unions. Where do you think they got the money to build them? Right again—from you.

What do you think these institutions do with the money you put into bank accounts, insurance policies, or pension funds? They invest it for their own profit. The greatest percentage of these funds goes into real estate. Some of it goes into loans to property buyers, and some into the purchase of property itself. Much of it, however, is channeled into the buying, selling, and trading of discounted mortgages.

The profit from those investments is so great that these institutions can easily afford to build and own those high-rise buildings. Think about it. The interest they pay you on your accounts, the dividend they pay on your policies (including the final payoff itself), or even the pension they give you to live on when you retire is a tiny pittance when compared with the multibillion dollar fortunes they make—using your money. They're using leverage—other people's money—*your money!* You've been their lender for years; you just didn't realize it.

Serious private investors work the very same way, and they also have become titans of wealth. They were smart enough and had guts enough to build their empires by borrowing the working capital from others.

The Part Debt Plays in Leveraging

Will you be going into debt? Sure, you will! In fact, you'll find yourself going deeper and deeper into debt as you continue to build your fortune. But how many truly wealthy people do you know, or have you heard of, who became rich without going into debt? You've got to accept the fact that without your willingness to borrow, and to continue borrowing, you can't possibly make it. The best you can hope for is to live from day to day, while watching helplessly as inflation keeps eating away at what little you have.

Before you start to panic, remember what you've just learned. By following these suggestions, you'll be using other people's money to make the payments on your debts, just as if you bought an apartment building and used the rents to pay off your loan.

Leveraging Requires the Purchase of Income-Producing Mortgages

In Chapter 2, when we were discussing the flexibility of terms in any given mortgage, we mentioned a "straight note." As you will recall, this was the type of note that called for no payments until the entire loan was due. We don't believe in buying a note that has no steady income. You, however, for one reason or another, and from time to time, may elect to invest in this kind of mortgage. Fine—*but don't borrow on it!*

The idea is to have a steady income from one note and to use that income to cover the payments on a loan for the purchase of another note. Obviously, if you borrow on a note that doesn't bring you a monthly income, you're stuck with making the loan payments out of your own pocket.

Also make certain that the duration of your loan is at least as long as the duration of the mortgage you're borrowing against. This way, you won't have to pay off your loan to the lender until your mortgagor has to pay off that loan to you. Then, because the amount you borrowed was a percentage of the full face amount of the note and because you've now received the face amount in cash, you can use the balance to purchase another mortgage, which will be larger than the one that you just paid off.

When you get to the point where you're holding quite a few mortgages, you might decide to bunch three or four of them together and use them at their *combined* full face value as the down payment on income property, such as an apartment building, a shopping center, or anything else that appeals to you and fits in with the long-range plan you've set up for yourself.

USING OTHER PEOPLE'S MONEY: THE MOST COMMON SOURCE OF LEVERAGED FUNDS

It's truly amazing when we consider how so few people have made really big money using their own funds. Most big money makers got an idea and developed it to a point where they were able to get someone else to back it financially.

Nowhere is this truer than in the area of real estate investments. Those who have become millionaires in this field did so by using high leverage; that is, using other people's money. Thus, a basic goal of the knowledgeable investor is to finance the major portion of the purchase price. This not only permits control over a large amount of real estate with minimal personal investment, but it also provides the opportunity of paying back the loans with inflation-created cheaper dollars.

How a Mortgage Can Be Used As Collateral

Remember when you used to play Monopoly™? What did you do if you owned some property, had very little cash, and suddenly landed on another property you wanted to buy? Because the bank wouldn't loan you money without collateral, you mortgaged the property you already had. The mortgaged property became the security, the bank loaned you the funds, and when you had a new cash reserve, you paid the bank and took back the mortgaged property. In the meantime, you were collecting "rent" on the property you purchased with the borrowed funds, and that rent helped to build up the new cash reserve you used for the payment to the bank.

You do the same thing with discounted mortgages. When you've held one long enough for the note to become seasoned, you then use *it* as collateral by borrowing against it for the purpose of buying another discounted mortgage. Now you have *two* monthly payments coming in. The first will cover all, or most of your loan payments, while the second is a net profit. When the second note is also seasoned, you use *it* as security, borrowing once again to buy yet another discounted mortgage. You can keep this up indefinitely and still adhere to the basic rule of judicious leverage. This is because each time you borrow to make another investment, the return generated by the mortgage purchased with the borrowed funds is greater than the cost of those funds.

The mechanics are simple. You buy a mortgage at a *discounted price*, but the amount you borrow on it is a percentage of the *face amount*, which gives you more capital for your next purchase.

A simple example will show you how this works. Suppose you own a seasoned note with a face value of $7,500. You bought it at a 30 percent discount, paying $5,250 for it. By borrowing 80 percent of the face value, you have $6,000 with which to buy another mortgage for $8,500 at a 30 percent discount.

If the payback on the first note is 1 percent of the face amount, you're receiving $75 monthly. Even if you have to pay 15 percent interest to obtain the $6,000, those payments would also come to $75. Therefore, the income of your first note is covering your *cost* to buy the second, and the income from *that one* is a net return to you.

Additionally, you've now increased your real estate interests to $16,000, and your total cash out-of-pocket is still only $5,250! By continuing this procedure you're constantly investing in more expensive properties, receiving larger monthly incomes, thereby increasing your net worth. Your out-of-pocket cost? Still the original $5,250.

How to Begin With Little or No Capital

Up to now, we've been talking about purchasing additional discounted mortgages by borrowing on those that are already paying you an income. In other words, those mortgages you already own become the collateral, or security, for new loans. But what do you do when you're first getting started, before you have an income-producing mortgage to use as security? And what if you have very little cash—or none at all—that you can afford to use for your first purchase? What then?

Almost everyone owns something that has a cash value and could be used as collateral for a loan. It might be some possession lying in the attic for years, which you've either forgotten or never considered of any value. Or it could be an item that, because of its known value, is locked away in a safe deposit box. In either case, you're deriving no benefit from it. Find it and use it for the purpose of making money—lots of money.

Alternative Collateral Sources: A Case in Point

Sandy once had a client, whom we'll call Michael, who for years engaged in the hobby of collecting gold coins. Michael had purchased them, one by one, during a period when gold was selling at $35 to $48 an ounce. At about the time Sandy and Michael first met, Michael had approximately $800 invested in his collection, but he had very little cash. When the price of gold started its astronomical rise, he placed the collection in a safe deposit box at his bank. Now and then he'd go down and look at it. Sure, the collection was increasing in value but unless he decided to sell it, he was getting no direct benefit from the collection.

One night while Michael and his wife were having dinner at Sandy's home, the conversation turned to a particular mortgage of Sandy's that had been paid off that very morning, bringing in quite a large sum of money. Michael remarked, a bit sadly, that he would give anything if he, too, could invest in something that would bring him a decent return. But things hadn't gone well for him recently, and his available cash was practically nonexistent. Then a thought struck him. Why not sell the collection and use the proceeds for investment capital? Sandy suggested, instead, that he consider pledging the collection as collateral for a loan and using the proceeds to buy a few small discounted mortgages.

The first step was to find out what the coins were worth. By this time gold was selling at $250 an ounce. Michael had always used great care in selecting each coin, paying attention to its condition, availability, year, and place of minting. Because each coin was very special, it was worth more than its proverbial "weight in gold." Even so, he was stunned to learn that his collection was worth $25,000.

He obtained a loan of 80 percent of the collection's value. With the interest rate on the loan at 10 percent, the $20,000 he borrowed would cost him $2,000 a year.

Within three days, Sandy and Michael were able to find four well-secured mortgages with a combined face value of $35,000 that could be purchased for a total of $20,000. Each note had a payback of 1 percent of its face value per month, including interest of 10 percent, which meant that Michael would receive a monthly total income of $350, or $4,200 per year. As the cost of the loan was only $2,000 a year, he was making a net profit of $2,200.

Meanwhile gold continued going up in value. When it reached $350 per ounce, Sandy suggested that Michael borrow another $25,000. Again Michael invested in discounted mortgages, and again he showed huge profits on the money he was borrowing.

He repeated this procedure many times while gold kept rising in value. Therefore, his collection, which he had pledged as security *but still owned*, was also increasing in value. Each time he paid off a loan with the proceeds of a mortgage, he invested the balance in a larger investment. He also started investing a portion of his monthly income from his notes in additional mortgages, making even more profit. (This involved a technique known as *pyramiding*, which is explained later in this chapter.) Finally, he began grouping mortgages together, and by using them as cash at their full face value, started buying many commercial buildings on tax-deferred exchanges.

Sandy hasn't seen too much of Michael the past several years, as he's usually out of town. He now spends most of his time flying all over the country, buying hotels and hiring chains such as the Hilton and Sheraton to manage them for him. Needless to say, he now owns millions of dollars worth of prime property and is collecting a fortune in monthly income. All this started with an $800 investment. Perhaps even more importantly, *he still owns his coin collection!*

So what if you don't have gold or silver to use as security? You don't need them. You'd be surprised to learn how many different assets can be used. Real estate, stocks, bonds, insurance policies, and personal loans on cars or furniture are only a few of the possibilities. Accounts receivable are often used as security for loans. If you have good credit, a promissory note may provide you the funds you need to get started. If this isn't enough for the lender to gamble on, get a guarantor for your note and pay a small fee for the service.

LEARNING WHAT EQUITY IS

Almost everyone thinks they fully understand the meaning of the word *equity*. And yet, we've been surprised at the number of people who couldn't give a simple, clear-cut definition of the word. Because this book is concerned with the ownership of interests in real estate, and because equity is what ownership is all about, let's here and now eliminate any confusion regarding its meaning.

Equity is the amount, or percentage, of something you *own*, over and above any amount, or percentage, you may still *owe* on it.

How Leverage Affects Equity

Obviously, if equity is the portion owned, over and above the portion still owed, the more leverage (borrowed capital) you use, the less equity you have. As you make your payments on the loan, your debt decreases, and your equity rises proportionately. (At the moment, we're only talking about the ratio between the amount paid on the principal and the balance on the loan. We'll bring in the matter of appreciation in a moment.)

So far, this seems simple enough. You purchase a property for $85,000, paying $17,000 down and obtaining a loan for the $68,000 balance. If you didn't borrow that down payment under conditions creating an additional lien on the property, your $17,000 cash investment starts you off with an equity of 20 percent and a debt of 80 percent. As your payments are made, whatever amount goes to pay off the principal reduces the debt that much, automatically increasing your equity percentage-wise.

If you had paid the entire purchase price in cash from your own personal funds, that $85,000 investment would have given you a 100 percent equity in the property from the moment you became the legal owner.

Because leverage is the borrowing of other people's money with which to make the purchase, and because the greater the borrowed amount the smaller your equity, it would seem that the smaller the loan, the better your equity position. *Wrong*.

How Increasing the Leverage Results in Greater Profits

Believe it or not, the smaller the amount you invest of your own funds, the more profit you'll make and the faster your equity will increase. This is true unless you have no loan whatsoever, in which case you'll always have a 100 percent equity. But this is *not* a wise investment move.

Let's take that $85,000 property we were talking about. What if you *had* paid all cash for it? You now have a 100 percent equity in it and you feel great because you own it free and clear. A year passes; real estate values appreciate 20 percent and your property is now worth $102,000. Based on your $85,000 investment, you've made $17,000 profit, or a 20 percent return on that investment. This is calculated by dividing your profit ($17,000) by your investment ($85,000). Now, while a 20 percent return is not bad, the reality is that you can do better—much better.

What would happen if you paid down only $17,000 on the property and financed the rest, giving you a 20 percent equity? At the end of a year, the property has appreciated, the same 20 percent still being worth $102,000. But there's a difference—a *big* difference. Your monetary profit hasn't changed. It's still $17,000, but the *percentage of profit* has changed drastically. Now when you divide your profit ($17,000) by your investment ($17,000) you see that you've made a 100 percent return on that investment.

In other words, add the profit to the investment to see how much that investment is now worth in dollars. Divide the profit dollars by the investment dollars to get the percentage of return. Which would you rather see: your $85,000 appreciate in value to $102,000, or your $17,000 appreciate to $34,000?

We'll take it one final step. So far, we've been talking about the return on your original investment. Now let's see how this affects the rate of increase in your actual equity.

Take the same example. The property costs $85,000; you paid $17,000 down and have a 20 percent equity. The year passes during which the value has appreciated $17,000 and your original $17,000 is now worth $34,000, or double its original amount.

To find out how much equity you now have in the property, divide that $34,000 by the present $102,000 value of the property. You'll find that your 20 percent equity has increased to 33 percent.

One more year goes by and again the property appreciates 20 percent ($20,400) making it now worth $122,400. Add that $20,400 to the $34,000, which is the present worth of the $17,000 you originally paid, and that $17,000 is now worth $54,400. Divide this $54,400 by the current value of the property ($122,400) and you'll see that you now have a 44 percent equity. In other words, in just two years, your equity position has gone from 20 percent to 44 percent because you used leverage.

Because leverage means the use of other people's money, and high leverage means the use of *mostly* other people's money, we arrive at another of real estate's best kept secrets:

> *The less you invest of your own money and the more you borrow from someone else, the higher the return on your investment and the faster the increase of your equity.*

Remember, the word *investment* means the use of *your own money*, not borrowed money, and the phrase, *return on your investment*, means the profit you make on *your own money*, not on borrowed money. Therefore, when you buy a mortgage at a discounted price and are paid back the entire loan balance, plus the interest on that balance, you've increased the amount of profit as well as the percentage of equity in the property. The less of your own money used in that purchase, the faster that profit and equity will increase, and should you have to foreclose, that equity will be substantially greater than what you paid for it.

HOW TO DETERMINE THE RISK ELEMENT IN LEVERAGING

Yes, there are risks involved in any investment, whether you use your own capital or leverage, but this book is specifically designed to help you recognize and eliminate most of them.

What are your alternatives? Surely there must be ways of helping your money grow in a totally safe environment. What about a savings account, a Treasury bill (T-bill), an All Savers Certificate, or other risk-free, fund-growing accounts? They'll earn interest, and although you wouldn't make an enormous profit, you'd still end up with more than you put in without worrying about it because they're government protected. Right?

Wrong. Let's see what would really happen. You put $5,000 into a T-bill paying you 15 percent compounded interest per year for a two-year term. First of all, you have to pay out the full $5,000; you don't buy them at a discount. Also, your money would be tied up for the full two years unless you want to be hit with a heavy penalty for early withdrawal. By the end of the second year, you'll collect a little under $6,700, which means that you've made a total annual return of 17 percent on your investment. So far, that doesn't sound too bad as there was no risk involved.

How Inflation Affects Investment Strategy

But how about inflation? Everyone knows that inflation is constantly decreasing the value of the dollar, day by day. This means that
the purchasing power of that dollar is progressively less than what it
used to be.

What most people don't understand, however, is the relationship
between the purchasing power of the dollar and the actual price of an
item. If the dollar is worth 100 cents (the way it used to be), it will take
only one to buy something that has a value of 100 cents. But if the
dollar is worth less than 100 cents, then it will take *more* than one to
buy the item, which still has the same value of 100 cents. In other
words, the value of the item hasn't really changed; it just takes more
dollars to equal that value.

Inflation is an economic problem that has been confronted—in
one fashion or another—by every administration in memory. The
obvious goal has been to find an acceptable method of bringing the
inflation rate down, or failing that, to at least slow the rate of its
growth. Varying conditions and attempts have served to create wide
fluctuations in the growth of our rate of inflation, but one fact remains
constant—the dollar's purchasing power is gradually declining. During certain periods, that decline may be at a faster or a slower rate, but
overall, inflation remains with us, and as time goes by we may be sure
that it will take more and more dollars to equal the same value or cost
of an item.

Now, let's return to your $5,000 T-bill and see how inflation
might affect your return. We've shown a $1,700 profit, or a 17 percent
annual return on your investment. But is this really the true figure?

The dollars you'll get will be cheaper, more inflated dollars than
those you invested. Suppose the inflation rate were 10 percent during
the two-year term of investment. This would mean that the purchasing
power of the dollar dropped 20 percent during the two years your
money was tied up.

Deduct that 20 percent from your $1,700 "profit," and you'll find
that the money you finally receive will have an effective purchasing
power of only $1,360. Now, divide that $1,360 by your original
investment of $5,000 to see what the total return is. It comes to a little
under 28 percent for the two years, or only 14 percent per year. That's
quite different from the 17 percent annual return you *thought* you were
making.

It's obvious that inflation creates a direct relationship between the purchasing power of the dollar and the actual cost of living. Thus, it becomes axiomatic that, if we're to survive financially, we must amass as many dollars as possible, as quickly as possible. If an investor insists on keeping money in "safe" accounts, the luxury of that safety will slowly but surely move the investor toward a position where even the bare necessities of life can no longer be afforded. Not a very pleasant prospect, is it?

So, what's the answer? Is it worth the risk—this going ever deeper into debt in order to invest in real estate? Is it worth the risk to use leverage in order to buy, sell, and trade discounted mortgages secured by that real estate? When you finally realize that this is the best security in the world, you can't help but come to one conclusion: You bet it is!

Developing an Understanding of What Happens When the Real Estate Market Softens

Even if the real estate market were to soften, as it does periodically, your mortgage *income* won't be affected. As long as the mortgagor is reliable, your investment remains intact and secure. This is because the balance of the loan doesn't drop, even if the value of the property does. Also, history has shown that any loss of value in real estate is always temporary, and its worth never fails to bounce up to a level higher than before.

While a soft real estate market will have little or no effect upon your mortgage income, you should understand that such market conditions would likely result in a depreciation of real estate *values*, thereby decreasing (for a time, at least) your equity and percentage of profit. What's important to remember here is the *relative* security that your mortgage investments will always enjoy. The only way you can lose in the investment of discounted mortgages is by getting involved in poor risks based on unwise decisions. Our purpose here is to provide you with sufficient information to make that a virtual impossibility.

Three Steps to Minimizing Risk

Nothing is guaranteed when you're investing in the future, not even real estate. But there are many ways you can minimize that risk.

1. *Know the Market.* Never allow yourself to lose touch with the market. This will enable you to develop and maintain an acute sense of value, both as to the mortgage itself as well as the property securing it.

Let's face it. If you have no idea what a comparable mortgage can be purchased for, you can't make an intelligent decision regarding the price you should offer for it. And if you don't know how to compare the property's value with other comparable properties, how will you know if the security is worth the amount of the investment?

2. *Study the Mortgage and Note.* As previously mentioned, a mortgage and the note that accompanies it contain numerous provisions, terms, and clauses, the inclusion or omission of which may or may not be advantageous to you.

3. *Plan Your Work and Work Your Plan.* The fact that you've heard this a million and one times doesn't make it less important. You must have a short- and a long-range plan so you'll never lose sight of where you're going. As you build your investment portfolio, make certain that every transaction you become involved with becomes another step closer to achieving the success of those plans.

Take the Risk: How Investing in Mortgages Compares with Investing in T-Bills

Now, what if you used that same $5,000 that you put into a T-bill and invested in a mortgage that was well secured by real estate? What are the differences between the two, and which is more advantageous to you?

First of all, unlike a T-bill, you *can* buy a mortgage at a discount. Second, you wouldn't have to keep the note for the full two-year period. You could sell it, trade it, or even borrow against it thereby increasing your return even more, as discussed earlier in this chapter. As we also discussed earlier, you could even use it at its full face value for the purchase of other investments. But if you *did* decide to hold it for the full term, let's find out what your profit and percentage of return would be on that investment.

As you read through the following illustration, keep in mind that the figures are *deliberately* conservative. The purpose of doing this is to help you understand there is no mathematical sleight-of-hand at work here.

Your $5,000 will buy at least a $6,250 mortgage at a minimum 20 percent discount. Just to keep it equal in all respects, we'll say that the term is for the same two years as the T-bill. We'll make the interest rate a low 12 percent instead of the 15 percent paid in the above example. To complete the picture, the payback is a monthly payment of 1 percent of the face value, which comes to $62.50. Now, let's figure it out together.

By the end of the second year, you will have received (at $62.50 per month) a total of $1,500, all of which is pure interest. At maturity, you'd get a lump sum of the entire $6,250, which is $1,250 more than what you paid for the note in the first place. Therefore, your profit for the two years would come to $2,750. Now, divide this amount by the $5,000 you invested, and you'll have a return of 55 percent, or 27½ percent annual return.

The next step is to deduct the same 20 percent inflation factor from your profit of $2,750, which shows that you have received an effective purchasing power of $2,200. The last step is to divide that $2,200 by the $5,000 original investment figure. As you can see, you end up with an annual net return of 22 percent.

Which would *you* rather have: a 14 percent return or a 22 percent return for the same amount of investment and for the same period of time?

For those with the inclination to carry leveraging one step further, pyramiding can be an exciting adventure in investing.

PYRAMIDING: AN INVESTMENT SCHEME WITH AN UNDESERVED REPUTATION

It's been said that the word *pyramid*, as used in investment circles, comes from the ancient pyramids that have stood the test of time as being among the most durable structures known to man. During the past decade, however, investment pyramiding has received considerable "bad press" and has been labeled as highly speculative and somewhat dangerous. But for those who invest in discounted mortgages, pyramiding has been found to be much safer than the nefarious schemes and exotic financing that have given it such a poor rating.

In this chapter we will look at the ways pyramiding has been applied to investments in discounted mortgages to accelerate and amplify investment dollars. We will demonstrate three different financial concepts essential to an understanding and appreciation of the pyramiding process—compounding, credit buying, and early paybacks. And 22 step-by-step building blocks gleaned from hundreds of investment experiences will be set out for you.

Learning What Pyramiding Is

Simply applied to discounted mortgages, pyramiding consists of financing additional investments by using existing equity as collateral and by reinvesting monthly mortgage income. This allows an investor to acquire real property with little or no capital outlay and retain ownership of the original property. As you may recall from the earlier part of this chapter, you start with a base—capital. You invest it, you nurture it, and when it is ready, you take the appreciated value and borrow against the initial investment. Now, in order to pyramid, you add to this leveraged capital the monthly mortgage payments you have accumulated and purchase another mortgage of greater value. When you use leverage with pyramiding in this fashion, each investment grows faster than the cost of borrowing.

How to Determine the Risks Involved

Admittedly, pyramiding is not for the faint-hearted. There is no investment plan that requires greater confidence in one's abilities than is experienced in pyramiding. However, when the dynamics are thoroughly understood and appreciated and the investor has had a little exposure to the mathematics of real estate financing, then prudent investments in a pyramiding plan can reap sometimes phenomenal results.

Pyramiding under these circumstances can be an extraordinary investment technique in good and in bad times. It is best achieved in a high-growth economy, but a declining economy will also enhance and multiply your chances for growth. In "tight" money circumstances you can be more selective and discriminating as there are a greater variety of mortgages offered. (If you have forgotten why this is so, you should reread the section on leveraging—found earlier in this chapter—as the same principle is at work here.)

It is most important to remember that your pyramid at all times will be based upon prudent and careful investments in real property. The most that you stand to lose is the amount that you have invested.

How Pyramiding Differs From Leveraging

Exactly how does pyramiding differ from leveraging? It doesn't, really. Pyramiding is a form of high leverage—you might say it is *leverage upon leverage*. It means you take the income from one leveraged mortgage and reinvest it again at high leverage, selling it soon and reinvesting it at still higher leverage. The object is to turn over the growing equity and income as quickly as possible and at the highest possible income rates.

How Pyramiding Works: A Simple Example

The easiest way to explain how pyramiding can work is by the use of a simplified example. Let's assume that at the start of Year One you invest $5,000 in a mortgage (Mortgage A) carrying a face value of $7,500. The note is for 18 months, the monthly payments are set at 2 percent (or $150), and the interest rate is 12 percent. At the end of Year One, then, you would have accumulated $1,800 for twelve monthly payments of $150 each. Now, if at the start of Year Two, you were to borrow $3,200 from the bank at 15 percent using your equity in Mortgage One as collateral and add to that sum your first year's accumulated earnings of $1,800, you would have a total of $5,000 to invest.

Assume that you learn of a second mortgage (Mortgage B) involved in a probate where the estate is desirous of liquidating that asset. The face amount of the note is $7,500, and the note carries monthly payments also of $150 with interest set at 12 percent. Most significantly, this note falls due in six months. Midway through Year Two both notes, thus, become due. Here is an accounting of your proceeds at the end of the 18th month:

$ 900	Six months' income from Mortgage A
900	Six months' income from Mortgage B
4,800	Principal balance due on Mortgage A
6,600	Principal balance due on Mortgage B
1,350	Eighteen months' interest on Mortgage A
450	Six months' interest on Mortgage B
$13,200	Total Income
$ 3,200	Bank loan repayment
240	Interest paid to bank (6 months at 15%)
3,440	Total Expenses
$13,200	Total Income
3,440	Total Expenses
$ 9,760	Net Profit

The Three Conceptual Bases of Pyramiding

This very simplified example demonstrates several things. First, it shows how a $5,000 investment can pyramid in a relatively short time to very nearly double that amount. Second, it illustrates three important concepts that play an integral part in any pyramiding plan. These three concepts are compounding, installment buying, and early pay-backs. Although each of these concepts will be explained in more detail in later chapters, their application to pyramiding is slightly different and extremely important.

1. *Compounding*. The concept of compounding will be discussed later in Chapter 11 on yields, but the principle involved is equally applicable to pyramiding. Here, we want to consider compounding in terms of the effect that it has on a pyramid plan with respect to time and yield.

For example, if you were to invest $10,000 at 12 percent, how long do you think it would take to earn the equivalent of your original investment? How long do you think it would take to double it? The table below will demonstrate the importance of timing to a pyramiding investment plan. As you can see, the chart illustrates the approximate lengths of time it takes to equal and to double an original investment at varying levels of interest return (yield) when compounded annually.

Yield	Approx. Years to Equal Original Money	Approx. Years to Double Original Money If Compounded
10%	10.0	7.2
12%	8.3	6.0
15%	6.6	4.8
18%	5.5	4.0
20%	5.0	3.6

Table 3.1

Carefully consider the meaning of these figures. If you purchase a 15 percent second mortgage and spend the income from that invest-ment as you receive it, it would take almost seven years for you to earn the equivalent of your original investment. But if you reinvest your earnings as you receive them, you would double your money in less than five years!

The chart also demonstrates the dramatic results that are possible when your money is reinvested at higher and higher yields. Obviously, the time required to double your original investment decreases as the yield increases. Thus, when all of your mortgage income is kept in circulation by continuous reinvestment at progressively higher yields, your investments will enjoy the fruits of this compounding effect.

2. *Installment Buying*. Does installment buying ever pay? Can borrowing money in order to purchase additional mortgages result in a

net profit? The answers to these questions are emphatically, "Yes!"
Serious investors are aware of this simple rule: The less of your own
money that is invested in a particular property, the higher your yield.
For the mathematical explanation of this rule, simply consider the two
illustrations that follow.

In order to illustrate this point, let's look again at the hypothetical
investments set out at the beginning of this chapter. You will recall that
Mortgage A had a face value of $7,500, cost $5,000, and bore interest
at 12 percent. Its term was for eighteen months, and the monthly
payments were set at $150. At the end of Year One, the investor had
accumulated $1,800, which represented twelve monthly payments at
$150 each.

Let's assume our hypothetical investor took these accumulated
earnings and invested them in a 15 percent bank savings account. Six
months later, our investor would have earned $135 in interest, and the
yield on the investment would have been almost 13½ percent.

If, instead, our investor had added to the $1,800 accumulated
earnings $3,200 borrowed at 15 percent, as outlined at the start of this
chapter, consider the different result. By investing $5,000 in Mortgage
B ($7,500 note with monthly payments of $150 and interest at 12
percent) instead of only $1,800, on this investment alone our investor
would have earned the following:

$7,500	Principal (face amount of Mortgage B)
450	Interest (on remaining six months)
7,950	Total Income
1,800	Original investment
240	Bank interest
3,200	Bank loan
5,240	Total Expenses
7,950	Total Income
5,240	Total Expenses
$2,710	Net Profit

The yield on this investment was *150 percent*. Obviously, it
behooved our hypothetical investor to spend $240 in interest in order
to earn a net profit of $2,710. The point to be understood here is that
cases do arise when borrowing money to take advantage of an outstanding investment opportunity can be advantageous and profitable. When
interest rates are generally low, and you can borrow money at a rate
that is less than you can earn, you will obviously be on the road to

wealth. The investor who can borrow at 10 percent and earn at 12 percent will probably retire very early indeed.

But investments that are funded with money borrowed at a higher rate than is earned will *only* be profitable when the loans are of short duration. In this example our investor was borrowing money at an interest rate of 15 percent and earning money at 12 percent, yet a profit was possible. This anomaly was the result of the early paybacks involved in the facts. The advantages of early paybacks are our next subject.

3. *Early Paybacks.* In Chapter 11 on yields, you will be shown how early paybacks operate to increase yield. By now, you should be aware that reinvesting your mortgage income and leveraged funds at increasingly higher and higher yields is one of the bases of a successful pyramiding plan. Let's briefly review, then, the early payback principles that will enhance your likelihood of success in pyramiding.

Basically, a loan can be repaid in any number of different ways. To promote a pyramiding plan, however, you will want to utilize payments that are fully amortized or that have a high payback. The rationale for this is that you will have more money back earlier to reinvest.

Some of the different payback methods are compared in Table 3.2 below. To illustrate the payback principle, assume you have just purchased a $10,000 second mortgage for $8,000. The note is for a term of two years. Compare the varying amounts you would have at the end of the first year depending upon how the payback is structured.

COMPARISON OF PAYBACK METHODS ON $10,000 MORTGAGE

Method	Money Collected During Year One
2% monthly	$2400
1% monthly	1200
Fully amortized	5649
Interest only	1200

Table 3.2

Between the choices of fully amortized and interest-only payback methods, the former is more advantageous to a pyramiding plan. This is because you have a larger amount to reinvest at an earlier time. The interest-only loan earns more interest in the long run because the interest is always computed on a current balance. When a loan is amortized, the balance is progressively declining thereby reducing the total interest. This monetary difference is compensated for in the amortization scheme by the time factor—a lender with an amortized loan gets money returned at a faster rate to reinvest. In the long run, the returns are about equal. You can also see from Table 3.2 the advantages of structuring a loan with a fixed percentage payback at the highest percentage possible.

One last word with respect to early paybacks. The pyramiding effect will be greatly amplified whenever loans are paid off early in full. Numerous incentives may be offered to mortgagors to encourage early payoff, such as waiving all or part of any prepayment penalty. Utilizing these inducements, our experience has been that one-year notes will usually pay off in 10 months, two-year notes in 19 months, and three-year notes in 30 months. When the property is sold, you will usually receive immediate, full payment plus penalty payoffs. Also, you should take note of the fact that the older the primary financing, usually the sooner it will pay off; this is because a larger equity build-up often facilitates refinancing. Finally, if a note is not fully paid off on the due date, the investor can renegotiate a new loan on whatever terms she or he specifies.

TWENTY-TWO BUILDING BLOCKS FOR PYRAMIDING SUCCESS

For many years now we have been personally involved, either for ourselves or for clients, in literally hundreds and hundreds of mortgage investments. From that background of experience, a number of selected suggestions have been collected for clients. Let us share some of these ideas with you now at the commencement of your pyramiding plan. This list is a compilation of ideas that are expanded upon throughout this book.

1. Plan your goal at the time of your initial structuring.

2. Weigh the risks carefully.

3. Consider your equity and evaluate it carefully.

4. Look for investments with little or nothing down and with substituted equities.

5. Sell your equity at a profit.

6. Where there is a substantial profit, take it if it can be replaced with a property of higher quality or greater security.

7. Use newly borrowed or obtained funds to purchase more mortgages by refinancing your investments.

8. Seek more secure investments by selling or trading to properties of higher value or quality while you continuously seek a greater return.

9. Tolerate no time lag in turning over your income. Money being accumulated from mortgage income should at the very least be invested in interest-bearing bank accounts until a sufficient amount is collected to purchase an additional mortgage.

10. Use a tax specialist when you trade up real estate for like investments and your capital gain taxes are being deferred.

11. Figure the rate of your return, both as to cash flow and percent of profit per year.

12. Structure the deal carefully and consider the various types of financing available.

13. Don't be hesitant or timid when you are ready to make your offer.

14. Consider a tax-deferred exchange if applicable.

15. Use your assets in a new investment and new income to find another investment.

16. Have your agreement ready and organized with photographs, charts, appraisals, financing, and commitments. Be ready to present your proposal so that you can make a quick deal and reinvest.

17. Diversify your investments.

18. Use the information on planning to increase your investment opportunities.

19. Consider using syndication to obtain an interest in a venture and for finding and financing new deals.

20. Consider earning and charging a management fee in your various investment transactions.

21. Consider the many ways to pyramid through use of governmental funds.

22. Consider obtaining governmental properties with little or nothing down.

CONCLUSION

Understanding leveraging is the first stepping stone to an appreciation of the possibilities of creative financing. Once you have mastered this background information and become adept at these financing fundamentals, you will want to read very carefully the final chapters in this book that explain the more sophisticated and creative possibilities in yields and selling.

Leverage is the use of other people's money that enables you to control large amounts of real estate while investing as little of your own capital as possible. This works to increase the yield on your investments. It can be accomplished as long as the return obtained from the use of the borrowed funds exceeds the cost of the loan. The return can be any kind of benefit, not necessarily money.

You actually make an extra profit when you finance a purchase rather than paying all cash. Because inflation is constantly decreasing the power of the dollar, the loan you make today will bring you dollars that can be used at their current value, but you'll be paying the loan back with dollars that are worth less than those you received.

A discounted mortgage earns not only a return on its own, but it can earn an additional return when it's used as security for a loan for the purpose of buying another mortgage. This further increases the total yield to the investor without necessitating any additional investor dollars. The monthly income from the collateralized note pays off the loan against it, and the income from the new note becomes net profit.

Almost anything can be used as security for the purpose of obtaining loans. *You don't need cash.* Coin and stamp collections, furniture, real estate, stocks and bonds, insurance policies, accounts receivable—these and almost anything else you own with a monetary value can be used as collateral. They can all make money for you if you put them to work.

Equity is the amount or percentage of something you own over and above any amount or percentage you still owe on it. Even so, when you talk about a commodity that appreciates in value, the less you use of your own money and the more you use of someone else's, the greater your profit and yield and the faster your equity will increase. This is especially true in real estate because profit, yield, and equity are based on the amount you actually pay out-of-pocket, rather than on the amount you borrow. As the property appreciates, the difference between its new value and the amount owed on it increases, giving you a higher percentage of equity.

In this chapter we have also taken a look at the investment phenomenon that is known as pyramiding, and we have shown how this phenomenon can be advantageously applied to investments in discounted mortgages.

Three of the most important elements in successful pyramiding —compounding, installment or credit financing, and early paybacks —were explained and illustrated in considerable detail. Finally, numerous down-to-earth suggestions and building blocks drawn from personal experiences with hundreds of investments were set out in order to assist you in your own successful pyramiding plan.

For many years, banks, insurance companies, and unions have been borrowing money from you, paying practically nothing for the privilege of using it while they've made billions of dollars investing it for their own account. Now it's time for you to turn the tables by using their methods to make that profit for yourself and your family.

Investing in discounted mortgages is a business, the bottom line of which is profit, whether in money or other benefits. Therefore, it's essential that you carefully judge those factors that determine how much value others will place on the property and mortgage, rather than allowing yourself to be influenced solely by your own personal taste and preference.

Ideas regarding borrowing have changed drastically during this century. Today, if you're afraid of going into debt you don't stand a chance against inflation. So-called "safe" accounts don't make you money; they *cost* you money because they don't pay you enough to make up for the amount inflation takes away each day. If you believe this and act on it before it's too late, you can beat inflation and insure your future.

4. Getting Started: Prepurchase Considerations Every Mortgage Investor Must Know

UNDERSTANDING THE GOOD TIMES AND BAD TIMES FOR MORTGAGE INVESTING

Picture a high school student trying to fight her way through geometry without first understanding simple concepts of elementary math. Picture an architect trying to sell his ideas for a new multistory office building when the diagrams and blueprints prove that he has no conception of design, material stress, or the needs of the future occupants.

Picture you, attempting to become a millionaire by investing in discounted mortgages before obtaining a working knowledge of real estate, mortgages, and leverage. That's what the beginning of this book was all about. Without it, you'd have found it difficult—if not impossible—to utilize the rest of the material to your greatest advantage.

Now, we get to the reason why you bought this book in the first place. Here's where we begin to explain in minute detail the actual steps toward making your dreams become a reality.

The purpose of this chapter is to answer your most immediate questions such as how to begin, when to invest, what to start with, where to find it, how much money is needed, which terms in the note you should look at first, and how to project the image of a serious investor in order to attract more potentially lucrative opportunities.

Later chapters will build on this foundation by taking you on a

45

hypothetical shopping trip where you'll contact your first mortgage sellers, examine all the various mortgage clause options, and become familiar with the effect on profit caused by the terms of the mortgage you're interested in. You'll learn how to judge, not only the value of the property securing the mortgage, but also the credit and personal stability of the borrowers. And you'll also see how to calculate exactly what discounted price will net you the yield you want to make. For the moment, however, let's turn our attention to more immediate issues.

The Role of Timing in Mortgage Investing

About six months ago we conducted a series of discounted mortgage investing classes at one of our local universities. One evening during a coffee break a young lady came up and said that she had about $4,000 to invest. She wanted an opinion as to how long she'd have to wait until the time would be right for her to start looking for a good note to purchase. We can still see the look on her face when we suggested that, since it was already 10:30 PM, perhaps she should wait until the following morning.

We already knew that she shared a popular misconception with many others; namely, that there are good and bad times for mortgage investing. Let us tell you something that will no doubt surprise you as much as it did that young lady: Nothing could be further from the truth. *There are no bad times to invest in discounted mortgages.*

Stocks, commodities, and other speculative investments are constantly subject to changes in local and world conditions, politics, business cycles, and many other factors. Periods of inflation, over-evaluation, and recession create excessive fluctuations, sometimes drastically changing the values of these investments overnight.

Trading in discounted mortgages is an investment in real estate, and that's an entirely different ballgame. Since the 1930s, property values have gone steadily upward, not only keeping pace with, but far exceeding, the rise of inflation. While it's true that the *sale* of real estate has been affected by economic conditions, the inherent *value* of real estate, even though it may fall slightly and temporarily, has always bounced back to a level higher than before.

Barring unforeseen and catastrophic developments, this is unlikely to ever change. Once again, we're faced with the law of supply and demand. People will always want to own property, and there's only so much available that they can buy. This being the case, sales will continue to take place and values will continue to rise. Because an investment in a mortgage is made *after* the sale has been consummated, it isn't nearly as vulnerable to external forces as are other, more speculative, ventures.

We said above that "good" and "bad" economic times have no effect on the "right" time to invest in discounted mortgages. Let's see why.

The Need for Mortgage Financing in "Good" Times

During periods of a healthy, thriving economy there is tremendous construction activity. Single-family homes, multiple dwellings, commercial, and industrial complexes of all kinds are occupied as fast as they're completed—sometimes even before. This gigantic volume of sales results in a vast number of mortgages, created to provide senior and secondary financing. Those lenders who want to cash out and invest elsewhere (because it *is* a "good" time) are most anxious to sell these notes—usually at a substantial discount.

The Need for Mortgage Financing in "Bad" Times

Surprisingly, when the economy is slow, there is an even *greater* need for secondary financing because of the tight money supply. These mortgages are immediately available for purchase—also at a substantial discount.

In addition, another source of supply suddenly appears on the market for the benefit of the serious investor. Many people take back mortgages, content with the profit they'll make on the interest until the note matures and becomes due. Over a period of months these notes become seasoned. Now what happens when the economy has a change for the worse, perhaps even resulting in a loss of the mortgagee's employment? Bills have to be paid and money is needed immediately. The small monthly income isn't nearly enough to live on. There develops a desperate need to sell—again, at a *very* substantial discount.

Let's get back to that young lady who attended class that evening. She decided to take our advice. Within four days her $4,000 bought a $6,000 note with 13 percent interest and payments of $65 per month. If she does nothing else but keep it for its two-year term, she will have received a net profit of $3,560, which comes to an 89 percent yield for the two years. Even accounting for a 20 percent loss due to inflation, she would still come out with a 36 percent annual yield on her investment. Try doing *that* with any other investment.

See what we mean? *Any* time is the right time.

HOW THINKING RICH CAN INCREASE YOUR PROFITS

The first thing you have to do, before anything else, is to make a major decision. What are you really after? Do you want to be rich? If so, are you ready to embark upon a program designed to move you constantly closer to becoming truly wealthy? Or do you want to play it safe by investing in one mortgage at a time, collecting your monthly income, and depositing the final payment in the bank before buying another one?

Take a moment to think about this statement: You can't possibly *become rich* without training yourself to *think rich.* And if being rich is your ultimate goal, you should start your investment folio, not with one large mortgage, but with three, four, or even five smaller ones.

Take it easy and don't look so startled. There are logical reasons for this, and we assure you the additional purchases won't cost you a penny more than the original amount you had in mind.

First of all, why have only one monthly check coming in when (for the same price) you can have several? This makes good sense, especially when you realize that it safeguards your income.

Consider the following: You are now the mortgagee on a note that pays you a monthly income of $160. For several months the payments are made on time until one day your mortgagor calls to say that he has a small problem and would appreciate your allowing him to skip this month and send you two payments the following month to make up for it. Since he's never given you any trouble, and because you're a nice guy, you can't turn him down. The trouble is, you have nothing coming in that month.

What if you were holding four notes instead of only one, with an average monthly payback of $40 each? But in this case, at least you'd get $120 from the other three! Isn't it better to get 75 percent of what you counted on rather than nothing?

Let's examine another aspect of it. Mortgage investing is interesting and exciting, as well as being profitable. The activity of the investor can be absolutely exhilarating! Each situation is totally different—the people, the property, the potential, and the method of attaining that potential. You'll be learning something new with every involvement. Each time you add more knowledge to what you already have, you become a better investor with a sharper insight than before. This results in greater and faster profits.

On the other hand, if you hold only one note at a time, you'll have very little to do and you'll learn very slowly. Not only will it be boring, just sitting around waiting for the check to come in, it will also bring your journey toward wealth to an agonizing crawl.

WHY YOU SHOULD BEGIN WITH SEVERAL
SMALL SECOND MORTGAGES ON SINGLE-FAMILY RESIDENCES

For your first investments look for three, four, or five very small second mortgages on single-family residences (either homes or condominiums).

Although there are good reasons why you'll be picking up third, fourth, and even fifth mortgages in the future, now is not the time. When you're just beginning, you're not yet ready for the complexities of lower-priority notes. They have their place and can be extremely profitable, but you have to know what you're doing in order to protect your interests. Later, we'll show you how to profit on these, but for now, the most simple road is also the best and safest road.

The reason for single-family residences is the same as for second mortgages. They're easier to manage and to understand. Each one is a relatively small piece of property that you can keep your eye on without any difficulty. The mortgagor usually lives in the residence, so you don't have to be concerned with determining who's responsible for its maintenance. Perhaps most important of all, there aren't any complex financial details for you to become submerged in as you'll find in commercial enterprises.

You'll have plenty of time to learn about and get involved in more advanced investments as you gain experience. For the present, however, let's keep it nice and simple as you feel your way along.

HOW TO DETERMINE THE LENGTH OF TIME TO LOCATE
AVAILABLE MORTGAGES

We hope you're not under the impression that all of these recommended mortgages have to be located and purchased in one day or even in one week. This would be impossible while you're still learning. Take your time. Plan on spending an average of two hours each Saturday and Sunday for a month or so. It won't take you very long to realize that it's surprisingly simple to find one good note each weekend.

HOW TO DECIDE THE AMOUNT OF MONEY NEEDED TO GET STARTED

How much money is needed to start off with? That's the big question, isn't it? The old saying, "If you have to ask how much it costs, you probably can't afford it," doesn't apply here. If you bought this book, you have enough. No kidding. Unless you're reading this out of idle curiosity, you have access to sufficient funds to take your first step, because it doesn't take all that much.

As little as three thousand dollars can buy you a mortgage.

As we said before, one mortgage isn't the best way to begin, but it *is* a beginning and it *will* make a profit for you. When you're able to put together additional money, you can buy another. It's the slow way to go, but it's better than nothing. Of course, it goes without saying that the more you can start with, the faster you'll increase your holdings.

Let's say that you have a total of $15,000 to invest. Hopefully, you will have obtained most of this amount through any of the leverage methods that have already been described. Even if we were to assume that the average discount came to only 25 percent, you'll be able to start with several mortgages with a combined face value of at least $20,000. (And we assure you, it can be better than that.)

From the moment you purchased them, you've already made $5,000 on your investment, and you haven't been paid one cent of interest yet! Add to that an average of 13 percent interest over three years, and you end up with $12,800 profit! Even when you account for inflation, you have still netted a minimum of 23 percent annual return.

MORTGAGE CLAUSES VARY IN IMPORTANCE

There are many terms and provisions that may (or may not) be in any given mortgage. Of these, quite a few have a direct effect on the potential return of your investment. The inclusion or omission of any one of them could be—and often is—the reason why an investor may decide to buy a particular note.

In Chapter 5, when you're on your first shopping trip, you'll have the opportunity of becoming familiar with all the most prevalent mortgage clauses. At this point, however, you want to focus in on the three most essential ones—those you look at first.

There's a two-fold reason why we're bringing these up now. First, if these three terms don't fill your present need or fit in with your future plan, you won't bother with checking the rest of the terms or viewing the property. Instead, you'll usually decide then and there not to invest in that mortgage. Second, it's of vital importance for beginners to keep these three terms uppermost in their minds at all times. This is because these terms determine whether or not a particular acquisition will really net you a profit.

Understanding the "PIDD" Rule

The three most important mortgage instrument clauses for you to know about are the payback schedule, interest rate, and due date. We call it the "PIDD" Rule, where:

$$P \quad = \quad \text{Payback Schedule}$$
$$I \quad = \quad \text{Interest Rate}$$
$$DD \quad = \quad \text{Due Date}$$

Let's consider each of these variables in detail so that you can more readily understand their individual impact upon potential profit.

1. *Payback Schedule.* Each note you buy (especially at the start) must have a definite payback schedule, assuring you of an immediate and steady monthly income. It can be an amortized schedule of payments, consisting of interest plus a small amount on the principal, or it could be interest-only payments. Although the latter is preferable to you as the investor, either way will suffice.

Not only will you be assured of an immediate and ongoing return from your investment, but you'll also discover that the note will be much more attractive to someone else should you wish to sell it, trade it for another note or property, or pledge it as collateral for a loan.

2. *Interest Rate.* The interest rate on the note is another important fact to consider. Together with the discounted price, these two variables play the biggest role in determining whether or not your final profit (or yield) will be greater than that amount lost because of inflation.

To demonstrate, let's assume that the current inflation is devaluating the purchase power of the dollar at a rate of 10 percent each year. You agree to make a $2,000 loan to a very close friend. Because you've practically grown up together, you're too embarrassed to ask for interest, so you don't charge any. The loan is due and payable in two years. By the time your friend pays you back, you've lost 20 percent of your purchasing power. The $2,000 she pays you back two years later is now worth only $1,600! Had the loan included 10 percent annual interest, you would have done no better than to break even.

Therefore, the interest rate on the note you buy, combined with the amount you saved by getting it at a discounted price, must bring you a return on your investment that is greater than your loss caused by inflation and your costs resulting from leveraging. Otherwise, you will find yourself with more dollars than before but they won't buy nearly as much as the dollars you originally had before making the investment.

To safeguard against this possibility, be cognizant of the current and projected inflation rates, not only at the time of the investment but also during the holding period until the note becomes due. As long as the interest rate is practically equal to, or not more than, the current and projected inflation rates, you will be in a good position to realize a profit.

3. *Due Date.* The due date obviously refers to the date the face amount of the loan becomes due and payable. The durations of your first mortgages should be no longer than a maximum of five years, preferably three years or less. When you're first starting out, you'll be better off looking for short-term, rather than long-term investments. It won't be beneficial for you to tie your funds up too long in one venture. Knowledgeable investors try to keep their money constantly moving, constantly working. Fast turnovers result in fast profits.

Another advantage to you at this time will be the purchase of notes with varying durations, rather than all coming due at the same time. Your goal should be as close as possible to the following formula: one note for four years, a second for three, a third for two, and one more coming due in one year. If you can achieve this, you'll have large sums of money coming in at different times, enabling you to continue reinvesting your profits on a steady basis. This is the way to keep your money working for you.

HOW TO LOCATE AVAILABLE MORTGAGES

Now that you know what to look for, where do you find it? Fortunately, this is the easiest part of all. Mortgages available for purchase at a discounted price are all around you.

We'll never forget a phone call we received about a year ago from a novice who was anxious to start an investment program. His problem was that he had no idea where to start looking or who to contact. When we volunteered to give him several suggestions, he got some paper so that he could write them down. We were still going strong when, after about a half-hour, he interrupted, saying that it would take him forever to act on only half of what he had already written.

The sources for locating and buying good discounted mortgages are so unbelievably numerous that you could spend eight hours a day, seven days a week for a solid year, and still come nowhere near contacting all the potentials in your own area. No matter where you live, as long as there is real estate, you'll find mortgages for sale.

The following list includes only a few of the unlimited potentials available to you. Admittedly, some of them will be easier to contact than others, depending upon how much time and effort you want to spend. However, all of them are accessible, within or very close to your own local community. To approach these sources, all you have to know is the face amount (or balance) of the note you want to invest in, the approximate yield you're looking for, and the type of property you want as security. For the present, remember, we are considering only single-family residences.

You'll see that in many cases your source will be a personal one. You'll have the opportunity to build up a working relationship with that person, and that relationship can easily lead to future referrals and investment transactions.

A Checklist of Sources and Contacts

1. Your local newspaper is by far the easiest source of available mortgages. Almost every classified and business section contains ads placed by lenders (either private parties or companies) who want to sell their notes. You can also place your own small ad in these sections, specifying the price and type of mortgage you're interested in buying. Even if the responses you get aren't what you're looking for at present, you'll be amazed at how many contacts you'll make for the future.

2. Financially oriented publications, such as the *Wall Street Journal*, as well as legal and real estate papers (available at metropolitan newsstands), contain "Mortgages For Sale" and "Mortgages To Buy" columns.

3. Contact your local real estate brokers and their agents. After all, their daily business is the selling of property. Most real estate sales require the creation of a mortgage between seller and buyer. The great majority of these sellers, being anxious to cash out as soon as possible, are happy to sell the note at a good discount.

After all, who is more aware of mortgages *about to become*

available than the professional agents who are putting these transactions together. In fact, quite often they'll take back a mortgage on the property themselves as part or as all of their commission, just to help the sale go through. In most cases, they're more than willing to sell the paper at a discount because practically all real estate agents work strictly on commission and would rather give up 25 to 30 percent of that commission than make nothing at all.

Ask these brokers and agents to keep your name and phone number for the future. Also request that they post it on their bulletin board (every real estate office has one) offering a 10 to 15 percent finder's fee to anyone who is instrumental in referring you to a mortgage that you buy. You'll get action—*fast*.

4. Most commercial banks and savings and loan associations have real estate departments where they keep and service mortgages they own, plus real estate trust departments where they cash out for the estates they handle. Contact them all. Speak to the managers of these departments explaining what you're looking for. Each one will probably offer you a choice of five at the very least. Because their job is to keep the bank's money moving from one investment to another, they're glad to talk with prospective purchasers.

5. Loan and finance companies constantly loan money on mortgages. Many of them look for an investor to sell the note to, even before they take it. By charging a small percentage to the seller and servicing the loan when requested, they turn their money over as quickly as possible, making a small profit on each transaction. Build up a personal rapport with the officers of these companies, and you will have gained yourself a treasure chest for the future.

6. Somewhere in your area there are title companies that have complete lists of every real estate transaction made. The information comes from the County Recorder's office, and the lists contain the date of sale, names and addresses of the seller and buyer, address of the property, sales price, down payment, and all mortgages involved.

Do you realize that a list from this source alone would give you hundreds of sellers who have taken back paper, each of whom could be contacted by phone or letter?

7. If you live in an area where escrow companies are used, talk to all the escrow officers in each company. Each officer handles his or her own escrow, doing all the paperwork until the title is recorded in the name of the new owner. As in the case of real estate brokers and agents, escrow officers know *up front* what mortgages either are, or soon will become, available, plus all the terms of those mortgages.

A great many mortgages are actually sold while the primary sale is still in escrow, and if you build up and maintain a good working relationship with these professionals, you can have your pick of the best before any other investor even gets wind of it.

8. If escrow companies aren't used in your area, find out which attorneys specialize in real estate transactions. They can not only provide you with the same information as the escrow officers, but also are usually looking for investors to buy those notes their clients want to sell.

9. Talk to friends and neighbors who have sold or who are in the process of selling their home. See if they've taken back a mortgage, or if they will, in order to make the sale. In either case, let them know that if they want to sell it for immediate cash, you might be interested in buying it.

10. Get into the habit of reading the bulletin boards at your local supermarket. People who live in the area are always placing notices on them, not all of which are limited to apartments for rent, puppies for sale, or baby-sitting jobs.

Put your own notice up, letting your neighbors know that you're looking for mortgages to buy. Placed in the right spot, such a notice will keep your phone ringing.

11. Check for pending foreclosure and bankruptcy sales by contacting credit, finance, and mortgage companies, by reading those lists that are always posted in courthouses, and by finding them when they're published in legal journals. The holders of these mortgages would much rather sell the paper at huge discounts than have to rely on the sale of the property in order to get their money.

12. Builders and land developers often take back mortgages just to make a sale. In most cases, they would like to sell them as quickly as possible so that they will have the funds to continue building and developing other projects.

You'll find builders listed in the phone book. Call to find out the location of the job they're working on, then drive out and speak with them in person. Even if they don't have a mortgage to sell at the present time, when a future sale depends upon their taking back paper as part of the purchase price, they'll call you to see if you'd be interested in buying it.

13. People and places you'd never think of accept mortgages as payment for their services or products. One client bought several mortgages from a local hospital that had taken them as paid bills owed

by various patients. Retailers and wholesalers who deal in expensive luxuries such as boats, art objects, jewelry, and antiques are often paid in mortgages. We know of one investor who even bought one from a house mover who had taken it as the fee for moving a home from one lot onto another.

Although we hope you'll never have need of bail bonding services, those professionals are also a wonderful source. It's not unusual for one of their clients to sign a mortgage as security for posted bail. If that bail is forfeited, the bonding professional wants nothing more than to sell the note as fast as possible for whatever possible.

This checklist is only a starting point. When you consider how many thousands of real estate sales are made each and every day, and when you realize that most of them require secondary financing to put them together, you begin to understand why there is such an incredible number of mortgages constantly becoming available to the astute investor who's looking for them.

You can probably sit down right now and come up with a list of your own, at least three times as long as the one already given you. The best part of it is you can use most of these sources time and time again. It's like any other business. Have an organized system, build a relationship with personal contacts, become a steady customer, and you'll find yourself on the receiving end of the best possible investment opportunities.

HOW IMAGE IMPACTS UPON INVESTMENT OPPORTUNITIES

At the risk of appearing redundant, we must repeat again what has already been said several times: *Investing in discounted mortgages is a business for profit, and although you'll get tremendous fun out of it, in order to be exceedingly successful at it, you must never stop treating it as a business.*

From now on you must become a part of the financial world. Each transaction will involve many thousands of dollars—eventually, hundreds of thousands. You'll be communicating with and meeting many different types of people from many walks of life.

Some of these will be private investors like yourself. Some will be major investment corporations such as banks, insurance companies, and pension fund administrators. Some will be, not investors *per se*, but catalysts who bring investors together. And some will be people who simply need cash and are ready to sell a mortgage to get it.

The better the professional image you project, the more you'll be respected as a serious investor who knows what he or she is doing. This will prove beneficial to you, inasmuch as others won't try to take advantage of you.

Let's face facts: Some mortgages are going to be bad risks. Because trading in discounted mortgages is a business just like any other, you will do well to let your colleagues know right from the start that you know your business. Being taken seriously is the first prerequisite for a successful investor image.

HOW COMMUNICATIONS CAN ENHANCE INVESTOR IMAGE

The right or wrong image can be projected in numerous ways. Your goal is to achieve the appearance of a professional at all times. The remainder of this chapter will explore the areas in which your professional investor image can be enhanced; we have no doubt that you'll be able to come up with many more.

The Right Time to Write a Letter

The three most utilized methods of communicating in this business are writing, telephoning, and personal meeting. Ask any successful business professional, and you'll be told that of these three, the most effective is an "eyeball-to-eyeball" contact. The reasons are obvious.

A letter communicates only *your* thoughts. Because there's no dialogue, there's no instant feedback. Also, without hearing someone's voice, there's no way of determining interest or the lack of it. Whenever possible, a letter should be used only as a first step in setting up an appointment for a meeting. Then follow up with a phone call.

The Right Time to Phone

Don't use the telephone for an in-depth discussion. Although dialogue *is* created, you could lose an opportunity to make an advantageous transaction if your call is received at a time when the recipient is unable to engage in a detailed conversation. Use the phone as you would a letter—to introduce yourself and arrange for an appointment. This is particularly true when you're contacting business establishments.

Three Important Advantages of Personal Contacts

A personal meeting when properly arranged can accomplish three important goals for each party. First, the conversation quickly establishes whether or not the meeting can be mutually productive. Second, when people are in other's presence, communication tends to be as complete and honest as it can be. A voice can be disguised to reflect whatever the speaker wants to project, but it's not easy to control one's eyes, actions, and body movements. All of these, of course, are excellent communicators that every wise investor learns to read and take advantage of. Third, a face-to-face meeting with someone will usually enable you to make your mind up as to whether or not you want to do business with him or her.

What the First Contact Should Accomplish

Whenever applicable and possible, the first contact should be for the purpose of setting up an appointment for the parties to meet each other in person. Speak to the person who handles the mortgages. Don't go into too much detail on the phone; that's what the meeting is for. Just say that you're an investor in mortgages and would like to get together to discuss possible transactions.

If the possibility of doing business exists, an appointment will be set and sufficient time allotted for the meeting. This way, your arrival won't be unexpected, resulting either in your being squeezed in between other duties or being told that no one is available who can speak with you.

On the other hand, even if the meeting proves to be of indirect service, the chances are that your business-like approach will still serve to make a good impression upon the person you're speaking with. In the future, not only will your name come to mind when something comes up, but you might even be referred to another source you didn't even have on your list.

HOW INVESTOR IMAGE CAN BE IMPROVED WITH ORGANIZATION

Keep an up-to-date prospect file. Whenever you make a contact who can be helpful to you in reaching your goals, either now or in the future, include that person or company in your file. Alphabetically arranged four- by six-inch cards will work perfectly.

For each source have one card that includes all pertinent data, such as the date of contact, a word or two pertaining to conversations held (including anything of a personal nature), and the type of mortgage with which the contact is usually involved. Reviewing each card periodically will be of great assistance to you. When your interests coincide with this contact's, you won't have to waste time wondering who to call.

IMPROVING INVESTOR IMAGE BY SYSTEMATIC FOLLOW-UP

Start building a personal relationship with the people or companies in your prospect file. If you anticipate working with them in the future, it wouldn't be wise to let them forget that you exist. Call them now and then, even if you're not looking for a transaction at the moment. Say that you just wanted to touch bases with them and find out what the market activity is.

Believe us, it helps. The more often they hear from you, the more apt they'll be to think of you when an interesting investment opportunity presents itself to them.

ENHANCE INVESTOR IMAGE WITH A BUSINESSLIKE APPEARANCE

Consider having cards printed with your name, phone number, and the fact that you buy, sell, and trade in mortgages. Keep it very simple, not gaudy or busy. A card adds to your image as a professional, and it can be given during a meeting or enclosed in a letter. In fact, it's not a bad idea to have personal stationery printed up with the same type letterhead.

After all, you're not the only one who will be keeping a prospect file for the future. All the professionals you'll be dealing with keep one also. You might just as well be included in theirs, as they will be in yours. For a very few dollars, you will have greatly increased your image as a serious investor.

Yes, the right image certainly helps, and if you follow the few suggestions above, and add more of your own, you'll soon find that you'll be regarded with the respect due a person seriously involved in the financial world of mortgage investments.

CONCLUSION

Any time is a good time to invest in mortgages. Unlike speculative investments, events, politics, and economic conditions have no adverse effect on either the availability or the face value of mortgages secured by real estate. In fact, when the economy is slow and money is tight, more mortgages are created to provide needed secondary financing, and investors have even better choices to pick from.

If your investment program is for the purpose of making you truly rich, you must keep your money and your profits working for you at all times. You can't accomplish this by purchasing one note and waiting for it to pay off before buying another. Begin by investing whatever funds you have or can get in a few small second mortgages, each one on a single-family residence. They should be purchased within as short a period of time as possible, run concurrently, and have varying durations on the loans.

Become thoroughly familiar with each variable in the "PIDD" Rule. Remember: P = payback schedule, I = interest rate, and DD = due date.

Make certain that each note has an immediate and steady monthly payback schedule. It can be either amortized or interest-only payments. This will not only assure you of a monthly income, but the seasoning of the note will become an important factor should you wish to sell, trade, or pledge it as security.

Investments are worthless unless they make a profit. If the number of dollars you receive is less than the number of dollars you lose in purchasing power, due to inflation, you not only haven't made a profit—you've actually lost money.

Therefore, the interest rate on the loans must be at least equal to, if not more than, the rate of inflation. As long as it is, when combined with the profit made because of the discounted price paid, you've protected yourself against the probability of being paid a larger number of cheaper dollars. Cheap dollars, of course, won't buy as much as the lesser number of more valuable dollars you originally invested.

The due date will tell you how long you have to wait until the note reaches maturity and becomes due and payable. Don't invest in any long-term investments at this time. It's not beneficial for you to have your funds tied up too long in one venture. It's better to be ready to take advantage of other opportunities as they come along.

Long-term investments will come later when you become involved in large commercial and income properties. For now, the maximum duration of the loans should be no longer than five years, preferably less, with each one coming due and payable at a different time. This constant ability to reinvest will propel you toward "The Good Life" more quickly than any other method known—short of robbing a bank or having a rich relative leave you a fortune in her will.

With the great majority of real estate transactions requiring secondary financing, the sources from which you can obtain discounted mortgages are limited only by your imagination. A few of these are local, legal, and financial newspapers, real estate brokers and agents, commercial banks, savings and loans, credit and finance companies, mortgage brokers, title company or County Recorder lists, escrow officers, real estate attorneys, friends and neighbors, bulletin boards, lists of pending foreclosure and bankruptcy sales, builders and land developers, private investors, investment clubs, and just about anyone else you can think of who might have taken a mortgage as payment for services rendered or products sold.

The right professional image will greatly enhance your appearance as a serious investor. Appointments to set up personal meetings, prospect lists periodically recontacted, rapport based upon ongoing relationships, plus business cards and stationery are only a few of the simple but effective ways by which you can gain the respect of other professionals.

5. What to Look for in Selecting Your Mortgage Investments

Today's the day! It's finally time to start using what you've learned thus far. As promised in the previous chapter, you're going on a shopping trip. Your goal will be to locate, and maybe even purchase, one or more mortgages that will comprise your first investment group.

You may not be successful on your first attempt. You might be offered opportunities that aren't suitable, whether in price, terms, loan duration, discount, type of property, or any number of other reasons. If this should happen, don't get discouraged. There's always tomorrow —hundreds of tomorrows—and thousands of mortgages.

For the present, your main concern is not allowing your natural excitement to get in the way of your sound judgment. These are investments we're talking about, not turn-of-a-card gambles. Your purpose is to *make* money, not to throw it away on a loser that someone is trying to get rid of. Therefore, as you talk to the sellers you'll be contacting, show interest but stay cool. Don't buy *anything* until your brain, calculator, and gut feelings convince you that you can profit by it.

Four Elements That Insure Profitable Return

Remember that your investment is not in the note alone, but in the real estate it represents. That's the *real security*. To be reasonably certain of an acceptable return on that investment, you must carefully consider each of the following four areas:

1. *Loan Terms.* The provisions spelled out in the mortgage and note will tell you how much money you can anticipate over what period of time, as well as which clauses and provisions are included for your protection.

2. *Property Value*. The property and surrounding area must appraise out at a present, as well as a projected future, value that assures the safety of your investment in the event of foreclosure.

3. *Mortgagor's Credibility*. Borrowers must be financially and personally stable. They should possess a good credit history and have enough equity in the property to guarantee that they'll do whatever is humanly possible to keep up the payments on the loan, so as to avoid foreclosure and the loss of that equity.

4. *Discounted Price*. The discount you receive must not only help to attain your desired yield, but must also be competitively priced with other discounts being offered on comparable mortgages.

Because of the importance of the above areas, don't ever make a purchase until you have had the time to analyze and make a reasonable judgment on each of them.

Where To Begin: Your First Contact

Turn to the classified section of your newspaper. Find the column headed "Mortgages For Sale." If you live in a large city, there will probably be at least ten ads listed. On any given day, for example, the *Los Angeles Times* will likely have fifteen or more. But we'll assume you find only three. Let's see what they say and how to handle them.

AD 1

$6,000

MORTGAGE FOR SALE

Negotiable Discount

Seller needs immediate cash!

Call 555-1234

Usually an ad will offer more information than this one does —duration of loan, interest rate, note priority, expected yield, monthly income, and more. This ad doesn't tell you any of those things, but it tells you something almost equally as important. There is a desperate need to sell. This is clearly evident by the wording, the exclamation mark, and by the seller's willingness to negotiate the discount.

(You should be aware that a discount is *always* negotiable to a certain extent. Although there are so-called "going rates," motivation will greatly determine the final price. A seller may offer a specified discount or even refuse to sell it for less, but that doesn't mean you have to accept it.)

The fact that the seller in this ad wants all investors to know that the percentage of discount is open to discussion proves that the money is needed badly—and quickly. Information you still need includes the following: The most important terms of the loan (remember the "PIDD" Rule—payback, interest, due date), the priority of the mortgagee, the location of the property, the size of the property (a single-family residence, hopefully), and the status of the seller as a private party, investor, or broker.

Don't wait to read the rest of the ads at this point. Telephone the first seller and introduce yourself as a possible buyer for the note. Let's assume that the conversation brings forth the following information.

The seller's name is David Randolph. Eighteen months ago he sold his previous home for $60,000, taking back a second mortgage for $6,000 with interest-only payments of 13 percent ($65 per month), all due and payable five years from close of escrow. Originally, he intended holding the note until maturity but a serious illness has resulted in a large hospital bill that is now due.

So far, the information coincides with your present interest. Set up an appointment to meet Randolph (not tomorrow, but within a couple of hours, if possible) for the purpose of going over the mortgage and note in detail.

Why You Should Learn to Act Immediately

You'll notice that we've had you set up the meeting with Randolph that *same* day. There's a reason for that—a very good reason. There's no better time than when you're first starting out to learn and practice the following rule: When interested—act! This is a habit you should get into immediately.

As soon as you hear of a mortgage that appears to be what you're looking for, speed is absolutely essential. If you're too slow in demonstrating interest to the seller, you'll find yourself losing the good ones and ending up with the marginal prospects.

You're not the only investor in the market. You must let the seller know that you're a serious buyer, genuinely interested in what the seller has to offer and ready to take action in pursuing the matter.

In our example Randolph is obviously in a financial bind, and you can bet that your call isn't the only one he's receiving from his ad. If you were to say that you'll think about it and call him in a day or so, you can kiss this investment good-bye. By that time he will most likely have already sold the note to the first investor who made him a halfway decent offer.

Okay, now that you've made your first appointment, let's go to another ad.

AD 2

INVESTORS

$3,000–$20,000

Mortgages taken on home improvement

jobs. Many to choose from. High returns.

ABC HOME IMPROVEMENT CO.

Call 555-7890

You call and reach a Betsy Troyan, the company manager, and learn that the only notes they're presently holding that could fit into your budget are on homes in areas you're not interested in. They are simply too far away for you to be able to service easily. However, your conversation with Troyan clearly indicates that you can most likely do business together in the future.

What do you do? Of course! You commence your prospect file, making out a card with Troyan's name, her company, the types of notes they generally have, the date of this contact, and any other information that might help you to approach Troyan on a more personal basis next time. (Naturally you're going to send her a follow-up note, enclose your card, and make reference to your conversation. Let her know that you are looking forward to doing business with her another time and that you hope she'll contact you when she acquires the next mortgage that fits your needs.)

AD 3

50% DISCOUNT!

31.5% AVERAGE ANNUAL YIELD

Private party forced to sell second

mortgage, secured by residential real

estate in prime area. $5,000 cash will

buy a $10,000 note!!

Call 555-5432

Sounds great, doesn't it? You're almost ready to buy it over the phone, sight unseen. Almost—but not quite. *You* know better.

How quickly your excitement disintegrates as you speak with the seller. The property *is* in a prime area. But it's not a home; it's a vacant lot. The note is for *ten years*, with interest at 10 percent. You quickly calculate what inflation will probably do to that.

The only way you'll ever make that 31½ percent average annual yield is if you get all the money due you. It will take ten long years for that to happen if, indeed, it happens at all. Taking all these facts into consideration, obviously you would be well advised to forget this prospective investment altogether.

Now that you've exhausted today's ads, you phone a local real estate broker and learn that she's just completed a sale in which she accepted a $7,500 second mortgage as her commission. She wants to sell it as soon as possible. You ask a few questions, get a few answers, and you both agree to meet after lunch to discuss the investment.

You've done extremely well. In less than thirty minutes you've spoken to four people, have two possibilities for the present, at least one excellent source for the future, and you haven't even begun to tap all the possibilities listed in Chapter 4.

In case you're getting the impression that we are making this appear ridiculously easy, let us assure you that we are—*because it is!* Finding mortgages for sale is probably the simplest thing in the world to do. There are so many of them, all around you. However, knowing if any one of them is a good, safe investment that will net you a fair return is another matter. That takes knowledge and foresight. The purpose of this book is to provide you with the former, plus the ability to develop the latter.

CLAUSES THAT ARE COMMON TO ALL MORTGAGES

Before you meet any prospective mortgage seller, you should become familiar with some of the most common clauses included in notes and mortgages, as such clauses spell out the actual terms and conditions of the loan. Some of these are in all mortgages and represent universally accepted lender protections without which no lender would grant the loan.

Most mortgages contain the same "boilerplate" materials. These are preprinted clauses covering items such as: using the property for legal purposes only, maintaining it properly, keeping up the tax payments, insuring it sufficiently to protect the lender, as well as a multitude of other conditions guaranteeing the lender that the security won't be impaired. The exact language in which these guarantees are expressed may vary from one instrument to another, but the intent and legal effect of the language remain the same.

Four Requirements of *Every* Mortgage

Every mortgage must include the following:

1. A proper identification of both the mortgagor and mortgagee.

2. An identification of the subject property that leaves no room for confusion as to which property is being secured. Although the legal description isn't absolutely necessary, it's the best.

3. A warrantee that the mortgagor is in legal possession of the title and will defend the property against all lawful demands.

4. A release of the mortgagor's dower in the event of foreclosure. The dower is that part of the real property that the law allows the wife of a deceased owner. If the mortgagor is unmarried, that fact should be stated in the mortgage.

As a rule, you won't have to be concerned with any of the above because they're practically always included in all mortgages that have been drawn up properly.

MORTGAGE CLAUSES THAT HAVE A DIRECT FINANCIAL IMPACT UPON INVESTMENTS

What we're interested in now is that other material—the filled-in blanks and special clauses that have a direct financial effect on the investment in that particular mortgage. You must know what to look for and how to analyze what you see, if you want to be reasonably certain of ending up with your desired yield.

When you're the original mortgagee, for example, the lender who makes the loan and draws up the documents, you can put whatever terms and provisions you want into the mortgage as long as the mortgagor agrees to them.

But when you invest in an already existing mortgage, the terms, conditions, obligations, and payback schedule have been set and you can't change them. If you're going to buy it, therefore, you do so in its existing form. So be smart: *Know what you're getting and get what you pay for!* Check each mortgage carefully, and make certain you understand each of the following provisions that directly affect the investment. Illustrations of each of these mortgage clauses can be found in Appendix A. Take the time to study them carefully as you read through the explanation for each. Familiarize yourself with the various terms and provisions and see how each one may be worded. This will enable you to scan an actual document quickly, know where to find what you're looking for, and understand the meaning of alternative wording.

Principal (or Face) Amount

This is the original amount of the total debt owed by the mortgagor (or maker) on the note to the original mortgagee (or holder) of the note. We used the words "original mortgagee" because the present holder may not have been the actual lender who funded the loan. The note might have been sold one or more times until finally purchased by the present mortgagee.

The existing balance at the time of your investment may be less than the original face amount. This will be the case if the payback schedule has been set up on an amortized basis where each payment includes a small portion of the principal as well as the interest. Even if this is so, that amount paid on the principal will be almost always infinitesimally small.

The "PIDD" Rule

Remember our old friend, the "PIDD" Rule? You'll find all its elements here. The note will clearly spell out the date of the first payment, the amount, the schedule of subsequent payments, the character of payments, whether amortized or interest-only, the interest rate, and finally, the date the note is to be paid off in full.

The date of the first payment immediately lets you know how long the mortgagor has been making payments. When payments have been made regularly and in full over a long period of time, the note is then considered to be seasoned.

The *payment amount* obviously determines your monthly income from the investment. Once again, bear in mind that if the payments are made on an amortized basis, the final balance when due will be for the original principal amount less whatever has been paid on that principal over the life of the loan.

As mentioned earlier, you are urged not to invest in any note that doesn't pay you a steady monthly income. If you do, you'll have a serious problem should you wish to use it in a sale, trade, purchase, or as collateral. Also, if you're not holding income-producing notes, you'll be denied the exciting opportunities outlined in Chapter 3 on pyramiding and compounding.

The *interest rate* is one of the most important considerations of the loan. We've already seen how the combination of interest and discount can work together to nullify any loss due to inflation. Now it becomes clear that if the interest rate doesn't come close to compensating for the inflation factor, it's going to take a much larger discount to make up for it.

The *due date* tells you how much time is left until the note becomes due and payable. Obviously, if it's a three-year loan and seventeen payments have been made on a monthly basis, the note will become due in another nineteen months.

Acceleration Clause

This clause allows the mortgagee, at his or her option, to demand payment of the entire balance of the loan upon the default of any payment then due. Because this would result in a foreclosure action, most mortgagees prefer to delay exercising this option until after the mortgagor has had two to three months to catch up and has still failed to do so.

Although the usual practice is to cooperate with the mortgagor during financial difficulties, for your protection this clause should be included in the note in case it becomes necessary to make use of it.

Due-on-Sale Clause

This means exactly what it says and, in fact, is often included in the above-mentioned acceleration clause. If a due-on-sale clause is included, the holder has the right to call the entire balance due upon the sale, conveyence, or other transfer of the title to the property prior to paying off the loan. In some cases the clause may include words similar to, "The lender agrees not to withhold reasonable approval of the new title holder." This means that the lender may allow the new owner to take over the existing loan without forcing payment of the balance.

Investors should be aware that the validity of due-on-sale clauses has been the subject of much recent litigation in several jurisdictions, much of which has turned upon the status of the lender as commercial or private. Important issues have been raised by these lawsuits, such as whether these clauses are in the public interest, and if not, whether or not they can be enforced. If a question arises in your potential investments relating to the validity of such a clause, you should refer the question to legal counsel for the most current advice.

Prepayment Penalty

This is a fee charged to the mortgagor if the loan is paid off before it's actually due (the longer the term of the loan, the more months during which interest is paid on that loan). The faster the mortgagor pays off the note, the less interest is paid. The prepayment penalty is for the purpose of compensating the lender for a portion of that lost interest.

Most junior mortgages contain a provision that allows the borrower to pay off the loan without incurring a penalty. This is done by including the words, "... or more ..." into the payment schedule wording. For example, the wording might be, "Monthly payments of $87.50 *or more*, including interest at 14 percent. . . ." Inclusion of the words "or more" allows the mortgagor to pay any amount above that which is due, whenever and as often as she or he pleases.

Although most first mortgages do have a prepayment penalty clause, there can be (and usually are) various exceptions depending on the lender's policy, especially those of banks, savings and loans, insurance companies, and so on. Two of these exceptions include allowing the borrower to pay a maximum of a certain percent of the principal (usually 20 percent) each quarter or each year, or having the clause be of no further effect five years after origination of the loan.

Should you invest in a note that allows the mortgagor to pay off the loan at any time? Of course! First of all, your funds are tied up for a shorter period of time, which means you can reinvest that much faster. Secondly, you're greatly increasing your yield by receiving the profit in less time than originally anticipated. (You'll see what we mean in Chapter 11 on yields.) In fact, you might even offer the mortgagor a small discount on the loan for any amounts on the principal paid in advance of the due date.

If the note does contain a prepayment penalty clause, it will state how much is to be paid as penalty. Usually the amount is somewhere around six months' unearned interest. For example: You hold a note for $5,000 with interest at 12½ percent. The monthly interest comes to $52.08. If the note calls for a six months' prepayment penalty, you would receive $312.50 unearned interest if the borrower pays off the note before it's due.

Late Payment Charge

This is self-explanatory. Not every note has this provision but it should. As an investor, you anticipate a certain amount of income on a specific day every month. You make plans for that income, and timely payments help you carry out those plans. A mortgagor is more apt to make payments on time if she knows it will cost her extra money when she's late. At present, the normal charge is 7 to 10 percent of the payment amount after ten days past the due date.

Subordination Clause

This clause will often be included when the property is a vacant lot or a building that will be torn down for the purpose of rebuilding. When you see this in a mortgage, it spells trouble. It's a very important clause that will rarely, if ever, benefit you. Any exercise of it by the mortgagor will automatically place your note into a lower position. If this clause is included, and unless it specifies differently, the borrower can place your note lower down in priority whenever he wants to put another loan in front of it. You may very well experience serious difficulty when you try to collect. Remember, you're looking for safe investments with reliable income.

Request for Notice of Default

This is an extremely important clause for you to be aware of as no junior mortgage should ever be without one. If you're holding a second mortgage and the borrower defaults on the first, the holder of that first has the right to foreclose on the property so that she can get her money. Once this action takes place, you're stuck with a piece of paper that may be worth absolutely nothing. The mortgagor isn't going to pay you another cent. Why should he? He's already lost the property. Your only hope of getting paid will depend on whether or not any money is left over from the foreclosure sale.

The only way you can protect your investment is by stopping the foreclosure. You accomplish this by *curing the default.* This means that you have to make up not only payments on the senior loan that are past due but also all incurred fees, penalties, unpaid taxes, and insurance premiums.

How do you discover that the property is going into foreclosure? That's easy. Just make certain that a clause requiring a "Request for Notice of Default" is included in any junior mortgage you're interested in. When the superior mortgage holder files a default notice with the County Recorder (which must be done according to law), you'll automatically receive a copy of it and can take the necessary steps.

FIVE OBJECTIVES TO MEET IN PERSONAL INTERVIEWS WITH SELLERS: A CASE STUDY

Now that you have reviewed the major clauses in notes and mortgages that may impact upon your investment decision, you're prepared for the two appointments you made on the telephone. Let's go see what these sellers have to offer. At the appointed hour, you arrive at the Randolph home. How do you act and what is your attitude?

Always Remember the Human Factor

Everyone has needs, from the president of a major corporation to the janitor in your local laundromat. If you have no concern for the other person's problems, you can't expect to achieve real success in any field. We hate using clichés, but it's true, one hand *does* wash the other. Show some understanding of the other person's position, and they will usually reciprocate.

The seller of a mortgage needs money. It could be for any number of personal or business reasons. Quite often, only a certain minimum amount will serve that purpose; anything less won't fill the need.

Like most sellers, the original asking price will probably be somewhat on the high side in order to leave room for negotiation. The more you show that you understand and care about the problem, the more the seller will be willing to understand yours. This leads to a more flexible negotiation than if your attitude were, "I don't care what your needs are—this is strictly business."

Naturally, negotiations can only proceed to a point, beyond which one of you will not be filling your need, thereby making a transaction impossible. But if each of you treats the other with respect and consideration, it's more than likely that you'll both reach your individual goals. The seller will get the money that is really needed, and you'll receive a larger discount than that which was offered originally. Always give the other person a chance to make a profit, and you'll make one as well.

With this thought in mind, let's get back to Randolph and his problem. You already know that he has to pay a large hospital bill. As soon as you meet, therefore, you might want to show that you're a considerate human being by expressing your hope that the person who was sick is now getting well. *But don't fake it—mean it!* You'll find that you're conversing immediately on a much more personal level that will result in a more productive price discussion later on. Randolph may even tell you how much his bill is. If he does, you'll know the minimum price he can possibly accept.

Always ask a seller why the mortgage is for sale. It's a fair question. You may not always get the truth. On the other hand, you may end up knowing just enough to give you a ballpark figure as to that seller's bottom line. Try it. You'll find it often works.

Ask About the Property

Before you look at the mortgage and note, you'll want to know something about the property. As we stated several times before, you might be buying a piece of paper but your investment is in the value of the property. If you have to foreclose, what will you own and how easily can you sell it?

As a result of your inquiries, you learn that the Randolph home has three bedrooms, a den, a dining area, plus one and three-quarter baths. That's a good beginning because it's what most people are looking for today. It's twenty-eight years old and was updated seven years ago when Randolph put in a custom kitchen and converted the floor furnace to forced-air heat. There are approximately 1,700 square feet, plus an attached double garage and a small yard.

The tract where the Randolph home is located consists of something over 50 one-story homes. It is in a desirable area of town, and the property owners are mostly young couples who are buying their first homes.

So far, it sounds like a worthwhile investment. If you're satisfied with the documents, you'll follow up with a personal visit to the home and see that a proper and objective appraisal is made.

Determine the Loan-to-Value Ratio

Now you turn your attention to the details regarding the actual loan. A prime consideration is the *loan-to-value ratio,* or how much equity the borrower has in the home. In Chapter 3 you read a definition of *equity.* It bears repeating: *Equity is the amount, or percentage, of something you own, over and above any amount, or percentage, you may still owe on it.*

The greater the equity, the less chance the borrower will walk away from the debt when faced with financial difficulties. You already know that the sales price of Randolph's home was $60,000. Now, check the face of the mortgage (not the note). See if there was any other lien on the property other than the first mortgage at the time the second was recorded. Every junior mortgage should state what other mortgages are superior to it. But just to be safe, you should always research this information later at the County Recorder's office.

The mortgage you're now looking at makes reference only to one other lien—the first mortgage for $48,000. This amount, plus the $6,000 note held by Randolph, shows that the buyer had a $6,000 or 10 percent equity in the property at time of purchase.

Notice that we said, ". . . at the time of purchase." The fact that the buyer had a certain equity in the property when it was purchased doesn't necessarily mean that the same equity exists now. It could be more or less, depending on several factors:

1. The home has most likely appreciated in value during the 18 months since Randolph sold it. If we assume a conservative 12 percent appreciation factor, the present value would be $70,800. Because the first few years of amortized payments do little else but take care of the interest, the $48,000 first mortgage hasn't decreased much. You can see by the documents that payments on the second are for interest only so the $6,000 loan hasn't decreased at all.

Therefore, the buyer still owes approximately $54,000 on a property now worth $70,800. His $6,000 down payment is now worth $16,800, and he's increased his equity from 10 percent to almost 24 percent. This increase in equity makes you happy. Randolph's buyers are not going to turn their backs on a built-in $10,800 profit. And if they do, you'll have a more valuable piece of property without spending any extra to get it.

2. On the other hand, the buyers may have taken a new loan any time *after* the second mortgage was recorded. This would *decrease* that equity as they would now owe a larger percentage of the property's value.

For example, let's say that they ran into problems at a time when the property's worth had increased to $68,000. If they borrowed an additional $6,000, their new total debt would be $60,000, leaving an equity of $8,000 or 12 percent.

Therefore, you make a mental note to check the County Recorder's office, which is easily done, to check *all present liens* on the property. Even though subsequent loans wouldn't affect the priority of the second mortgage, it might mean that the mortgagor is having financial problems and is becoming overextended.

Study the Documents

The documents show the terms of the loan to be exactly what Randolph said they were. It's a five-year note (due in three and one-half more years) for $6,000, payable interest-only at 13 percent with monthly payments of $65. All the necessary clauses are included for the mortgagee's protection. Also included is an insurance policy with Randolph as the co-insured, which will be changed to your name should you buy the note.

After studying the mortgage and note, you ask to see the record of the buyer's payments. Every mortgagee should keep one. Randolph shows it to you, and it's clear that the mortgagor has made every payment on time.

The note is obviously seasoned, and the terms and price bracket are exactly what you hoped to find for your first investment. There's no question in your mind that if the value of the property and the mortgagor are both satisfactory, you'll be ready to make an offer. The next question becomes: How large a discount can you get?

Determine the Amount of the Discount

Earlier in this chapter you learned that it's important to convey your interest to a seller immediately, before the seller becomes involved with another buyer. That's why you're here now—only two hours after talking to Randolph on the phone. Now you have to let him know that you're even more interested than before.

First of all, you should be taking written notes on whatever is said regarding the property, the loan, and the mortgagor. These notes will be invaluable to you when you want to either check out a fact or refresh your memory. Also, ask permission to get all documents copied so that you can study them in detail. These two actions will show that you're a serious investor.

Ask Randolph how much he wants for the note. Whatever his answer, remain noncommittal, even if the discount reflects a mere 10 to 15 percent. *Don't* laugh hysterically as if that's the funniest joke you've ever heard. Seriously. A verbal, "Uh, huh," works much better than a "Huh???" You don't want Randolph to realize just yet that you think his asking price is more than you're willing to pay.

Don't quote any figure of your own. That will come later after you've done the necessary research and figured out the yield you want to make. While he's still of the opinion that you'll meet his price, he probably won't sell to someone else for less. But as soon as he knows the amount you have in mind, Randolph will sell the note to the first investor who offers something better. You, on the other hand, will have lost what might have been a great investment opportunity.

Tell Randolph you want to see the property and meet the mortgagor personally. You'll also want to check the title report and arrange for an appraisal on the home. All this will indicate that you're an interested, serious buyer and know what you're doing. Take the mortgagor's name and phone number, and tell Randolph that if you're satisfied, you'll be ready to discuss the purchase of the note within three to four days.

After all, you're really being totally honest with him. If the property's value and the mortgagor's credibility satisfy you, you'll most likely make an offer on this note.

Remember, as you leave, Randolph should be practically convinced that he has a sale and that you're the buyer.

PUTTING IT ALL TOGETHER: ANOTHER CASE STUDY

After lunch, you keep your appointment with the real estate broker who took back the $7,500 second as her commission. Because you've already been through the procedure, you know exactly what to do and what to ask.

Once again, you begin by inquiring about the property. You learn that the sales price was $87,500 and that it's an older home having two bedrooms and one bath. You also learn that the house is situated on a huge lot. When you learn the location of the area, however, you're just about ready to chalk up this visit as a wasted trip. You remember that location from several years ago, and it was run down and seedy looking even then. There's no way it could have improved.

But wait! The realtor mentions something you didn't know. That entire area has been rezoned for multiple units. Builders have started buying the homes, tearing them down, and replacing them with condominiums and apartment buildings. That old home on its huge lot could become a very desirable property that could very well be the reason why the buyers purchased it in the first place.

When the realtor goes over the paperwork with you, it gets even better. The buyers put $30,000 down (34 percent equity!) and assumed the existing $50,000 mortgage. The payback schedule calls for 14 percent interest-only payments of $87.50 per month, and the entire note is due and payable in *one* year.

Obviously, being a new note, there hasn't been time for it to become seasoned, but the broker had run a credit check on the buyers and shows you the result. You couldn't ask for a more impeccable credit reference.

When the broker offers you this note at a 20 percent discount, you're tempted to take out your checkbook. But again you recall and follow our previous advice: show interest but stay neutral. As you did with Randolph, you demonstrate that interest by assuring the broker that you'll be in touch with her as soon as you've appraised the property, met the mortgagor, and checked the title report.

Once you've told a seller that you'll call back, *do it,* even if you've decided against purchasing that particular mortgage. *You* wouldn't enjoy waiting for an answer that isn't coming, and neither will the seller. Besides, you may want to do business with this person in the future, and this is one way you can prove your reliability.

You leave the broker's office, hardly able to believe what you've accomplished in less than two hours of actual work. Not only have you located two potential investments, each of which fits into your present plan and budget, but you've also made a personal contact with a home improvement company that may turn out to be an excellent source for the future.

FACTORS THAT WILL DETERMINE
THE ADVISABILITY OF A PARTICULAR INVESTMENT

It takes about four days to get a title report and to have a property appraised. The materials in the following chapters will explain exactly how this is done. After these are completed, you might decide to make an offer on either, or both, of these hypothetical mortgages.

That decision will ultimately turn upon your analysis of the projected yield on each of the investment possibilities. Yield is simply the measure of the actual profit you've made or hope to make. The words *yield* and *discount* go together: In order to attain your desired yield, you must acquire the mortgage at a certain discounted price.

Chapter 11 will concentrate on this area. You'll find mortgage yield tables accompanied by easy-to-follow instructions on the use of them. For those of you who might fear mathematical gymnastics, let us assure you that this will be no more difficult than using a ruler and an inexpensive calculator to do the work for you. It won't take you long to become skilled in the use of the material, after which you'll be able to calculate—quickly and easily—what discounted price to offer for any mortgage.

CONCLUSION

There are innumerable mortgages constantly available on the market. Be selective, taking care that your choice for an investment is compatible with your present need and budget, as well as with a future plan and goal you can live with. Don't get discouraged and be talked into something unprofitable for you, just because you haven't found what you're looking for. Wait for the next time. Every day, more mortgages became available. Always remember that you're an investor, not a gambler.

The underlying security is in the real property, represented by the mortgage investment. Thus, that property's value, both present and future, as well as the specific terms of the loan, the financial and personal credibility of the mortgagor, and the discounted price you pay for the note, all combine together in determining whether or not you're making a wise and safe investment. Study each of these areas carefully, and make no purchase until you are fully satisfied with all of them.

Your initial contact with a seller who has advertised a note for sale should quickly determine if a personal meeting could be beneficial to you. To accomplish this, inquire about the following information: type of property, mortgage priority, face amount, monthly income, duration of loan, interest rate, and discount being offered. Unless these important variables are what you're looking for, there's not much sense in wasting time by pursuing it any further.

If the obtained information is in line with your present need, show genuine interest and arrange an immediate meeting. If an investment is a good one, you don't want to lose it because some other investor acted faster than you did. You must show the seller that you're a serious buyer, and you can do this by asking to see the mortgage and note at the seller's earliest convenience.

When you accept an existing mortgage and note, you are also accepting all the terms and provisions contained therein. These have already been set, and you have no control over them. The general provisions are preprinted and are pretty much the same in all mortgages. These include such stipulations as legal use of the property, maintenance, tax payments, insurance coverage with the mortgagee as co-insured, and many others.

The filled-in blanks, added material, and special clauses contain those terms relating specifically to that particular lien. Become familiar with all of the following terms: principal (or face) amount, income schedule, interest rate, due date, acceleration clause, subordination clause, due-on-sale clause (often included in the acceleration clause), prepayment penalty, and especially a request for notice of default.

By giving sellers a chance to fill their needs, you'll be giving yourself a better chance to fill your own. Don't try to be such an overly sharp negotiator in your attempt to "steal" the note that you make it impossible for the seller to sell it to you. When you make an offer, it should be fair to both of you. If the price you insist on is so low that the money won't serve the purpose for which it's needed, you might very well lose out on what could have been one of your best investments. And if the seller is one whose business is dealing in mortgages, you might eliminate any possibility of future transactions.

This is a "people" business. Mutual respect and consideration are essential ingredients of equitable transactions. Give the other person a chance for a decent profit and you'll end up making one also. This is especially true when you hope to build an ongoing relationship for future transactions.

When first meeting with the seller, ask about the property before going over the terms and provisions of the mortgage and note. Because the ultimate security of the loan lies in the property itself, you should have a mental picture of it while studying the financial documents.

Loan-to-value ratio means the amount or percentage of *equity* the borrower has in the property, over and above what the borrower owes on it. This is one of the most important considerations of the wise investor. Unless you're purchasing the note with the hope of foreclosing on the property, you want that equity to be as high as possible. The higher it is, the more difficult it will be for the mortgagor to face losing it by not keeping up the payments on the loans.

It's imperative, therefore, that you know *all* the liens against the property, not just the ones as of the recorded date of the mortgage you're working on. If you're seriously considering this investment, you'll want to check the title report at the County Recorder's Office to see if any additional liens have been recorded subsequent to that date.

Once you've checked the loan provisions, if you're genuinely interested, let the seller know it by asking the price. Don't give the impression that you won't pay it or that you have to think about it. Show that you're a serious buyer and know what you're doing by telling the seller that you'll be in touch as soon as you've appraised the property and met the mortgagor.

The seller must be convinced that you are most likely going to make an offer on the note. If you're a procrastinator, unable to make fast decisions, the seller might accept another offer before you can get back with your own offer.

Your next step is to determine the value of the property and the reliability of the mortgagor. As previously mentioned, if the mortgagor defaults and you end up as the owner of the property, you haven't lost a thing as long as the value is great enough to be easily converted to an acceptable amount in cash or other benefits. Therefore, an objective appraisal is essential, and that's our next subject.

6. How an Appraisal Can Insure the Reliability of a Mortgage Investment

HOW YOU CAN BE ASSURED OF THE REAL PROPERTY VALUE OF A POTENTIAL INVESTMENT

Because real estate is used as the security for investments in discounted mortgages, it is essential for the investor to know the value of real estate in order to analyze intelligently the relative safety of an investment. In this chapter, therefore, you are going to be exposed to the various principles that must be applied in evaluating real estate, to three specific methods by which property may be qualified or appraised, and to a structured, five-step process to be utilized in creating an appraisal file that should assist in condensing and ordering all of the appraisal data so that a more reasoned evaluation may be reached. Finally, a pair of hypothetical investors will be taken on an appraisal "tour" of an investment property under consideration.

TEN GENERAL CONSIDERATIONS REGARDING PROPERTY VALUATION

Before delving into these specifics, however, perhaps it would be instructive to reflect upon the following general considerations and suggestions:

1. Always remember that the point of an appraisal is to minimize the risk of loss of capital, principal, or equity *and* simultaneously to further your goals by providing an adequate buffer or security for your investments.

2. Keep in mind the ability and willingness of the mortgagor to pay.

3. Learn the standard methods of determining approximate market value so that, first, there is little or no chance of a foreclosure, and second, in the event of foreclosure, you will receive not only your capital and equity, but a profit as well.

4. Don't look for shortcuts in appraising. At the beginning, appraising is a matter of digging and hard work. The beginner should proceed step by careful step. Shortcuts are more appropriately utilized when you become more knowledgeable.

5. Make your appraisal work a pleasurable task, not an odious one. Involve your mate, members of the family, partner, or joint venturer. Each will have something unique to offer and may become an expert in some phases of appraising.

6. Seek out realtors, bank appraisers, savings and loan appraisers, mortgage brokers, government appraisers, insurance company appraisers, real estate brokers, and others who are usually more than willing to assist in this process and to answer questions. Also, make it a point to seek out anyone who has previously made an appraisal of an investment property you are considering.

7. Remember that governmental records concerning investment property may be available to you without charge. These records might include appraisals for taxes, assessments, and other legal documents.

8. Avoid homes in high fire, flood, erosion, or landslide areas as a beginning appraiser. Avoid as well the following: properties adjoining commercial areas, garbage dumps, mortuaries, cemeteries, and properties adjoining railroad tracks, railroad sidings, airports, factories, or school playgrounds.

9. Remember that appraisals can be obtained for greater or lesser sums than the property may be worth to you. Never accept appraisals offered by other interested parties at full face value, as an obvious conflict of interest may exist. There are as many approaches to appraising property as there are reasons for appraising it. A particular piece of real estate can have different values; for example, among many estimates of value are insurance value, replacement value, tax or assessed value, market value, book value, and income value.

10. Be aware that the rules and regulations of commercial lenders often force them into a position of refusing loans on sound, but junior or small, mortgages. This occurs when the expense of investigating and maintaining the mortgages outweighs the income. This situation provides the small investor with a great opportunity to buy perfectly good mortgages that a commercial lender would not consider. Private

investors, unlike commercial lenders, are in a position to take the risk inherent in owning second or third mortgages where they can be assured there is sufficient equity or where the risk is small and the return is great. Remember, for the purpose of mortgaging, small investors may view appraisals from an altogether different angle than large financial institutions do.

It is essential that these general suggestions be kept in mind throughout your involvement with the remainder of this material on appraisals. Turning now from the general to the specific, let's consider some of the fundamental principles that must be mastered by the prospective investor before attempting to master the methods of appraising.

THE FIVE PRINCIPLES OF EVALUATION

In buying discounted mortgages, every investor must fully integrate five principles of evaluation into his or her thinking processes: substitution (or replacement value), change, highest and best use, conformity, and progression. Although these may sound imposing, they are, in fact, quite simple to understand.

Substitution (or Replacement) Value

Where real property is replaceable, a value may be set for it by determining the cost of acquiring a substitute. Such a value should not exceed the value in the marketplace where, within a reasonable time, the property can be replaced. The substitution value must be based upon the current market value or upon a comparison approach to value. The substitution principle requires that you think of a replacement of equal value that is similar in design and function.

Change

Working with real property also requires a recognition of the fact that all real property goes through three major changes: growth (or development), stability (or maintaining the *status quo*), and decline. It is imperative, therefore, that an investor consider a broad area surrounding the property under investigation at various times of the day and week in order to ascertain the social and economic trends occurring in the neighborhood. Such trends will greatly assist in setting a correct value on the property.

Highest and Best Use

Consider whether the real property under consideration is likely to produce the best and greatest net return during your holding. In order to do this, take into consideration the development of the area surrounding the property in question. Determine if it is currently being put to its highest and best use because changes can be costly. For example, a single-family residence surrounded on all sides by commercial retail establishments might call into question the principle of highest and best use.

Conformity

There should be harmony and similarity to other nearby pieces of property. Residences, especially, should generally conform to the design of adjoining structures regarding style, use, and population. The suburban ranch house tract surrounding a single, three-story Victorian should call to mind the principle of conformity.

Progression

It is generally known that properties of substantially greater value than the adjacent properties will be adversely affected (and *vice versa*). Thus, the mansion that is constructed adjacent to the garbage dump will suffer a reduction in its value, and a modest home in the midst of affluent homes will enjoy a proportionate increase in its value.

These five basic principles of evaluation should be so engrained that they are consistently and automatically analyzed each time a piece of property is under consideration. Once these concepts are fully mastered, you are ready to focus upon the three specific methods by which you can appraise property in order to protect your investment.

QUALIFYING THE PROPERTY: THREE APPRAISAL TECHNIQUES

It's already been pointed out that the purpose of appraisals is to provide an important tool that can be used to determine the safety of an investment. The three appraisal techniques that are about to be discussed will show you various ways that you can appraise property to accomplish this protection. Consider what we really mean by the word, "protection."

Suppose Jean is looking at a $20,000 second mortgage for investment purposes. The mortgage is on a house that also has a first mortgage of $90,000. Jean thinks the house is worth $150,000. She would have a false sense of security if the house were, in fact, worth only $95,000. If Jean had to foreclose to recover her investment, her note with a face value of $20,000 may have no value whatsoever. If the borrower were to let the first mortgage go into default, the cost of making up the payments to cure the default as well as the cost to sell the property could easily cost her more than the $5,000 equity on the property.

This example demonstrates the importance of understanding how to determine accurately the property value so that the amount of "protection" that is the real security on the property is positively known.

Effectively determining property value is accomplished through the appraisal process. The relative complexity of this process should not be underestimated. It has already been shown that there are just as many approaches to appraising as there are reasons for appraising. Of all the approaches that exist, however, there are three that will be most useful to you in investing in mortgages. These techniques are the cost approach, the market data approach, and the income approach. Each method has its own peculiar purpose, but all of them can help you to assess accurately the value of mortgage security.

The Cost Approach

Of the three approaches under consideration, the cost approach will tend to produce a high estimate of value. It is determined from the cost of reproducing the improvements at the current market price and deducting from that cost the depreciation on improvements. To this figure is then added an estimated value of the land. Look at the following example:

Suppose a ten-year-old house has 1800 square feet of living space plus 300 square feet of garage space. Further, assume that the house is built on a lot with an estimated value of $25,000. If, after checking with a local building contractor, it is found that the cost of building a new house would be $51 per square foot and a new garage $25 per square foot, then it would cost $91,800 to replace the house and $7,500 to replace the garage. Thus, the total replacement cost would be $99,300. Adding this to the value of the land, the estimated value before depreciation would be $124,300. Assuming that the property had depreciated 1 percent a year, its replacement cost would be approximately 10 percent less, or $114,370. (Notice that the land is not depreciated.)

The Market Data Approach

Using the market data approach to value property produces a medium range in property appraisals. It's the most logical way to appraise a house that is situated in a neighborhood of other houses, and it is effectively used to determine the value range of a single-family dwelling. Also, it's easy for an alert student to master this technique in a short period of time.

Recall the earlier discussion on the principle of substitution; this is the essence of the market data approach. If a similar home has sold for $135,000 in the neighborhood of the house you desire to evaluate, then the house in question is also worth approximately $135,000. Adjustments would have to be made, of course, for any differences between the two houses. For example, if an otherwise identical $135,000 house had a $3,500 fireplace, and the house in question did not, then the investor would subtract $3,500 from the value of the prospective investment.

Similarly, adjustments should be made for *all* major differences between the properties. Some of the usual adjustments to be made include differences in location, lot size, building site, condition of the property, and any time differences between the sales. One of the houses may be backed up to a highway, while the other is at the end of a cul-de-sac. One may have a nice, large, pool-size lot, while the other may have a small yard. One may have an extra bedroom and be well-maintained, while the other needs painting and new carpeting and lacks the extra floor space. By comparing recent sales in the same neighborhood, an investor will soon learn to spot the trends in selling prices. Actually, the more comparable sales you obtain, the more certain will be the results.

The Income Approach

This approach produces a low estimate in value and does not lend itself very well to obtaining the value of single-family residences. However, it is very effective in arriving at a reasonable price for commercial real estate; thus, it is wise for the would-be investor to be familiar with this information.

In principle, the concept is very simple. The investor looks at the income stream produced by the property the same as he or she would look at money earning interest in the bank. Consider this example:

John is earning $1,000 per year on a sum of money at 10 percent interest. The money, thus, has a 10 percent capitalization rate, and the income stream is worth $10,000. The income stream is calculated by dividing the capitalization rate into the annual income stream ($1,000) to obtain a principal value of $10,000. Now assume that John must pay $50 annually in bank service fees. All such expenses must be deducted from the annual gross income ($1,000) to arrive at a net operating income of $950. Now, to arrive at the true value of the investment, divide the net operating income ($950) by the capitalization rate, which equals $9,500.

Using the income approach to value, a piece of real estate is basically the same as this bank example. In order to do this, first look over the books and records of the property to determine the income stream due to rents or lease payments, but disregard concessions, laundry room services, and other related income. (You disregard these other items because you are appraising the value of the real estate's income stream and not, say, a washing machine's income stream.) Be careful to avoid basing a value on an owner's projection of rental increase in the future. This can be disastrous as the vacancy caused by a rental increase can be costly.

Next, a review of the annual expenses must be undertaken. It is advisable that these figures for expenses be compared with other similar rental properties in the area. There are eight basic expense categories to be considered: vacancies, taxes, insurance and licenses, manager fees, utilities, maintenance and repairs, services (gardeners and such), and replacement reserves.

If either the income or expenses is too high or too low, try to find out why. Mistakes carry directly over to the value of the property and can grossly bias a true estimate of value. For example, a 10 percent error in the income will cause *more* than a 10 percent error in the evaluation of the property. (Selection of the capitalization rate is even more sensitive. Because this rate is divided into the net income, a 1 percent difference can alter the estimated property value by up to 10 percent or more!)

To demonstrate the income approach to appraising real property, consider the following hypothetical case:

Janet is interested in purchasing a discounted mortgage on a small apartment house near her home. She learns that the apartment house was sold to the new owners just three months ago, and the new owners are in need of immediate cash. The sales price was $99,500, and the apartment house has steadily produced an annual income of $25,000.

Janet thoroughly reviews the owners' books and sees that annual expenses come to $13,000, which leaves a net operating income of $12,000 per year. In order to determine the capitalization rate, Janet visits her friend, Jack the realtor, who produces for her the figures from the sales of three comparable apartment houses within the past few months. Here is a summary of Jack's findings:

	Sales Price	Annual Net Income
Apartment A	$102,000	$12,000
Apartment B	100,000	9,500
Apartment C	95,000	9,500

Janet quickly determined each of the apartments' capitalization rates by dividing the net income by the sales price:

Apartment A	11.8%
Apartment B	9.5%
Apartment C	10.0%

Janet decided to take the average of the rates to use for her own calculations. This came to just under 10½ percent. Now, to arrive at the true value of the real property, Janet divided the net operating income by the capitalization rate to arrive at the figure, $115,385.

Although the capitalization rate is useful in computing the property value, it's also important to consider the interest rate on any underlying mortgages. For example, if a mortgage is carrying an interest rate of 12 percent and the property has a capitalization rate of only 10 percent, then the property is, in essence, borrowing money at the rate of 12 percent and earning money at the rate of 10 percent. Under certain circumstances, it may be appropriate to loan money on such a property where there is sufficient protective equity.

THE ROLE YOUR INTUITION PLAYS IN APPRAISALS

To a very large degree, an experienced investor learns to rely upon a combination of intuition, knowledge, experience, and investigation in making each and every investment. Friends, brokers, realtors, and salespersons *all* view property in different lights for different reasons. The experienced investor learns to rely upon his or her own judgment.

In the final analysis this may boil down to nothing more than "gut feeling." Often, using all three different formulas for appraising property yields estimates that are very, very close. An average can be taken between the three of them in order to find a "true value" of the property. But when all of the figuring is done, the investigation complete, and discussion over, a prudent investor will do well to cultivate a consultation with that "gut feeling" or intuition. An investor should *know* right then and there whether he or she wants to deal. You, too, will develop that sixth sense with experience, and when you do, you should act upon it.

FIVE ELEMENTS IN THE APPRAISAL PROCESS

By now, you should be thoroughly acquainted with the general considerations, five principles of valuing, and the three methods of property appraisal. It is appropriate, then, to put this substantive knowledge to the test and to begin viewing real property for purposes of appraisal as a potential buyer of discounted mortgages. In order to manipulate the mass of data that will be generated by this process, an orderly appraisal procedure should be followed.

This ordered appraisal process will involve the creation of a file for each piece of property under serious consideration. The file will contain the five important elements described below. The final appraisal produced by this process may differ from a professional appraiser's *method* but should produce an equivalent *result*.

Identify the Property

So that there will be no misunderstanding about exactly which piece of real property is involved, identify the property in two ways

a. By proper legal description; and
b. By street address (including city, county, and state).

Identify the Title, Interests, and Liens

The file should show the nature of the title (fee simple, life estate, and so on) and the nature of each ownership such as single person, joint ownership, or joint tenancy. Of *primary* concern is the identification of all obligations and liens against the property (mortgages, attachments, liens, taxes, and other assessments) and of any adverse holdings or claims or actions pending against the property or ownership, as for example a *lis pendens.*

Provide a Narrative Description

Give an overall, general description of the property. Include at least the following information:

    a. type of dwelling (single, duplex, or triplex);

    b. style of house (ranch, Victorian, or whatever);

    c. number of floors;

    d. vacancy status; and

    e. photographs, if at all possible.

Appraise the Property

Follow the steps set out in this chapter to determine the market value of the property. Include in the file all of the data upon which the appraisal is based.

Utilize Other Appraisals

In many cases an investor will have access to past appraisals or even current appraisals made by loan companies, mortgage companies, and financial institutions. Be certain that you note the purpose of such an evaluation and the date of its making. Both of these factors should be taken into account before the information can be effectively utilized by the investor.

The appraisal file, once complete, should provide you with all of the pertinent information upon which an intelligent and accurate estimation may be made as to a property's "true value." It is an indispensable part of the appraisal process.

A HYPOTHETICAL TOUR ILLUSTRATES THE APPRAISAL PROCESS

Now that you are fully equipped to make a property appraisal, let's accompany a couple of experienced investors through a routine appraisal.

Jeff and Jennifer are a married couple who have been investing in discounted mortgages for over ten years. Their realtor friend, Jack, called to tell them about the availability of a discounted second mortgage on a single-family residence that looked like a good investment. Jennifer immediately took note of the street address of the property involved, the details of the transaction, and inquired if Jack was aware of any existing appraisals on the property. Because Jack's office had been involved in the transfer of this home just over three years ago, Jack said that he could provide them with copies of the last appraisal, instrument of transfer, and legal description.

Jeff immediately drove down to Jack's office and obtained copies of these documents. He returned home and picked up Jennifer, and together they drove past the property under consideration. They found that the home was a residential tract home surrounded by houses of substantially the same design. It was well-kept and well-located. Because of the terms of the proposed second mortgage, and because the property appeared to be a good investment, they decided to go in immediately and look over the house, the property owners, and the general circumstances of the property.

They approached the door and decided that Jennifer should be the first person that the homeowner would see. John, one of the homeowners, answered the door. Jennifer immediately introduced herself and Jeff and announced the purpose of their visit, "We understand that the holder of the second mortgage on your home wants to transfer that interest. We are interested in that investment and wondered if we might look at the house for evaluation purposes?"

As usual when Jennifer went along, they were admitted and given a tour of the home. Both Jeff and Jennifer have trained themselves to make mental notes of innumerable details: how the premises are kept, the furniture, the neatness and cleanliness of the whole house, the dress, demeanor and conduct of the owners and their children, and other things. Jeff and Jennifer make it a point to conduct these "tours" whenever possible *without* an appointment so that they can obtain a truer picture of the total environment.

In this case, John, the homeowner, apologizes for the mess as this is his housecleaning day. But the only "mess" visible to the eye is the floor polishing machine obviously in use upon a clean kitchen floor. Jennifer and Jeff contain their excitement as they are shown through an investor's dream house.

The only question nagging in the backs of both their minds by now is the status of John's employment. Why is he at home on a weekday morning polishing the floor?

This question was answered during the tour of the house when John showed them his office where he did at-home editing for his employer, a nationally recognized publishing house. Because his employment offered a flex-time situation and his wife, Jewel's, as an accountant, did not, John liked to spend his Fridays preparing the house for their weekend activities.

Jennifer and Jeff have seen enough. They take their leave of John and immediately retire to their car where they make a joint effort to note down every important detail about the house and owner that they can remember. As Jeff is driving to the courthouse, Jennifer is busy taking down all of the information the two of them can gather on preprinted appraisal forms. They note the good parts and the bad parts of the premises, the condition of the paint, the condition of the house, the nature of any building projects or new structures, the condition of the garden and yard, and the automobiles and recreational vehicles on the premises. In short, *every* detail, whether negative or positive, is noted.

Particular discussion ensues concerning the employment of the owners. Editors and accountants are adjudged relatively "safe" occupations. Their experience in the past with people employed in the aircraft industry, by comparison, had been particularly negative. Any occupation or company that is completely dependent upon the government for a livelihood merits special consideration. Certain industries have a "feast or famine" cycle, and this is a special fact to be taken into consideration in their appraisal process.

As they are scouting out a phone, they also make notes about the surrounding neighborhood. They look for churches, markets, transportation facilities, and schools, all of which assist them in their final evaluation. Finally, Jeff sees a phone and he stops to call the holder of the mortgage.

When Janet, the holder, answers, Jeff introduces himself and identifies the purpose of his call. He expresses his interest in the investment and sets up an appointment later that afternoon.

Jeff and Jennifer drive straight to the courthouse to finalize the details of their appraisal. They verify the legal description and learn that the only other obligation of record outstanding on the property is a first mortgage in the face amount of $50,000 on a note of thirty years duration at 11 percent interest.

Our investors return to their home to digest all of the information now accumulated in their appraisal file and to consider the terms of the proposed second mortgage transfer. By now they know that John and Jewel purchased the house three years ago for a sale price of $125,000. They had put down $30,000 in cash, had applied toward the balance $50,000 which they borrowed from JKL Bank, and had given the owner a second mortgage and note for the $45,000 balance. That second mortgage carried interest-only payments with a balloon payment in five years. The owner—for reasons as yet unknown—needed or wanted to sell her second mortgage. On the phone the holder had indicated simply that she wanted to dispose of the interest and was thinking that a discount of 18 percent would be fair.

Jeff and Jennifer agree that the house would have roughly appreciated 10 percent per year since the last appraisal. This meant that the house would be worth somewhere around $162,500 on the current market. With a total of $95,000 more or less still outstanding, they figured that John and Jewel had an equity worth about $67,500. Their intuition tells them that taking into consideration all of the information at their disposal, this is probably a close estimate of the value and that this is a very likely prospect for their investment portfolio.

During their conference with Janet, the holder of the second mortgage, they learn that, with an accountant's precision, every payment on the $45,000 second mortgage has been made on time. They also learn that Janet is 75 years old and wants to simplify her life and liquidate her holdings for estate planning reasons.

Before meeting with Janet, Jeff and Jennifer have discussed the amount of the proposed discount. They agree that they will try to push for a full 20 percent if they can expose any flaw whatsoever in the proposed investment. Upon discovering that the note is seasoned and that the holder is not particularly pressed for money, they agree that her original terms, under all of the circumstances, are completely fair. They relay to Janet their enthusiasm and willingness to purchase the note and indicate they will get back to her that evening with their response.

The only factor remaining to be considered in their analysis is obtaining a more precise appraisal on the property. When they return home, they immediately phone Jack to see if he can give them any more information on the value of other houses in the neighborhood. Jack says that he will check around with his associates and see what he can find out.

While they are waiting, Jennifer and Jeff go over their information one last time. Both of them feel intuitively that this is shaping up to be an excellent prospect; provided the final appraisal comports with their rough estimates, they are prepared to consummate the transfer that evening.

Jack calls back within a couple of hours and provides the details of the sales of two similar houses in the neighborhood within the past seven months. From these figures, Jennifer and Jeff compare the qualities of their prospective property.

The first comparison home had an additional bedroom and half-bath and was sold for $175,000. The second comparison home had the same identical floor plan as the house under consideration, but it was located on the subdivision boundary street that faced a busy highway. This home had sold just two months ago for $159,000.

Jeff and Jennifer concluded that they did, indeed, have sufficient and accurate information to make the decision to proceed with the transfer. They called Janet that evening and made arrangements to prepare the paperwork first thing the following morning.

Most likely, an investor will not often come upon a potential investment that seems to fall together quite this nicely. But the example of Jeff and Jennifer was intended to illustrate the appraisal process and to assist you in visualizing the way that an investment decision is pieced together.

The single most important point to be made is that these hypothetical investors had done their homework; they had totally assimilated all of the information in this chapter and were, therefore, perfectly capable of manipulating it to their maximum advantage. You should be able to see by this point that appraisals constitute an investment art form that involves all senses. It is an aptitude that can be developed with practice and hard work.

CONCLUSION

It has been shown that an accurate appraisal will operate to safeguard your investment. In this chapter you have looked at several general considerations to keep in mind when considering the value of a piece of real property as well as the value of a discounted mortgage. After that you looked at five basic principles of valuing to be mastered before trying one of the three different appraisal methods: cost approach, market data approach, and income approach. Finally, you took an overview of an orderly appraisal process before observing two hypothetical investors evaluate a piece of property as a potential investment by utilizing all of the information given in this chapter.

Now that our hypothetical investors have committed themselves to this transfer, the next step in the process is to meet with the holder and finalize the details of the transfer. Our hypothetical investors will then carry this information to their attorney in order to begin the escrow process. In the following chapter, you'll see how this is accomplished.

7. Uncovering the Role of Escrow in the Transfer of Real Property Interests

THE FUNCTION OF AN ESCROW

One of the most important elements to keep in mind about trading in discounted second mortgages is the relative safety of your investment. The information given elsewhere on appraisals and fraud will go far toward reducing the small element of risk that exists. But the single most important area where expert assistance can best be utilized to minimize your risk factor is in the area of escrow. Thus, this chapter will take a look at the legal requirements necessary for a valid escrow, the tasks that are performed in a standard loan escrow process, and the circumstances surrounding the termination of an escrow.

How to Determine if an Escrow Is Necessary

Through the years a relatively complex body of law and procedure has evolved that concerns itself primarily with the transfer of interests in real property. The processing of all the paperwork and funds in connection with such a transaction is involved and requires special skills in order to perform the work promptly and accurately. For this reason, the custom has grown in most states of entrusting these details and tasks to a disinterested third party who is authorized to act as the agent of both parties. This third party is known as the *escrow holder*, and during the time that the documents, funds, and instructions relating to a real property transfer are in the hands of that third party, they are said to be *in escrow*.

Understanding What an Escrow Is

Escrow defies simple, straightforward definition. In essence, it may be said to be a written agreement between two or more parties to deliver to a neutral third party (the escrow holder) certain documents, deeds, or other instruments to be delivered to the grantee named in the agreement upon the fulfillment of all of the conditions of the agreement. The escrow holder, thus, may be referred to as the "stakeholder."

A more formal description of an escrow is provided by the California Civil Code, which describes it as "[a] grant [that] may be deposited by the grantor, with a third person, to be delivered on the performance of a condition, and on delivery by the depository, it shall take effect."

Most states have laws strictly regulating and licensing escrow companies. These regulations typically require provision of securities and bonding of escrow holders as well as annual audits of all books and records. In California, for instance, individuals may not be licensed as escrow holders; the license must be held by a corporate entity that is organized for the purpose of conducting an escrow business.

Further, licensed escrow holders are prevented by law from paying referral fees to anyone other than regular employees of the escrow company. This law operates to prohibit the giving of commissions to brokers for sending business to any one particular escrow company. Fees in these cases have been construed to include gifts or merchandise or other things of value.

An escrow may be opened for any number of reasons, but we shall concern ourselves here strictly with the "loan escrow" that involves the placing or transfer of a loan on a piece of real property. It is not always a necessity to open escrow for the consummation of such a transaction, but until you are thoroughly familiar with the information in this chapter (and in the chapter to follow on fraud) and until you have considerable experience in such transfers, it is definitely advisable that you utilize the services of a competent escrow holder, attorney, or other real estate expert. Remember that an escrow will not only serve to minimize the possibility of misunderstandings arising between the parties, but it will also serve to expedite the closing of the transaction, and, most importantly, to minimize your risk.

THE LEGAL REQUIREMENTS OF A VALID ESCROW

A valid escrow is created when there exists a binding contract between the buyer and seller *and* there has been a conditional delivery of transfer instruments to a third person. The binding contract can appear in any form including a deposit receipt, an agreement to sell, an exchange agreement, an option, or mutual instructions of the buyer and seller.

UNDERSTANDING ESCROW INSTRUCTIONS

Traders in discount mortgages will most likely use a form that is known as "escrow instructions." This is usually an agreement drawn by the parties themselves or by their attorney or broker or escrow holder. Although a written agreement is not strictly required, it *is* advisable. (A sample escrow instruction document may be found in Appendix A.)

Both parties to the agreement must submit instructions, even though in some states both buyer and seller instructions may be in the same document. You should be aware that if there is an original contract and subsequent escrow instructions conflict with that document, a court will refer back to the original document and attempt to reconcile the two. If no reconciliation is possible, however, the terms of the instructions will usually control.

Thus, it is essential for the novice to appreciate this fact: When respective escrow instructions are submitted by each of the parties and they are identical in their material terms and effect, they will—in and of themselves—constitute a *binding and enforceable contract*. This is a very significant *legal* fact and should operate to alert the beginning trader in second mortgages to an area for caution.

What Should Be Included in Escrow Instructions

Before entering into an escrow agreement, it is essential that the parties at their leisure go over each and every item they propose be put into the instructions. Especial attention should be paid in the instructions to the disposition of fees and prorations. The cost of the escrow, structural reports, title insurance, broker's fees, filing or recording fees, and all other expenses involved in the transfer should be clearly spelled out at the beginning of the escrow process in the instructions.

Another consideration (at least in certain parts of the country) in conjunction with escrow instructions is a structural report on the property that may include a termite inspection. If either of these factors is a consideration for the making of the loan, then the escrow should be contingent upon a favorable disposition of these issues. The general rule is that the seller of a mortgage pays all of the costs involved in transferring a second mortgage, but this should be discussed and included in your escrow instructions as a part of your written agreement.

Once the parties can reach agreement, the instructions should be reviewed by an expert in the field of real estate. In fact, when possible, it would be a prudent practice to have your expert appear at the time of the drafting of the instructions instrument (where the escrow holder is drafting the document) so that each element of the transaction is integrated into the instructions.

This procedure will obviously minimize the likelihood of misunderstandings arising during the course of the escrow. It also minimizes the chance that subsequent changes will have to be made in the instructions. You should know that all changes or modifications that must be made to the instructions once they are submitted will have to be in writing and signed by all of the parties to the transaction.

THE TASKS PERFORMED BY AN ESCROW HOLDER

When the instructions are in agreeable form to all of the parties, the instructions will accompany the conditional delivery to the third party stating that the instruments are to be delivered upon the performance of the stipulated conditions. When the delivery is complete, then, the two requirements for a valid escrow have been met.

From this point on, the average loan escrow process will involve three distinct tasks to be performed by the escrow holder:

1. A preparation of all papers involved in the real estate transfer;

2. An assurance that the papers are properly executed, delivered, and recorded; and

3. An accounting of all disbursements of monies involved in the transfer.

Checklist of Documents Processed in Escrow

The legal requirements that must be met in order to protect an investor may vary in small but significant ways from one state to another. Therefore, it is advisable for the novice to work closely with an attorney or other real estate expert until he or she has gained experience with the paperwork trail that is involved in every such real estate transfer. Although the names of some of these documents may vary from state to state, the essential purposes of the documents that are required for these transfers are standard.

There are eight documents of legal significance that are of concern to a potential investor:

1. Mortgage or Trust Deed
2. Promissory Note
3. Assignment
4. Policy of Title Insurance
5. Owner's Offset Statement
6. Insurance Endorsement
7. Request for Notice (of Default)
8. First Mortgagee's Statement

Each of these documents is described in detail below, and a sample of each form may be found in Appendix A. The intent of this discussion and these samples is to acquaint you with the *basic* information you'll need in a loan escrow. This isn't intended to substitute for the advice of competent counsel. To the contrary, we suggest that you familiarize yourself with these documents thoroughly and then invest in some advice from your local attorney in order to learn your state's variations. Generally remember, however, that there is a definite legal purpose for each of these documents and that for the most part they are protective of your rights and of your investment.

Mortgage or Trust Deed. As you may recall from the description of these instruments in Chapter 1, the original mortgage or trust deed is a printed document with certain filled-in information: the name of the mortgagee, a legal description of the property, and the total of the debt that refers to a certain promissory note "of even date." This document will be signed by the homeowner(s)-mortgagor(s) and notarized. Most such instruments also contain their share of "fine print" or "boiler-plate" that spells out in minute detail the rights and duties of both parties to the mortgage.

Promissory Note. The second important document to the escrow is the original promissory note. This is the signed promise to pay that accompanies the original mortgage. Such a note may be in one of several forms (demand note, installment note, and so on), but generally it is an installment note that will refer to the mortgage of the same date that secures the note.

It, too, is signed by the homeowner(s)-mortgagor(s) who thereby promises to pay the total indebtedness shown on the note, together with a specified amount and rate of interest, with payments to be made at specified times. It will state how the payments are to be credited; usually, payments are credited first to interest then due and the remainder to principal. It may state that the entire balance falls due at a certain date, or it may state that the payments are to continue until all principal and interest have been paid.

As part of the escrow, the original note must be endorsed over to you by the previous mortgagee. This endorsement will appear on the back of the note exactly as if it were an endorsement on a check. Naturally, all of the signatures must match those on the earlier note and mortgage. A note signed by more than one party must be endorsed by *all* original signers.

Assignment. The third important document to the escrow is known as the assignment of the mortgage. It is usually a printed document with spaces for your name and a legal description of the property. This interlineated information should also be checked for accuracy.

The assignment will be signed by the party who is transferring the mortgage to you, and that name and signature should be identical to the name and signature on the mortgage and promissory note endorsements. Where a mortgage has been through several transfers, there will appear many such endorsements, and each of these should be checked for accuracy of legal description and signatures.

Policy of Title Insurance. The fourth important document is a policy of title insurance. In some areas this is known as the abstract of title. It will consist of a folder of information relating to the amount of insurance coverage on the validity of title, a legal description, a list of easements, status of mineral and water rights, a list of liens against the property, and the status of taxes.

You should verify that your name and the legal description are correct. Most importantly, verify that there are no liens prior to your own mortgage of which you were not aware and that there are no delinquent taxes owing on the property.

Owner's Offset Statement. The fifth important document is known as the owner's offset statement or the estoppel agreement. This form contains the information you need to insure that the amount represented to be owed on the property is correct. It's a statement that shows the balance due on the note, the amount of the regular monthly payments, the rate of interest, and the date to which interest has been paid. Most importantly, it bears the owner's signature.

Insurance Endorsement. The sixth important document is an insurance endorsement changing the name listed on the fire or householder insurance policy from the former mortgagee's to yours. This may be, instead, in the form of a letter from the former mortgagee to the insurance carrier requesting that this change in names be made.

Request for Notice (of Default). This is the seventh important document, and for traders in discounted second mortgages, it is one of the most important. This document, which is to be signed by the former mortgagee, asks that you be notified if the property is to be sold as a result of foreclosure action by the holder of the first mortgage. This document must be recorded to be effective, and once it is, it is a powerful protection for you. This is true because the first mortgage holder must prove that you were notified prior to any foreclosure action if any such purported foreclosure were to be effective.

First Mortgagee's Statement. This is the eighth and final document that will be important in an escrow of a second mortgage, and like the Request for Notice, it's *essential* for your protection. Roughly, it is equivalent to the owner's offset statement described earlier. This document, however, is obtained from and signed by the holder of the first mortgage, and it sets out the date to which interest has been paid and the amount of the principal balance remaining on the first mortgage. The seller of a second mortgage may have submitted in the escrow instructions an estimate of the approximate balance on the first mortgage, but this document will *insure* that the balance on a first mortgage is not much greater than you were led to believe.

Although this array of legalistic documents may seem imposing, each and every one serves a unique purpose in the transfer of interests in real estate. After you have been through the escrow process several times and are more familiar with these documents, you'll incorporate them very easily into your thinking.

But until that time arrives and you feel quite comfortable with each of these documents and their variations, remember that it's advisable to have an expert backing you up. With expert input relating to those variations, you'll soon learn that there are a few shortcuts that may safely be taken. You will also learn what procedures are required in your state when any of these eight documents are lost or destroyed. But, as mentioned earlier, because of the state-to-state variations in real estate law and escrow procedures, it is most advisable that these questions be directed to your local expert.

The Universal Escrow Steps

The basic steps in the escrow procedure are universal. When the parties have agreed upon the escrow instructions, the paperwork described above is initiated. The monies that are called for are deposited with the escrow holder, and all of the papers necessary to the instructions are obtained and handed over to the escrow holder.

A preliminary title search is then conducted, and a report is made for the purpose of immediately ascertaining the legal ability to sell, transfer, or convey the property. The preliminary title search will also report on the conditions of the title and any liens, investments, bonds, or other matters that may hamper the completion of the escrow instructions.

Once the title search is completed, the escrow holder proceeds to obtain all of the signatures necessary to the transfer. When all of the instructions, monies, and documents are collected in escrow so that it can be finalized, it is referred to as a "perfect escrow." It's at this point that the relevant documents are recorded.

Understanding Why Recordation of Escrowed Documents Is Necessary

Why is recording necessary? Some written instruments *must* be recorded in order to be legally effective. The reason for this is simply to "give the world notice" of the existence of the document, and therefore of the interest. In legal terms this is called *constructive notice*, which means that the law will *presume* that all the world has knowledge of any document that is recorded.

Most states (if not all) require that such documents relating to real property be recorded in the county where the real property is situated.

Thus, a purchaser of real property is stopped from coming into a court and claiming ownership of a parcel of land he or she has paid for when the record shows that it was purchased from someone who never had title and authority to sell.

Another kind of notice that you should be aware of is *actual notice*. This occurs when a person has personal knowledge of a situation that is contradictory to a transaction. A classic example of actual notice is where a party is purchasing some interest in real property from one person and then the purchaser actually goes to the real property and discovers an altogether different person in apparent possession of the land.

The law would say that the purchaser had been put on notice that there were persons who might have an interest adverse to the original understanding. Thus, a duty would be imposed upon the purchaser as a result of this actual notice to determine the true nature of the ownership before proceeding with the transfer.

Recording serves another purpose, too, and that is to prioritize all of the legal instruments affecting a piece of real property. This prioritization will directly impact upon the amount of equity that is actually available to a parcel of land and to a potential purchaser of a second mortgage secured by that land.

The precise rules of priorities will definitely vary from one jurisdiction to another. Thus, unless you count yourself among the other real estate and legal experts in your state, it is highly advisable that you seek competent advice in this area.

The Part Accounting Plays in an Escrow

The third and final task in the escrow process is the accounting of all charges, disbursements, prorations, and net disposition of the funds that are involved in the transfer. In addition to the loan amount, a typical mortgage transfer may involve other expenses for both parties. Also, there may be expenses that will have already been paid in advance for a set period of time or that must be paid in the future. The responsibility for these expenses must be prorated (divided) between the parties.

For the typical loan escrow this proration will involve a tabulation of advance interest payments, fees for legal services, costs of recording and escrow, and possibly amounts to be applied against existing debts. The usual practice is for the escrow holder to account for all of these items by preparing a written closing statement that shows the amount of money the purchaser needs and the seller nets after expenses. While the format of closing statements may vary widely, the final result should always show this tabulation.

HOW TO CLOSE AN ESCROW

An escrow can be terminated in one of two ways: by full performance and closing, or by mutual consent and cancellation. The three-step process described above usually leads to a termination by full performance and closing. But there may arise an occasion where the escrow holder's examination of title discloses liens for which the seller is responsible (or unaware). In this eventuality, the instructions may provide that the loan amount may be used to clear the title so that the transaction may proceed to closing.

But in the case where the title cannot be cleared or for any other reason the sale cannot be completed according to the agreement, then the instructions usually provide that all documents and monies be returned to the appropriate party. Alternatively, an occasion may arise where the time limit on an escrow expires and neither party has performed in accord with the terms of the agreement. The general rule in these cases is that all parties are entitled to the return of their papers and documents and the escrow is thereby cancelled.

CONCLUSION

The information in this chapter has provided a detailed review of all phases of the escrow process. This review began with the general background and meaning of escrow, escrow holders, and escrow companies that are common to all states. It continued with a look at the requirements necessary to a legally valid escrow. Particular attention was devoted to suggestions for inclusion in the escrow instructions.

This analysis was followed by a comprehensive look at the three basic tasks of an escrow: the documentation, the execution and recording, and the accounting. Finally, we took a brief look at some of the circumstances that may arise to cause a termination of the escrow.

The purpose of this discussion has been to appraise you of the general information that every investor should master at the outset. The complexity of the legal documents and the serious ramifications of the various legal nuances involved in the transfer of an interest in real property support the suggestion that the beginning investor invest *first* in sound, expert advice applicable to the jurisdiction in which transactions will be occurring.

We hope that by now you appreciate the protection that a "clean" escrow can provide. As pointed out in the beginning, an escrow can operate as one of the most significant factors in assuring the safety of your investment. Another source of insurance is educating yourself with respect to common fraudulent practices. This interesting and informative topic is the subject of our next chapter.

8. How to Size Up and Limit Your Investment Risk in Discount Mortgages

HOW TO DETERMINE IF FRAUD OCCURS IN THE DISCOUNT MORTGAGE FIELD

The theory upon which this book has been based is that investing in second mortgages produces high profits at a relatively low level of risk. You have already been shown that the risk factor can be reduced with accurate appraisals and expert help at the escrow stage of your investing. We believe that there is one other area where a little education at the outset may stand you in good stead; that area, of course, is fraud and deceit.

At a real estate class held in the Los Angeles area by one of the realty departments of a prestigious bank, the instructor warned: "If you deal with a crook, you are going to be crooked!" He went on to describe how he and his bank had twice been "done in" by unscrupulous "wheeler-dealers."

Although there can be no guarantees, the information in this chapter should go a long way towards educating you in the fine art of uncovering possible frauds *before* you invest your hard-earned money. In this chapter we will consider first the legal background underlying a cause of action for fraud or deceit. Next, we will list the primary deceptive practices that occur in the mortgage trading field. After that, one specific case of mortgage fraud will be described. Finally, we will take a look at twelve safeguards that you can take to protect yourself from fraudulent practices.

107

THE COMMON LAW ELEMENTS OF FRAUD AND DECEIT

The common law rule is that a cause of action for deceit will lie where there has been a fraud resulting in damage. The elements for such a cause of action are:

1. A material representation was made as a statement of fact that was known to be untrue.

2. The statement was made with the intent to deceive and to induce the other party to act upon it.

3. The other party did rely upon it and was damaged thereby.

HOW TO USE CASE LAW TO DEFINE THE PARAMETERS OF FRAUD

The question of fraud being committed by silence has received special attention by the courts. Here, the general rule is that mere silence does not constitute fraud. However, in cases where a special relationship of trust exists between the parties (such as broker to client), a duty to speak does exist, and silence (or nondisclosure) in this circumstance may constitute fraud.

In most states, if a material, false statement is made without knowledge of its falsity, but *recklessly* made without regard to the consequences, then a fraud action will also lie. And if a person makes an unqualified statement implying personal knowledge when none, in fact, exists, then he or she is likewise liable for the statement.

On the other hand, where a person expresses an opinion or makes a guess or an estimate that later proves to be untrue, no fraud may be said to have been committed. The general rule that a cause of action in fraud cannot be based upon the mere expression of opinion has been the subject of extensive litigation and is now heavily qualified. For example, there is authority for the view that fraud is committed where a person expressed an opinion where the other party had a right to rely on what was stated and was damaged thereby.

There is also support for the view that it is an act of fraud to purchase or obtain services or goods without any intention of paying for them. And an intentional misrepresentation as to the contents, nature, or terms of a contract or other instrument is considered an actionable fraud.

Finally, a person has no right to rely on a material, false statement if she or he had knowledge of its falsity or has reason to doubt the truth of it. This is related to a person's duty to use ordinary measures of caution to protect his or her own interests.

THE DIFFERENCE BETWEEN CIVIL AND CRIMINAL FRAUD

In *civil* litigation the deceived party is usually attempting to recover money damages to compensate for the harm resulting from the fraud. These actions are litigated by private parties and their own attorneys.

In all states there will also be *criminal* statutes defining a crime of fraud or deceit. The language of these statutes will vary from state to state. It's important for you to know that a case of civil fraud may also involve the commission of a crime. In these cases, the criminal portion of the litigation would be prosecuted by the appropriate state officer (District Attorney, Prosecutor, or Attorney General) while the civil portion would be conducted by private attorneys.

EIGHT DECEPTIVE MORTGAGE PRACTICES

Now that you are apprised of the legal bases for civil and criminal fraud, let's look at a few of the deceptive practices that periodically crop up in conjunction with mortgage trading.

1. False claims as to the financial ability of a person or business to meet its obligations.

2. False property appraisals.

3. False statements as to the position of the mortgage being traded with respect to other mortgages, liens, claims, taxes, obligations, suits and litigation, easements, and covenants relating to the real property.

4. False statements as to the condition of the title or ownership of the primary obligation and its security.

5. False statements as to the amount of the obligation, promptness of payment, the true payor, and the circumstances under which payments have been made.

6. False statements as to the financial condition of the senior mortgages.

7. False statements and claims utilizing charts, figures, graphs, and equations promising a particular yield that is not forthcoming.

8. False statements concerning the payments, duration of the note, and the terms and conditions therein.

This is a brief survey of some of the most frequently attempted deceptive practices that are sometimes seen in the trading of second mortgages. See how many of these you recognize in the following scenario.

A HYPOTHETICAL CASE OF FRAUD

Consider this fictitious example carefully: JKL Builders, Inc., develops a small, two-acre tract in moderately-priced suburban ranch-style homes at an average cost of $40,000. JKL obtains a commitment from the local bank to finance first mortgages of $35,000 and decides to sell the homes starting at $55,000. Because the buyer will have to come up with $20,000 cash for the down payment, and because few home purchasers for these particular homes are likely to have that much cash available, JKL is prepared to accept a down payment of $10,000 and to finance the remaining $10,000 on a second mortgage for the buyer.

The "good paper" ending to this story is that such a buyer appears and purchases one of the homes for $55,000 total—$10,000 cash down, a first mortgage to the bank of $35,000, and a second mortgage to JKL of $10,000. JKL then sells this paper at a 20 percent discount for $8,000 and nets a profit of $13,000.

The "bad paper" ending is dramatically different. The homes are built and the bank commitment is arranged. But the economy suffers a sudden, unexplained downturn. Buyers grow more conservative as well as more scarce. JKL, which has the bulk of its working capital tied up on the tract, finds it is in dire need of money if it is to stay in business.

A scheme is devised to produce that capital whereby a "buyer" is produced who "purchases" one of JKL's homes. The buyer signs for the $35,000 bank loan and the $10,000 JKL second mortgage, but no $10,000 down payment is ever made. JKL then sells the second mortgage, as above, for $8,000. JKL has now sold one house and received $35,000 from the bank and $8,000 from the sale of the second mortgage for a total profit of $3,000.

But the "buyer" (not too surprisingly) fails to make any payments.

In exchange for the use of the buyer's good name, he or she will receive free rent until evicted, which could take many months. The purchaser of the second mortgage has been, in the words of the real estate teacher, "crooked."

Or consider a slight variation on the "bad paper" ending. Suppose JKL builds the homes for $40,000 and wants to sell them at an over-priced value of $75,000. Again, there is collusion between JKL and a "buyer" with no intention of paying. If a first mortgage of $45,000 can be obtained and a second mortgage for $8,000, then JKL simply comes out that much more ahead.

Needless to say, variations on this theme can go on and on. The number and variety of fraudulent schemes are literally infinite. If this is true, you are undoubtedly wondering, how can you protect yourself from being a victim of such deception? Well, the answer is quite simple: Use your common sense, thoroughly equip yourself with the fundamentals outlined in this book, avail yourself of expert help when appropriate, and take note of the safeguards listed below.

TWELVE SAFEGUARDS AGAINST FRAUD

As attorneys guiding and advising innumerable clients who are trading in discounted mortgages, we have developed over the years a list of twelve important safeguards against fraud. If you are diligent in your efforts to abide by these rules, the chances of your being "crooked" will be effectively reduced.

1. Know the entire transaction. *Refuse* to be rushed. A fast talker should operate as a red flag to be cautious. If there is some element of the transaction that you do not understand and that cannot be satisfactorily explained to you, then insist upon taking the time to find an expert in the field that can explain it to your satisfaction.

2. Cultivate a strong working relationship with a dependable, knowledgeable expert and be guided by his or her advice.

3. Know the strengths and weaknesses of your seller, whether it be a private individual or a mortgage investment company.

4. Obtain a guaranteed title. Insist that your escrow include all of the documents pertinent to your state and to your transaction that are described in detail in the chapter on escrow.

5. Read every instrument and obligation connected with your

transaction. If there is *anything* that you do not understand, seek your expert's advice.

6. Always know the track record of the payor. This goes hand in hand with the advice to avoid purchasing any unseasoned note. If you question this advice, reread the hypothetical case of fraud given above.

7. Always fully inspect the real property that is securing the loan. Make your own appraisal or procure an independent, professional appraisal. Know the value of the real property.

8. Check out all of the representations that are made as much as possible. Especially look into any claims relating to yield. If representations are made orally, see that the party puts them in writing and have the document dated and signed by the maker of the statement.

9. Before you begin to invest in discounted mortgages, make certain that you are able to meet all costs and expenses in the event of a foreclosure.

10. If you are utilizing the services of a mortgage broker, look into his or her business background. Call the local Better Business Bureau and see what they have to say. You might even ask a prospective broker for two or three references. Call them and see what they have to say before entrusting your money to a total stranger. Go slowly. Let a broker who is unfamiliar to you handle one relatively minor matter for you. See how it feels. Build these relationships slowly and carefully.

11. Always keep in mind that the higher the return, the greater the risk. If a "fabulous" deal is offered to you, take the time to find out why. We already know there is no such thing as a free lunch, so try to find out why this is being offered to (or unloaded upon!) you.

12. Keep a full and complete record of the entire transaction for further reference in the event it becomes necessary.

CONCLUSION

In this chapter we have taken a long, hard look at the darker side of mortgage trading. We outlined in detail the legal underpinnings of a cause of action in fraud or deceit so that you would be familiar with all of the possible parameters of the problem.

The scope of fraudulent schemes is unlimited, and it is our intent here simply to apprise you of the possibilities. A description of all the variations that are possible would fill volumes, but we don't believe that it's necessary at all to belabor this point. Simply being aware that there are plenty of unscrupulous people out there who would love to take your money is sufficient.

We have attempted to bring about this awareness by listing some of the primary deceptive practices and then by describing in detail one specific case of mortgage fraud. Finally, we listed the twelve most important safeguards we share with clients who are investors.

Now that some of the seamier possibilities of mortgage investing have been revealed to you, we feel it incumbent to point out that we have assisted or advised literally dozens of mortgage investors over a span of several decades and, to our knowledge, not a single one has been a victim of a fraudulent practice. This brings us back to a very important point that it's easy to lose sight of: It's all relative. The more conservatively you proceed in your investing career, the less likely it is that you are going to end up being "crooked!"

9. How To Manage Mortgage Investments

THE PRIMARY GOAL OF MORTGAGE MANAGEMENT

Once you have begun the process of acquiring mortgages, your focus will begin to shift from purchasing to managing. This is an appropriate and sometimes subtle change. You will find that here, as in no other area of the investment field, your personal style and philosophy will come into play.

Managing an investment refers to the innumerable unexpected things that must be done in order to insure proper seasoning of a mortgage. A simpler way of putting it is to say that it is the collecting of rent. But it is the *way* in which you ultimately elect to pursue this goal that will determine not only your success but your pleasure in the process as well.

As you gain experience, of course, you will develop your own style. It's our purpose in this chapter to share with you an approach to managing investments that has evolved through many years in the business. Some of these ideas and suggestions may prove useful to you, especially at the start, as a model of one style of management.

The basic premise upon which this management approach is based is to do everything reasonably possible to obtain the mortgage payment so that the investment will be kept up and seasoned. As you already know, this is the surest way to obtain excellent equity, thereby constantly enhancing the investment. Additionally, from the chapter on leveraging, you know that the other component to regular and timely mortgage payments is that the investor has available at his or her disposal greater and greater funds for *other* investments.

THE PART THAT PERSONAL STYLE PLAYS IN MORTGAGE MANAGEMENT

The element of personal style comes in when you decide just exactly *how* it is that you are going to go about insuring the timely

115

payment of your mortgage investment. We have elected to follow a more personal approach in this regard, emphasizing to the borrower that we are "in the same boat together." Anything that can be done to assist a borrower in trouble only serves to reciprocate in kind.

Thus, rather than set up stiff and artificial boundaries between the borrower and the investor, it is preferable to keep the relationship on a more personal basis. For example, we have driven mortgagors to different places, procured doctors, baby-sat, found jobs, and written letters—all for the ultimate purpose of seasoning investments. Other lenders send mortgagors birthday or holiday cards. (Information of this sort can be obtained from original loan applications.)

At the other end of this continuum of styles, we are all familiar with the heavy-handed, aggressive, and litigious landlord style. Somewhere between the extremes each investor must learn through experience to strike an agreeable balance.

Checklist of Management Factors to Consider in Formulating Your Style

In formulating your own philosophy of management, consider the following suggestions:

1. Do all you can to see that payments are made. Be a nursemaid, if necessary, until you have sufficient equity in your investment.

2. Each monthly payment usually means a payment on the senior obligations as well as on your own, which also serves to enhance *your* equity.

3. Each payment on the senior obligation helps to season and strengthen your mortgage and investment so that a future sale can be made at a smaller discount.

4. Properties in good areas for the past forty years have advanced approximately $8\frac{1}{2}$ percent each year, giving equity that much more protection. This fact should inspire every investor to continue to make certain that payments are made, especially on the senior obligations.

5. The more equity the borrower has in the property, the more he or she will make every possible effort to keep up the property and its payments. You'll find few foreclosures where the borrower has a good equity.

6. The nearer to maturity a senior obligation is, the easier it is for the mortgagor to obtain new financing and to pay off your loan. This

is also true where property is sold and your mortgage contains an acceleration clause.

7. When you assist your borrower in paying off the loan, you have money available to use in obtaining new and larger discounted mortgages.

8. Do all you can to obtain larger monthly payments by offering a good size discount for larger payments or for a payoff (as long as the discount you give is less than the discount you receive). Remember you are being paid on the face amount of what is due and not on what you paid for the mortgage.

9. Remember, too, that in a payoff or refinance situation you receive the full face amount due and not what you paid for the investment.

10. The more equity you have in your mortgage investment, the more you can borrow upon it and at lower interest rates.

11. If a borrower can't make a payment, consider a substitute payment, such as a coin collection, stamps, automobile, or other personal or real property.

12. Never lose your temper. It's sometimes appropriate to be stern, but never get so carried away that you say something you later regret.

13. If you make promises, keep them if at all possible.

14. Likewise, if you make threats, be prepared to follow through.

15. If new arrangements are made for the payments, make a note of the agreement and mail a copy of your note to the borrower to avoid misunderstandings.

16. Always make detailed notes of important conversations.

17. Keep on top of your investment by periodically discussing the situation with the borrower and senior lien holders, and neighbors when necessary. Periodically view the premises to ascertain how it is being maintained.

ALTERNATIVE WAYS OF MANAGING INVESTMENTS

You should be aware that there are alternative methods of managing investments. Most notably, professional mortgage or loan brokers, banks, and savings and loan associations will do the collecting for you should you so desire. If you are a good depositor, some will do it at no charge; others will perform this service for a small percentage charge. If for whatever reason you are not in a position to actively manage your investment, you should discuss this service with those businesses in your community that provide it and compare the offerings and charges.

PRELIMINARY STEPS TO BE TAKEN BY ALL MORTGAGE MANAGERS

No matter which route to managing your investments you decide to follow, there are a few preliminary steps you should take. We would suggest to the beginner that he or she set aside some time to sit down with an accountant in order to set up books for recording monthly transactions in the most orderly and efficient manner. Once this format is established, you will be able to utilize it for each new acquisition you make.

Next, set up an orderly filing system that you can also utilize for all future additions. For each separate mortgage, use an accordion file that contains three or four compartments at least. In this file keep all notes of discussions, pictures of property, appraisals, copies of mortgage and note, copies of all correspondence relative to the property or mortgage, credit reports, listings, escrow documents, and whatever else is pertinent to that particular piece of property or loan.

Once these housekeeping tasks are organized, you are then in a position to concentrate your energy on the active servicing of your properties.

How Forms Can Be Used in Standardized Situations to Streamline Management

Some of the correspondence involved in mortgage investment management is routine and common to each new transaction. For these types of letters, you may wish to utilize forms, either copied or stored on word processing equipment. (Several of the forms that we have found useful in mortgage management may be found in Appendix C.)

The first form letter that is useful is a letter to the borrower advising that you have purchased the mortgage and note and giving the borrower payment information. This information should include the address for payment, a payment book (which can be obtained from your bank or escrow company), and your phone number at the very least.

We usually go a little further than this and advise the borrower of our own filing system number and enclose a self-addressed envelope with the payment book filled out showing the balance due and the due date.

We also point out in this introductory letter that prompt payment is expected and that there is a late charge if the payments are not made within five days of the due date. This letter usually concludes with the observation that we are now "co-investors" in this transaction and that as lenders we stand ready to assist the borrower in any way possible to insure the continued safety and growth of the investment.

This introductory letter may be followed up with a personal call to the borrowers to emphasize that they, too, are making a wise investment and are on their way to accumulating a good asset. Again, we advise the borrowers that we will cooperate with them if they will meet their obligations.

The next form letter you may utilize is to the senior and junior mortgage holders and lien holders advising them of the transfer of ownership. Remember that a senior or junior lien holder may be a good prospect for selling at a discount in the future.

Other lenders use form letters to send to borrowers who fail to make timely payments or meet some other obligations due under the mortgage contract. We have seen separate form letters for every conceivable violation and default.

Alternatively, we have seen letters with a heading similar to the example below where the lender simply checks the appropriate category and writes an explanation when necessary in the lower half of the page.

_____ Failure to pay

_____ Late charge

_____ Late on tax payment(s)

_____ No copy of insurance coverage

_____ Failure to pay senior mortgage or lien holder

_____ Failure to keep premises in good repair

_____ Failure to lift mechanic's lien

In addition to these types of form letters, you may wish to adapt for your own use a set of forms for the eventuality that a borrower is in default in payments. These letters should be followed up with a telephone call. If no payment is forthcoming, you may use a form letter that advises the borrower of the date you will file for default if no arrangements are made to pay. Such communications will keep you advised of your investment status at all times.

CONCLUSION

In this chapter we have looked at the meaning of and necessity for the management of mortgage investments. Numerous suggestions were enumerated for consideration. In particular, we have looked at the impact that one's personal style will have upon the manner in which investments are serviced, and we have set out some of the details of our own management systems. Suggestions were made for the beginning investor as to the preliminary steps to be taken in setting up a management format. Finally, we looked at some of the standardized forms that may be utilized in the course of managing mortgage investments.

10. How to Cure Delinquencies and Turn Foreclosures to Your Advantage

HOW TO MINIMIZE INVESTMENT RISKS BY GOOD MORTGAGE MANAGEMENT

You have already observed that there is an element of risk involved in *any* investment but that the risk is considerably reduced when an investment is made in mortgages secured by real property. For those particular investments, the risks are generally limited to time requirements and capital exposure. The philosophy of our approach to mortgage investing has been to minimize risk in both of these areas. We have shown you how to educate yourself to the maximum extent possible, analyze potential investments for yield and risk, and appraise accurately the value of the equity securing your investments. Assuming that you put these practices to work for you in your own investment program, your exposure will also be minimized.

But, of course, the exception remains. It is for that case that we must turn our attention now to the management of a mortgage that gets into trouble. The well-educated mortgage investor, like the boy scout, should—after all—always be prepared.

HOW TO DETERMINE WHEN A DELINQUENCY OCCURS

In theory, a payment is delinquent if it is not made by 5:00 o'clock on the due date specified in the loan documents. In practice, however, most investors consider a payment to be delinquent if it has not been made five to ten (or even fifteen) days after the due date specified. This determination will depend upon the management style that you adopt, as was discussed in the previous chapter.

121

Delinquency can also occur in another way. Most borrowers in trouble will attempt to pay the larger, first mortgage and hope that the holder of the second will be patient. A few, however, will meet the payment of the second (because it is smaller, presumably) and fail to make the payment on the first mortgage. When this occurs, the investor will be unaware of the delinquency on the first until notification is received *vis à vis* the Request for Notice clause. (Refer to Chapter 7 on escrow if you need to review this important mortgage clause.) Such a delinquency is obviously a very disturbing situation to the mortgage investor because the default must be cured either by the borrower or the investor in order to protect the investment.

HOW TO HANDLE DELINQUENCIES

In the previous chapter you took a look at our rather informal system of mortgage management. This informality is possible, of course, only because you have done your homework *prior* to the investment. During the course of mortgage management, experienced investors have developed a sixth sense for the delinquency that is simply an oversight and the delinquency that is the forerunner of serious trouble. Before you have developed that sixth sense, however, you should take care to study carefully *every* delinquency. You may conclude that a conservative approach is more appropriate than informality, depending upon the circumstances you find.

Conduct an Immediate Investment Analysis

Should you conclude that you have a problem on your hands, it would be a good idea to conduct an immediate investment analysis to ascertain the seriousness of your position and to determine the appropriate course of action.

Your analysis should at the very least include the following items:

1. The remaining principal balances on all outstanding loans against the property,

2. An outline of the costs that are currently mounting against the property,

3. A determination of the status of all loans recorded prior to yours,

4. A determination of the status of tax payments relating to the property,

5. The charges accrued for late payments on either loans or taxes,

6. The time frame within which you must pay these protective costs, and

7. A determination of the condition of the property.

This analysis should help you determine your immediate equity position and project that position four months hence when a foreclosure can be completed.

Determine the True Cause of the Delinquency: Is it Minor or Major?

To help you analyze the situation, try to determine if the true cause of the delinquency is a major or minor problem. You will discover that some payors simply have bad payment habits. They really do not intend to default; they simply are disorganized. This is a minor problem that can be handled by the prompt and certain use of your late charges. Other minor problems you may encounter include delays in receiving expected monies, being away on vacation, changing jobs, sickness, and other unexpected expenses.

Major problems, on the other hand, usually fall into one of six categories:

1. Death of the breadwinner,
2. Separation or divorce,
3. Serious health crises,
4. Drug dependencies (especially alcoholism),
5. Loss of a job, or
6. Deliberate delaying tactics.

Take the Appropriate Corrective Action

Once you have ascertained the true cause of the delinquency, you will be in a better position to take the appropriate corrective action. This action may be one (or some combination) of the following:

1. Exercising the late payment penalty,
2. Corresponding with the borrower,
3. Contacting the borrower personally,

4. Cooperating with the borrower by developing a plan to cure the default,

5. Filing a foreclosure action.

Let's consider each of these options in detail.

When to Exercise the Late Payment Penalty

Provision for this penalty should be written into every note in which you invest because the exercise of this penalty can operate to nip many annoying delays in the bud. Every investor sooner or later encounters a borrower who tries to test mortgagees. If this is the case, firm action is called for by the investor. You do not have to accept a late payment that does not include the penalty fee. Such a payment can be returned and the fee deducted out of principal. Notification that this action has been taken will generally serve to place testing borrowers on notice that you are fully aware of your rights and intend to protect them. Routinely late borrowers, additionally, receive pocketbook impetus to become more organized when they begin to appreciate the actual cost in late payment penalty dollars for their disorganization.

When to Correspond with the Borrower

Most experienced mortgage investors have developed a series of three or four letters of increasing severity that can be used in cases of unexplained delinquency. Typically, the investor establishes a fixed time interval for sending such letters and hopes that one such letter will jar the borrower's consciousness to at least contact the mortgagee with an explanation of the delinquency and work cooperatively toward a resolution of the difficulty. (See Appendix C for letter samples.)

When to Contact the Borrower Personally

The borrower should be contacted personally when there has been no response by the borrower to your inquiries within your own personal time period limitation. This contact can be accomplished by a simple phone call in most instances.

When to Cooperate with the Borrower in Curing the Delinquency

When you are certain that the borrower's need for a grace period is genuine, you can reasonably wait for the borrower to bring the account current as quickly as possible. And there will be many cases where you can exercise this degree of confidence in your borrower. In the alternative, you may prefer to work out an informal repayment schedule with the borrower.

In those cases where you are not so sure of your borrower's integrity, however, you may want to agree to a specified grace period beyond which you will file a foreclosure action. The utilization of this deadline threat will help the borrower to understand that serious financial penalties will accrue—not to mention damage to credit —should the delinquency continue. Needless to say, failing to follow through on such a threat will seriously erode any remaining investor control over a delinquent borrower.

A particularly useful cooperative tactic can be applied where it is apparent that the borrower cannot cure the delinquency. This involves structuring a transfer of the real property to the mortgagee. In exchange for an agreed upon sum, the borrower agrees to transfer possession and ownership of the property.

When to File a Foreclosure

A foreclosure action should be filed as soon as your equity position is in peril. You must remember that you are in business, and where no other solution can be found, you must act swiftly and decisively to protect your own investments.

Acting quickly under these circumstances serves to protect your interest in several ways. First, it avoids additional (involuntary) liens being placed against the property, such as special assessments, real and personal property taxes, judgment liens, attachments, and mechanic's liens. Second, you may also prevent voluntary liens against the property. These may include homestead exemptions, easements, governmental restrictions, rights of way, and new leases.

Borrowers in marital trouble also merit swift attention. Investors learn very quickly that a divorce will ultimately lead to a change in title. Long legal entanglements may ensue with the unfortunate side effect of property neglect. Additionally, there may be disputes involving mortgage payments, and frequently creditors take action against such parties' real property.

HOW TO DETERMINE WHAT A FORECLOSURE ACTION ENTAILS

The actual mechanics of a foreclosure will depend upon whether you have invested in a mortgage or a trust deed. You may recall that in Chapter 2 the differences between these two instruments were outlined. In particular, you may want to review the broad differences between these two with respect to foreclosure before undertaking the detailed information below. Please note, too, that references in the following discussion to specific foreclosure time periods are given here for one typical jurisdiction. Those time periods may vary in your state.

Learning How a Mortgage Is Foreclosed

When a mortgagor fails to pay the loan according to the terms of the original agreement, the only legal method to force payment is to institute a legal action known as a suit in foreclosure. When a trial is held and the default proven, the court will order a sale of the property by the Sheriff or Court Commissioner. Specific time periods may vary from jurisdiction to jurisdiction; typically, however, a "Notice of Sale" is required to be posted for a period of twenty days and published once a week for at least three weeks, with the first publication at least twenty days prior to the sale.

At the expiration of the required time period, a sale is conducted and the property sold to the highest bidder. At this time the purchaser receives a "Certificate of Sale" that does not constitute either a deed or authority to take physical possession of the property. The certificate states, rather, that the mortgagor has the right to redeem the property within a one-year period. If the mortgagor fails to do so, then the purchaser will receive a Sheriff's or Court Commissioner's Deed.

During the one-year "Period of Redemption" the mortgagor may live on the property or sell the "Equity of Redemption" to another party. That grantee would thereby gain the right to redeem the property during the redemption period. If the mortgagor continues to occupy the home and fails to redeem, the purchaser is entitled to reasonable rent for that one-year period.

It may be important to remember that a deficiency judgment is possible where the foreclosure sale does not bring enough to pay the mortgage as well as the costs. And it is also important to be aware of the Statute of Limitations relevant to foreclosure actions. If a lender fails to file an action in foreclosure until after a period of four years has elapsed from the default, then the right of action is forever lost. Both the mortgage and the note securing it fall within the proscribed time limit.

Learning How a Trust Deed Is Foreclosed

A trust deed may be foreclosed as a mortgage or by a trustee's sale. In the former instance the procedure parallels that of a mortgage foreclosure except in one particular. If a deficiency judgment is not specifically asked for in the foreclosure, then there is a very limited time period (90 days) within which the trustor can redeem after the date of the sale. Otherwise, the time period for redemption is one year.

A foreclosure by a trustee's sale is initiated when the beneficiary notifies the trustee in writing that a default has occurred and requests steps be taken to foreclose. The trustee files a "Notice of Default" that must state with specificity the nature and extent of the default, identify the trust deed, and state that the beneficiary has elected to sell (or cause a sale of) the property. A copy of the Notice of Default must then be sent to the trustor, stating that the property may be advertised for sale three months after recordation.

If the trustor wishes to reinstate during this three-month period, the beneficiary must be paid the amount of all delinquencies including payment installments, taxes, assessments, actual costs the beneficiary has incurred in filing the foreclosure, and a fee to the trustee.

If the trustor does not wish to reinstate, at the expiration of the waiting period the trustee prepares a "Notice of Sale" which must be posted for at least 20 days in a public place in the city or district where the property is to be sold and additionally in some conspicuous place on the property itself. The Notice of Sale must also be published in a newspaper of general circulation at least once a week for at least three weeks. The first date of publication must be at least 20 days before the date of the sale. The published notice must contain all the pertinent data relating to the sale: the time of the sale, the location, a property description, and the occasion for the sale. Finally, a copy of the Notice of Sale must be sent to any person or entity who has previously filed a "Request for Notice of Default."

The trustor may prevent the sale at any time during the 20-day period of publication by paying off the entire loan, plus interest and costs. If the sale goes forward, the property is sold to the highest bidder and the beneficiary receives payment from the proceeds. Of course, all lien holders who are in a priority position are entitled to receive payment first. In order to protect your investment, therefore, you must initiate foreclosure and assume the obligations of prior liens. If another lien holder has initiated foreclosure, you must cure that default and then commence your own action. The purchaser receives a "Trustee's Deed" issued by the trustee, and may enjoy immediate possession of the property.

A foreclosure sale will call for bids to be paid in cash. The only exception to this rule is that the lender may bid up to the amount of unpaid balance without cash tendered.

The Statute of Limitations does not directly impact upon trust deeds. It is true that no foreclosure action may be maintained when filed four years after the default has occurred. However, because a trust deed can be foreclosed out of court by a trustee's sale, the statute has no effective impact.

By that same reasoning, no deficiency judgment is available in a trustee's sale. In other words, such a judgment can be obtained only in a court of law, and because the foreclosure proceedings do not take place within the court system, no judgment can be obtained.

But assume for the moment that a beneficiary perceived that there would be insufficient money at a trustee's sale to cover the loans against the property. Instead of selling the land through a trustee sale, the beneficiary could initiate a lawsuit and foreclosure through the courts, thereby obtaining the desired deficiency judgment.

But you should be aware that a deficiency judgment in court is allowed *only* in cases where the original loan did not originate out of a purchase money agreement. A *purchase money mortgage* arises out of one of the following circumstances:

1. Where a note is carried back by the seller as part or all of the purchase price on the property being purchased; and

2. Where a third person or party lends part or all of the purchase price of a dwelling with less than five units, at least one of which will be occupied by the purchaser. (Just for comparison, an example of a loan that would *not* be considered a purchase money mortgage would be one where a property owner mortgages real property for the purpose of financing a child's college education.)

HOW TO AVOID FORECLOSURES

Our experience is that most foreclosures can be avoided. Serious deterioration of investments can be ameliorated by the firm education of the borrower regarding timely payments. The investor has to make it clear that payments must be made on time. It is a serious mistake to fall into the habit of loaning borrowers money (on top of the original loan) in order to meet the original payment schedule. If a borrower cannot meet the payments, then the money should be borrowed from some other source. It is very easy for some borrowers to slide into an excessive debt position from which it is impossible to be extricated. This is to be avoided at all costs, and to a certain extent it is the responsibility of the investor to remember it may not be a favor in the long run to allow a borrower to miss payments.

But no matter how diligently you track your mortgagors, once in a while one of your investments may run into unavoidable trouble. Is there anything you can do to avoid a foreclosure in these cases? You can start by calling upon all of your *creative* resources. Consider the following as a small sampling of your options short of a foreclosure:

1. Approach the owner to see if any alternative payment can be arranged.

2. Consider accepting substitute payments—cars, property, other things of value.

3. Accept a quitclaim deed from the owner and cover senior mortgagees costs while awaiting a quick sale.

4. Offer the owner six month's free rent in exchange for such a quitclaim deed.

5. Offer the owner free rent in another property you own in exchange for such a deed.

6. Agree to wait for the owner to make the payments.

7. Obtain a deed in lieu of foreclosure (voluntary deed) from the mortgagor in satisfaction of the debt.

8. Assist the owner in the sale of the property.

9. Take a partial ownership in exchange for a reduction in the debt.

10. Agree to refinance the loan in order to get the owner back on his or her feet.

11. Accept a lump sum of principal and interest and adjust the mortgage to reflect the later payment of the overdue amount.

12. Allow the borrower to bring the interest portion current and agree to accept the late principal amount at some future date.

HOW YOU CAN UTILIZE A FORECLOSURE TO INVESTMENT ADVANTAGE

Most potential investors in real estate are aware of the large numbers of seminars available to the general public (and often at outrageous cost) purporting to demonstrate the way to wealth *vis à vis* foreclosures. We must admit a certain hesitation in this regard that is possibly grounded in personal preference. On a more concrete level, you should note that less that one and one-half percent of foreclosure actions filed actually go through to a judgment. Statistically, the odds are simply against you.

There are certain types of individuals, however, who seem perfectly suited to this avenue to wealth. They seem to enjoy the "game" of following the notices of default, contacting the borrowers in default, and arranging for a high-yield transfer of the property. It's just not a game that we have found particularly rewarding.

For those perhaps more knowledgeable or adventurous than we, it is interesting to consider the relationship between these two investment philosophies. For example, when you become knowledgeable in every phase of mortgage discounting and *if* you enjoy foreclosures, then you would be in an excellent position to service any discounted mortgage that fell into the category of delinquency.

It is not an aspect of mortgage investing that we can recommend for beginners. Foreclosures require a certain level of expertise, and a definite portion of success is dependent upon an investor's ability to act more quickly than other investors in gathering information and analyzing investment potential. But if you feel you may fall into this specialized category of investors, we should point out the advantages a combination of philosophies offers:

1. You are closer to the ground floor where you can learn about properties in distress before actually going into foreclosure.

2. You are familiar with the financial institutions that would want a responsible party to take over defaulting property.

3. Your financial institution contacts will give you leads and assist you in working out transfers.

4. You are in a favorable position to arrange package deals with excellent mortgages as well as distress mortgages with large discounts.

5. Your network of contacts is bringing you a constant source of mortgages that a more conservative investor in discounted mortgages would not consider.

6. You can buy distress property at a large discount, age the mortgage, and then have access to contacts where it can be sold at a small discount.

7. You can obtain a large inventory of mortgages for a small capital investment.

8. You can cultivate a larger clientele for buying and selling all kinds of mortgages.

9. Many key lots, homes, and other valuable property can be acquired only through foreclosure.

10. Very little money is needed to get into the foreclosure business.

11. There is little office expense necessary; many of the systems in use for your discounted mortgage investments will apply to foreclosure investments.

CONCLUSION

We know that investor risk is generally reduced by careful analysis of the borrower and the real property *before* a loan is made. The vast majority of borrowers are honest, decent people who would do almost anything to avoid a foreclosure.

But we believe that intelligent investing requires the realistic view that even honest, decent people can fall upon hard times and be unable to prevent a foreclosure. For these rare eventualities, a prudent investor must be prepared with the knowledge and techniques to limit losses to the maximum extent possible.

We have considered the problems of determining when a delinquency has, in fact, occurred, and how investor style can define the course of action to be followed upon that determination. The data that must be collected in an Investment Analysis were enumerated. Depending upon whether the borrower's problem is major or minor, five corrective actions have been set out.

In particular, you should be familiar with the mechanics of a foreclosure action so that you will not hesitate to initiate such an action where appropriate.

Finally, we took a moment to look at the business of turning a foreclosure loss situation into a high-yield profitable event. Although we do not recommend this avenue to the beginning investor, for those more experienced, we set out eleven ways that operating such a business in tandem with discounting mortgages could prove to be advantageous.

11. The Numbers Game: How Mortgage Yields Are Calculated

DETERMINING WHAT YIELD IS

In its simplest form, "yield" refers to the profit one makes on a given investment. This profit, or return on investment, may be calculated and expressed in a variety of ways, depending upon which of several variables and mathematical formulas are relied upon. Thus, you can readily see that the subject of yield, like the subject of interest, can be as complicated (or compounded, if you will) as you wish it to be. In keeping with the philosophy behind this book, we choose to look upon this subject in the simplest light possible.

WHY YIELD IS IMPORTANT IN DISCOUNT MORTGAGE PRACTICE

Yield is important because profit is important; the higher the yield, the higher the profit. And that—after all—is the reason why you are reading this book.

Consider for a moment the yield that would be earned on a simple savings account. If $10,000 is invested in a bank passbook account at 10 percent interest for one year, the yield would be 10 percent or $1,000. In this case, the yield is expressed as a *percentage* that reflects the relationship between the return on the investment ($1,000) and the amount invested ($10,000). Thus, the simplest formula expressing yield may be stated:

$$\frac{\text{Return}}{\text{Amount Invested}} = \text{Yield}$$

Now, suppose instead that our investor is considering an investment in a $10,000, one-year (interest only) second mortgage at 10 percent. Is there any way that a yield higher than the passbook account can be obtained on this investment? The answer depends upon several factors, but let's continue to look at the simplest case. If the investor must pay the face amount of the note (the full $10,000), then the return would be calculated exactly like the passbook example above. For example, the return would amount to $1,000 and the amount invested would remain $10,000. Using the formula above, we can see that the yield would be 10 percent.

$$\frac{\$1,000}{\$10,000} = .10$$

But how would the yield be affected if the $10,000 could be invested in a $10,000 second mortgage sold to the investor at a 25 percent discount, for example, for $7,500? In that case, the interest earned (10 percent of $10,000) would be the same as above, or $1,000, but the amount invested would be different. Using the yield formula set out above, that yield calculation would be as follows:

$$\frac{\$1,000}{\$7,500} = .13$$

You can readily see that discounting a note has a direct and positive impact upon the investment's yield.

THE VIEW FROM THE BUYER'S POSITION

For the sake of clarity, let's consider the significance of the yield from the buyer's point of view. Suppose you are a mortgage buyer with $10,000 to invest, and you want to produce a yield of 20 percent. You are able to locate a second mortgage seller with a $10,000 note at 10 percent, interest-only payments, for one year. How can this seller structure the sale of such a note in order to meet your needs?

Hopefully, you already understand the answer to that question —by manipulating the discount. If the mortgage earns interest of $1,000 per year and the yield demanded is 20 percent, then the formula for determining the amount the mortgage must be discounted is:

$$\frac{\text{Return}}{\text{Yield Desired}} = \text{Amount of Discount}$$

Plugging in our figures, we see that the seller must discount this particular note by $5,000 in order to meet your yield requirement of 20 percent:

$$\frac{\$1,000}{.20} = \$5,000$$

On the surface, this is only logical. If you were to invest $5,000 for one year at 20 percent interest, then you would, indeed, earn $1,000 in interest by the end of that term. But those readers who are already experienced in yield calculations will readily see that these simplistic examples do not take into account the *term* of the note. To frame the last example in more precise mortgage yield terms, it should be noted that a $5,000 discount would be required on a $10,000, 10 percent, *fully amortized* note. The impact that term has upon yield calculations is explained in more detail in the following section.

For the moment, however, these highly simplified examples illustrate the importance of yield in the mortgage investment field: Buyers of mortgages learn very quickly to analyze potential investments in terms of yield—it is the factor that will determine the discount that a buyer will demand. Sellers, on the other hand, can use the principles of yield and discounting to help them sell their mortgages. In this chapter, we will explore these subjects primarily from the buyer's point of view; the following chapter will complete the loop and consider yield and discounting from the seller's point of view.

THE TIME VALUE OF MONEY

If you were to lend $10,000 at 10 percent with interest-only payments for one year, then you would receive monthly the sum of $83.33.

Step 1: $10,000
             .10
            $ 1,000

Step 2: $\frac{\$1,000}{12 \text{ months}} = \$83.33$

At the end of the year you would have accumulated $1,000 in interest, which is, of course, 10 percent of the amount loaned.

But what if instead of monthly payments of $83.33, you were to receive the interest payment in one lump sum at the end of the year? The figures remain exactly the same, thus the yield would remain 10 percent. Technically, however, these are two different yields.

This is because of the time value of money. When you receive interest payments on a monthly basis, as opposed to an annual payment, you have an opportunity to put each successive interest payment to work earning *additional* interest, thereby increasing the total yield. If, as is often the case, the loan is fully amortized, there will be in addition to monthly interest payments a portion of principal repayment, further influencing the yield calculations. And just to keep it interesting, you should realize that for the most part, interest in mortgage lending is charged against the declining principal balance. If the loan is amortized, covering both interest and principal, then you are getting back some of your investment each month, but the portion attributable to interest is simultaneously declining.

Another way to look at the concept of the time value of money is by considering the future value of a fixed sum of money based on the principal of compounding. Suppose you have $10,000 in the bank at 10 percent annual interest. The first year you would earn $1,000, and at the end of the year you would have $11,000. At the end of the second year you would have accumulated $12,100. Carrying this out for a succession of ten years, you would have at the end of each successive year:

Future Value of $10,000 Compounded at 10 Percent Interest

Year 1	$11,000
Year 2	12,100
Year 3	13,310
Year 4	14,641
Year 5	16,105
Year 6	17,716
Year 7	19,487
Year 8	21,436
Year 9	23,579
Year 10	25,937

Table 11.1

If, however, you were to increase the interest rate to 15, 20, or 25 percent, your initial small investment could grow to amazing amounts.

For example, that same $10,000 invested for ten years at 15 percent would grow to $40,456; at 20 percent it would grow to $61,917; and at 25 percent it would grow to $93,132.

Look at Table 11.2 and see how a relatively small investment of $10,000 can grow to a multimillion dollar amount at different rates of interest, provided you do not touch the principal or interest over the holding period. By a slight stretch of the imagination, we can see that $361,000,000 can make life a bit more interesting than we can expect it to be existing on social security.

Future Value of $10,000 Compounded at Various Rates

Year	Future Value at 15%	Future Value at 20%	Future Value at 25%	Future Value at 30%
10	40,456	61,917	93,132	137,858
15	81,371	154,070	284,217	511,859
20	163,665	383,376	867,362	1,900,496
25	329,190	953,962	2,646,978	7,056,410
30	662,118	2,373,763	8,077,936	26,199,956
35	1,331,755	5,906,682	24,651,903	97,278,604
40	2,678,635	14,697,716	75,231,638	361,188,648

Table 11.2

THE VARIABLES THAT AFFECT MORTGAGE YIELD CALCULATION

The simple example just given points out the reason why there are *several* different ways of calculating yield, depending upon investor intent and the variables that are relevant. Thus, you may already be familiar with the calculations involved in figuring an internal rate of return, which can be applied where monthly payments are expended as they are earned, as opposed to mortgage yield calculations that attempt to account for the reinvestment of payments as they are earned. Because most second mortgages are traded on the basis of mortgage yield calculations, we will limit our discussion of yields to those terms.

Mortgage yield calculations involve the following parameters: the interest rate, the discount, the due date, the pay back rate, and the utilization of earned interest and principal. It may be said that mortgage yield is a method of computing a uniform rate of interest over the total pay back period taking into consideration all of the aforementioned variables. In other words, it takes into account the time value of money by giving greater weight to payments recovered earlier in the payment history and by giving less weight to payments received later in the payment history.

For the serious student of yield computations, the mathematical bases for the mortgage yield formulas may be found in Appendix E. For the remainder, which will include the vast majority of mortgage investors, the mortgage yield tables suffice very nicely. Let us turn now to a step-by-step illustration of the utilization of these tables.

HOW TO UTILIZE YIELD TABLES TO CALCULATE YIELD

As a rule, tables and statistics tend to discourage many people. You can become *very* interested in mortgage tables and statistics, however, when you learn how they can be utilized to increase your power to gain additional wealth and help you to become very rich. Just as an example, with a discounted, fully amortized note you can increase your yield and profit thousands of dollars by reducing the interest rate in exchange for a larger pay back rate, thereby recapturing your discount at a faster rate. Let's see how the yield tables can be used to help you save thousands of dollars with the proper manipulation of the terms of a note.

John inherited a $100,000, 10 percent, fully amortized mortgage from his grandmother. A few years ago she had taken advantage of the tax forgiveness law that allowed senior citizens a $100,000 tax-free profit on the sale of their residence. She used the $1,000 monthly payment generated by the note to supplement her social security check, and she moved into a nice apartment to avoid yard work.

John wanted to convert his newly acquired note into cash and did some investigation into its marketability. He called several mortgage brokers and spoke with one of his good friends in real estate and learned that on the existing market, the note could be sold at an 18 percent yield. John's friends explained that this figure would be based on risk, current market conditions, and the liquidity of the mortgage involved. (For example, a bank passbook account carries virtually no risk and is instantly liquid. It would, therefore, require no discount because it is on a par with cash. Similarly, a first mortgage is more secure than a second, and an investor would not require as large a return in order to compensate for the added investment risk of a second.)

John then used a mortgage yield table to find the cash value of the note under its existing terms. The tables John used were similar to those that can be found in the reference section of most local libraries. His first step was to compute the monthly pay-back rate by dividing the $1,000 monthly payment by the $100,000 face amount of the loan and then expressing that sum as a percentage (by multiplying that figure by 100 percent). Thus, John's pay-back rate was:

$$\frac{\$1,000}{\$100,000} \times 100\% = 1\%$$

A portion of the 10 percent yield table is shown below in Table 11.3 for your convenience in following through this example. On that table, you can see a 36.01 percent discount circled underneath the 18 percent yield column on the 1.00 percent monthly (No Accelerated Due Date) pay-back row. (Another useful tool for computing yield is the use of yield graphs, such as those found in Appendix F. If you are interested in seeing how the yield graphs differ from the yield charts, you may want to turn to Appendix F at this time and work through John's problem as it is set out there.)

10% INTEREST   MORTGAGE YIELD TABLE
SHOWING DISCOUNT PERCENTAGES
AT VARIOUS YIELDS, PAY-BACK RATES AND DUE DATES
10% INTEREST

YIELD →	10%	11%	12%	13%	14%	15%	16%	17%	18%	19%
Monthly Payback Rate										
				NO ACCELERATED DUE DATE						
1.00	0.00	6.12	11.67	16.71	21.29	25.47	29.30	32.80	36.01	38.97
1.25	0.00	4.39	8.49	12.33	15.93	19.31	22.49	25.47	28.28	30.92
1.50	0.00	3.46	6.73	9.85	12.82	15.64	18.34	20.90	23.34	25.67
1.75	0.00	2.86	5.60	8.23	10.76	13.18	15.51	17.75	19.90	21.97
2.00	0.00	2.45	4.80	7.08	9.28	11.40	13.46	15.45	17.36	19.22
2.50	0.00	1.91	3.75	5.55	7.30	9.00	10.66	12.28	13.86	15.39
3.00	0.00	1.56	3.08	4.57	6.03	7.45	8.85	10.22	11.55	12.86
4.00	0.00	1.16	2.29	3.40	4.49	5.57	6.63	7.68	8.70	9.71

Reprinted from the Realty Bluebook by permission of the copyright owner, Professional Publishing Corporation, 122 Paul Drive, San Rafael, CA 94903, © Copyright Professional Publishing Corporation 1976. For complete Yield and other Tables, readers can purchase the Realty Bluebook from Professional Publishing Corp.

Table 11.3

What does this tell us? This simply means that if John were to market this note under its present terms, he would have to discount the remaining balance of the note by 36 percent. As a consequence of such a discount, John would obtain less than $64,000 for his $100,000 note.

John intended to convert his inherited first mortgage into cash that he could then apply as a down payment on an excellent apartment investment, but he did not want to sell his note for a 36 percent discount. He wondered if there might be a possibility he could talk the mortgagor (the borrower on the house) into changing the terms of the first mortgage in exchange for a lower interest rate. John composed and sent the following letter to the mortgagor:

> Dear Mr. and Mrs. Mortgagor,
>
> I have recently acquired your note with a remaining balance of $93,036.36 at an interest rate of 10 percent with a monthly payment of $1,000. I would be willing to reduce the interest rate to 7 percent if you increase your monthly payment to $1,750 per month. At this lower interest rate your loan will be paid off in approximately 63 months. This means you will have no more house payments after 5¼ years, and you will save over $69,750 in interest on the remaining balance.
>
> If you are in agreement with these new terms, sign the attached amendment to the note. Otherwise, write reject on this letter and return it in the enclosed self-addressed envelope.
>
> Best regards,
> John

Mr. and Mrs. Mortgagor had a basic need to have their mortgage paid off and were excited about the large interest savings, the interest rate reduction, and the prospect of owning their house free and clear in just over five years. They signed the amendment of the note and returned it to John.

Now let's consider what John achieved by this maneuver. Converting the monthly payment into a pay-back rate, we see that the new rate becomes 1.75 percent.

$$\frac{\$1,750}{\$100,000} \times 100\% = 1.75\%$$

Because the interest rate has been changed from 10 percent to 7 percent, we must now consult the 7 percent yield table, which is set out in Table 11.4:

7% INTEREST		**MORGAGE YIELD TABLE** SHOWING DISCOUNT PERCENTAGES AT VARIOUS YIELDS, PAY-BACK RATES AND DUE DATES								**7%** INTEREST
YIELD →	10%	11%	12%	13%	14%	15%	16%	17%	18%	19%
Monthly Payback Rate										
				NO ACCELERATED DUE DATE						
1.00	14.41	18.53	22.36	25.92	29.24	32.33	35.21	37.91	40.42	42.78
1.25	11.17	14.50	17.64	20.62	23.44	26.11	28.65	31.05	33.34	35.50
1.50	9.14	11.93	14.59	17.14	19.58	21.91	24.15	26.29	28.35	30.31
1.75	7.75	10.15	12.45	14.68	16.82	18.88	20.88	22.80	24.65	26.44
2.00	6.73	8.84	10.87	12.84	14.75	16.60	18.39	20.13	21.82	23.45
2.50	5.33	7.03	8.68	10.29	11.86	13.38	14.88	16.33	17.75	19.14
3.00	4.43	5.85	7.24	8.60	9.93	11.23	12.50	13.76	14.98	16.18
4.00	3.32	4.40	5.45	6.49	7.51	8.52	9.51	10.49	11.46	12.40

Reprinted from the Realty Bluebook by permission of the copyright owner, Professional Publishing Corporation, 122 Paul Drive, San Rafael, CA 94903, © Copyright Professional Publishing Corporation 1976. For complete Yield and other Tables, readers can purchase the Realty Bluebook from Professional Publishing Corp.

Table 11.4

Looking across the 1.75 percent pay-back row and looking down the 18 percent yield column, we see that the new discount to sell the note is 24.65 percent. Thus, by using a simple letter, John has reduced the discount of his note 11.35 percent and thereby increased his profit over $10,000.

How You Can Manipulate Variables to Increase Profit

This example demonstrates how variables can be manipulated in order to increase profit. The key to successful investing is to increase yield so that more money can be placed back into circulation to make it grow. For fully amortized notes, this is best achieved by observing that the pay-back rate is more important than the interest rate because the investor is recovering the discount back faster than interest can be earned. Because of inflation, money received earlier in the investment has more value than money received later. It makes sense, therefore, to obtain the principal as well as the discount as soon as possible.

Now that you are familiar with the basics of mortgage yield calculations, let's analyze a few sample transactions to solidify your understanding.

How a Mortgage Purchaser Can Increase Profit

Suppose for a moment that John, in the example above, was not an astute investor. In fact, his "easy come, easy go" investment philosophy made him perfectly willing to sell the $100,000 note at a 36 percent discount and take the money and run.

A smart purchaser in this case could have picked up the note at the 18 percent yield and increased it to over 25 percent by sending a letter similar to the one above addressed to Mr. and Mrs. Mortgagor.

It would be good practice for you to try and figure this out for yourself at this time. The mortgage yield table that you will need has already been provided.

Ready to check your calculations? First, remember that the pay-back rate must be calculated by dividing the new monthly payment of $1,750 by the $100,000 face value of the note and expressing that number as a percentage.

$$\frac{\$1,750}{\$100,000} \times 100\% = 1.75\%$$

Now consult the 7 percent yield table (see Table 11.5) and follow the 1.75 percent pay-back line across to the 36 percent (discount) position. As you can see, there is no such point on the table. Rather, you must find the points on the table between which the discount lies. In this case, we see that 36.01 percent lies almost halfway between 35.95 percent and 38.71 percent. We, therefore, extrapolate that the yield lies between 25 and 27 percent, and conclude that the yield is slightly over 26 percent. This is indicated by the arrow drawn in Table 11.5.

7%
INTEREST

MORTGAGE YIELD TABLE
SHOWING DISCOUNT PERCENTAGES
AT VARIOUS YIELDS, PAY-BACK RATES AND DUE DATES

7%
INTEREST

20%	21%	22%	23%	25%	27%	29%	31%	33%	35%	← YIELD
										Balloon Payment
			NO ACCELERATED DUE DATE							MONTHS
44.98	47.05	49.00	50.82	54.15	57.12	59.76	62.12	64.25	66.17	150.53
37.56	39.52	41.39	43.16	46.46	49.46	52.19	54.69	56.97	59.06	108.09
32.20	34.01	35.75	37.42	40.56	43.46	46.15	48.63	50.94	53.08	84.68
28.17	29.83	31.45	33.00	35.95	38.71	41.29	43.70	45.96	48.08	69.72
25.03	26.57	28.06	29.51	32.27	34.87	37.33	39.64	41.83	43.90	59.29
20.49	21.81	23.10	24.36	26.78	29.09	31.30	33.40	35.41	37.33	45.69
17.36	18.51	19.65	20.75	22.90	24.97	26.95	28.86	30.70	32.46	37.18
13.34	14.26	15.16	16.06	17.80	19.49	21.13	22.72	24.27	25.77	27.10

Reprinted from the Realty Bluebook by permission of the copyright owner, Professional Publishing Corporation, 122 Paul Drive, San Rafael, CA 94903, © Copyright Professional Publishing Corporation 1976. For complete Yield and other Tables, readers can purchase the Realty Bluebook from Professional Publishing Corp.

Table 11.5

Using Yield Tables to Determine Advisability of an Investment

Remember Harry, back in Chapter 3? Let's assume for a moment that Harry's note is a possible candidate for your investment portfolio. We know from the terms of Harry's note that its face value is $50,000, with a 12 percent annual interest rate and a monthly payment of $514 amortized over 30 years. Harry is willing to sell the note at a 20 percent discount with a three-year due date.

In order to determine the advisability of this investment, you must first consider your own strategy. You have been very lucky indeed, the past few years, and your present investments are earning you a solid annual yield of 20 percent. It would be foolish to trade one good investment for another unless there was an assurance of increased profit. You decide, therefore, that any future investment, including Harry's, must bring you a 25 percent yield or you will not be interested. If that figure can be met, then you will want to invest in Harry's note because the mortgagor has a good job, is making improvements on the house, and has sufficient equity in the house to make it an excellent risk.

How can you know whether or not this investment will provide you with your required 25 percent yield? To determine the yield, you must reduce the components of the loan to terms that correspond to the yield table. From the information you have been given, you can see that the monthly pay-back rate is the only term that needs to be changed to match the mortgage yield table. You already know how to derive the pay-back rate by using our standard formula, thus:

$$\frac{\$524}{\$50,000} \times 100\% = 1.02\%$$

In this case, you must consult the 12 percent yield table, but this time it will be under the "3-Year Note" heading. Refer to Table 11.6 and see if you can determine the yield you could expect on the proposed investment.

12% MORTGAGE YIELD TABLE 12%

INTEREST — SHOWING DISCOUNT PERCENTAGES AT VARIOUS YIELDS, PAY-BACK RATES AND DUE DATES — **INTEREST**

20%	21%	22%	23%	25%	27%	29%	31%	33%	35%	← YIELD
										Balloon Payment
			DUE IN	2-YRS	(4.71)*					
13.10	14.60	16.06	17.50	20.30	22.99	25.57	28.06	30.45	32.75	100.00
12.72	14.13	15.60	17.00	19.72	22.34	24.86	27.28	29.62	31.86	93.26
12.35	13.76	15.15	16.51	19.15	21.70	24.15	26.51	28.78	30.97	86.51
11.97	13.34	14.69	16.01	18.58	21.05	23.44	25.74	27.95	30.08	79.77
11.59	12.92	14.23	15.51	18.01	20.41	22.73	24.96	27.12	29.19	73.03
10.84	12.09	13.31	14.52	16.86	19.12	21.31	23.41	25.45	27.41	59.54
10.09	11.25	12.40	13.52	15.71	17.84	19.89	21.87	23.78	25.64	46.05
9.33	10.41	11.48	12.53	14.57	16.55	18.46	20.32	22.12	23.86	32.57
8.58	9.53	10.56	11.53	13.42	15.26	17.04	18.77	20.45	22.08	19.08
			DUE IN	3-YRS	(3.32)*					
17.94	19.91	21.82	23.68	27.25	30.62	33.81	36.82	39.67	42.37	100.00
17.15	19.04	20.87	22.66	26.09	29.33	32.40	35.31	38.06	40.67	89.23
16.36	18.17	19.93	21.64	24.92	28.04	30.99	33.79	36.45	38.97	78.46
15.58	17.30	18.98	20.62	23.76	26.75	29.59	32.28	34.84	37.27	67.69
14.79	16.43	18.04	19.60	22.60	25.46	28.18	30.76	33.22	35.57	56.92
14.00	15.56	17.09	18.58	21.44	24.17	26.77	29.25	31.61	33.87	46.15
13.22	14.70	16.14	17.55	20.28	22.88	25.36	27.74	30.00	32.17	35.38
10.07	11.22	12.36	13.47	15.63	17.73	19.74	21.68	23.55	25.36	-7.69

Reprinted from the Realty Bluebook by permission of the copyright owner, Professional Publishing Corporation, 122 Paul Drive, San Rafael, CA 94903, © Copyright Professional Publishing Corporation 1976. For complete Yield and other Tables, readers can purchase the Realty Bluebook from Professional Publishing Corp.

Table 11.6

In order to make this determination correctly, you should have concluded that the 1 percent pay-back rate is the closest to the 1.02 percent that you are working with. Your next step should have been to follow the 1 percent row across to the nearest approximation of the 20 percent discount Harry is offering. As you can see, that will fall in between 19.91 and 21.82. The yield, therefore, will fall very close to 21 percent. This means that if this mortgage is paid off as scheduled, the ultimate yield will be very close to 21 percent. The note with its present configuration does not, therefore, meet your 25 percent yield criterion.

Are you still with us? The next illustration will test the mettle of any stalwart investor. By the time you have worked through this yield problem and all its variations, you will be as competent at mortgage yield calculations as an experienced broker.

How Refinancing a Seasoned Note Can Maximize Yield

Our next hypothetical situation involves George, a mortgagee, and Beth, a mortgagor. When George sold his house to Beth, he took back a $22,500 second mortgage with a five-year due date. He thought the interest rate was great at 9 percent, with an interest-only payment of $165. At that time, George could not get a better return at the local bank or savings and loan. After a couple of years, however, banks were paying as much as 18 percent for three-year certificates. George wanted to get his money back, but he was not willing to sell his note at the 45.43 percent discount necessary to achieve a 25 percent yield required of the market at that time. He held on to the note until it was due.

Near the time it fell due, Beth approached George asking him if he would be interested in extending the note. George told Beth he would think about it for a couple of days and get back to her.

George liked the monthly payments, but he was not very happy with what inflation had done to his $22,500 note while the value of Beth's house had increased inversely to the value of George's note. That is, the value of the note was decreasing while the value of the house was increasing.

By this time George had learned that he could invest in discounted mortgages, and so he took out his mortgage yield book to compute the size note he could purchase with his $22,500 principal payment that was soon due. Marketable yields for second mortgages at the time were at 18 percent. George decided to put the note at 12 percent interest with a three-year due date and a 1.5 percent pay-back rate per month.

George turned to the 12 percent yield table, given below in Table 11.7, and saw that the discount was 12.60 percent under the 18 percent yield column.

12% MORTGAGE YIELD TABLE 12%

INTEREST   SHOWING DISCOUNT PERCENTAGES   **INTEREST**
AT VARIOUS YIELDS, PAY-BACK RATES AND DUE DATES

YIELD →	10%	11%	12%	13%	14%	15%	16%	17%	18%	19%
Monthly Payback Rate										
			DUE IN 2-YRS (4.71)*							
1.00	0.0	0.0	0.00	1.75	3.47	5.16	6.81	8.43	10.01	11.57
1.25	0.0	0.0	0.00	1.70	3.37	5.01	6.61	8.18	9.72	11.24
1.50	0.0	0.0	0.00	1.65	3.27	4.85	6.41	7.94	9.44	10.90
1.75	0.0	0.0	0.00	1.60	3.17	4.70	6.21	7.69	9.15	10.57
2.00	0.0	0.0	0.00	1.55	3.06	4.55	6.01	7.45	8.86	10.24
2.50	0.0	0.0	0.00	1.45	2.86	4.25	5.62	6.96	8.28	9.57
3.00	0.0	0.0	0.01	1.34	2.66	3.95	5.22	6.47	7.70	8.90
3.50	0.0	0.0	0.01	1.24	2.45	3.65	4.82	5.98	7.12	8.23
4.00	0.0	0.0	0.01	1.14	2.25	3.35	4.42	5.49	6.54	7.57
			DUE IN 3-YRS (3.32)*							
1.00	0.0	0.0	0.00	2.47	4.88	7.21	9.48	11.69	13.83	15.91
1.25	0.0	0.0	0.00	2.36	4.66	6.89	9.06	11.17	13.22	15.21
1.50	0.0	0.0	0.00	2.25	4.43	6.56	8.63	10.64	12.60	14.51
1.75	0.0	0.0	0.00	2.14	4.21	6.24	8.20	10.12	11.99	13.81
2.00	0.0	0.0	0.01	2.02	3.99	5.91	7.78	9.60	11.38	13.10
2.25	0.0	0.0	0.01	1.91	3.77	5.58	7.35	9.08	10.76	12.40
2.50	0.0	0.0	0.01	1.80	3.55	5.26	6.93	8.56	10.15	11.70
3.50	0.0	0.0	0.01	1.35	2.67	3.96	5.22	6.47	7.70	8.89

Reprinted from the Realty Bluebook by permission of the copyright owner, Professional Publishing Corporation, 122 Paul Drive, San Rafael, CA 94903, © Copyright Professional Publishing Corporation 1976. For complete Yield and other Tables, readers can purchase the Realty Bluebook from Professional Publishing Corp.

Table 11.7

George knew, therefore, that he could purchase a 12 percent note with a three-year due date for 87.4 cents on the dollar. George then divided 0.874 into the face value of the note to come up with the new value he needed in order to achieve his desired yield:

$$\frac{\$22,500}{.874} = \$25,743.71$$

George rounded that amount to $25,750 and got back to Beth with his figures. He explained to Beth the reason for his new terms and told her to take a couple of days to make her decision either to get a new loan and pay George off or to take George's proposed extension at an increased face value of $25,750 at 12 percent interest, a three-year due date, and a 1.5 percent pay back of $386.25 per month.

Beth did a little shopping around and decided to go along with George's terms. George was happy with the new structure of the note on this piece of property as Beth's house had increased a great deal in value making the note even more secure than before.

What are some of the other mortgage yield lessons that can be learned from George's experience? First, if the term of the original note had been three years instead of five, his discount would have changed from 45.43 percent to 33.53 percent. (See Table 11.8.) Second, if he had negotiated a 1.5 percent pay-back rate on the original note, rather than an interest-only pay back of .75 percent, he would have further reduced the discount from 33.53 percent to 29.36 percent.

CONCLUSION: THE CALCULATION OF MORTGAGE YIELDS SHOULD BECOME SECOND NATURE

The figures given in the illustrations throughout this chapter demonstrate that the sooner you get your money back for reinvestment the better. Whether that timing is the result of a larger pay back or a shorten due date, there will be a stronger impact on your yield than will result from a higher interest rate or a larger discount. However, each aspect of the PIDD Rule should be used to your advantage to increase the yield. The shorter the due date, the larger the pay back, the higher the discount, and the greater the interest rate, the more you would expect to receive in your yield.

If you are to be successful at mortgage investing, it will be necessary for the calculation of mortgage yield to become second nature to you. For the reader who has just been introduced to the subject of yields, this undoubtedly appears more complex than it really is. To these investors, we would advise that you read and reread this material until you are satisfied that you understand it thoroughly. We have attempted to provide you with step-by-step instructions for yield calculation; the mastery of this material must be left to the individual.

MORTGAGE YIELD TABLE

9% INTEREST

SHOWING DISCOUNT PERCENTAGES
AT VARIOUS YIELDS, PAY-BACK RATES AND DUE DATES

9% INTEREST

20%	21%	22%	23%	25%	27%	29%	31%	33%	35%	← YIELD / Balloon Payment
				DUE IN 2-YRS (4.57)*						
18.01	19.46	20.88	22.28	24.98	27.58	30.08	32.49	34.80	37.02	100.00
17.50	18.91	20.30	21.65	24.29	26.82	29.26	31.61	33.86	36.04	93.45
16.99	18.37	19.71	21.03	23.60	26.07	28.44	30.73	32.93	35.05	86.91
16.48	17.82	19.13	20.41	22.90	25.31	27.62	29.85	31.99	34.06	80.36
15.98	17.27	18.54	19.79	22.21	24.55	26.80	28.97	31.06	33.07	73.81
15.47	16.72	17.96	19.17	21.52	23.79	25.98	28.09	30.12	32.08	67.26
14.45	15.63	16.79	17.92	20.13	22.27	24.33	26.33	28.25	30.11	54.17
13.43	14.53	15.61	16.68	18.75	20.75	22.69	24.57	26.38	28.13	41.08
11.40	12.34	13.27	14.19	15.98	17.72	19.41	21.04	22.64	24.18	14.89
				DUE IN 3-YRS (3.18)*						
24.67	26.54	28.37	30.14	33.53	36.74	39.77	42.63	45.34	47.90	100.00
23.61	25.42	27.17	28.87	32.14	35.24	38.16	40.93	43.55	46.02	89.71
22.56	24.29	25.97	27.61	30.75	33.73	36.55	39.22	41.75	44.15	79.42
21.51	23.16	24.78	26.35	29.36	32.23	34.94	37.52	39.96	42.28	69.14
20.46	22.04	23.58	25.08	27.97	30.72	33.33	35.81	38.17	40.41	58.85
19.40	20.91	22.38	23.82	26.58	29.21	31.72	34.10	36.37	38.54	48.56
17.30	18.66	19.99	21.29	23.80	26.20	28.50	30.69	32.79	34.79	27.98
15.19	16.41	17.60	18.76	21.02	23.19	25.28	27.28	29.20	31.05	7.41
				DUE IN 4-YRS (2.49)*						
30.12	32.29	34.38	36.40	40.21	43.75	47.04	50.10	52.95	55.60	100.00
28.41	30.47	32.46	34.38	38.02	41.40	44.56	47.50	50.24	52.80	85.62
26.70	28.65	30.54	32.36	35.82	39.05	42.07	44.89	47.53	50.00	71.24
24.99	26.83	28.62	30.34	33.63	36.70	39.59	42.29	44.83	47.21	56.86
23.28	25.01	26.70	28.32	31.43	34.35	37.10	39.69	42.12	44.41	42.48
21.57	23.19	24.77	26.31	29.24	32.01	34.62	37.08	39.41	41.61	28.10
19.86	21.37	22.85	24.29	27.04	29.66	32.13	34.48	36.70	38.81	13.72
				DUE IN 5-YRS (2.08)*						
34.60	36.96	39.22	41.38	45.43	49.12	52.51	55.60	58.44	61.05	100.00
32.16	34.38	36.51	38.55	42.38	45.90	49.13	52.10	54.84	57.36	81.14
29.72	31.80	33.80	35.72	39.34	42.67	45.75	48.60	51.24	53.68	62.29
27.27	29.22	31.09	32.89	36.29	39.45	42.38	45.10	47.64	50.00	43.43
24.83	26.64	28.38	30.06	33.25	36.22	39.00	41.60	44.03	46.31	24.58
22.39	24.05	25.67	27.23	30.20	33.00	35.63	38.10	40.43	42.63	5.72

Table 11.8

12. How to Price Your Mortgage and Sell It

HOW SELLING FITS INTO AN INVESTMENT SCHEME

Up to this point, we have been investigating the parameters of mortgage investment almost exclusively from the point of view of buying and building an investment portfolio. The inexperienced investor may think that this is, in fact, the sum and substance of mortgage investing. Nothing could be further from the truth—that is assuming it is your intent to create enormous wealth through your investments.

Once you have invested all of the capital that you can put together, should you sit back and simply reap the harvest? If you did follow that route, you could do so with the knowledge that you have at the very least invested your money in a relatively risk-free, high-yield area. On the other hand, the wise investor will see that the real work (and fun) has only just begun.

Let's review for a moment the ways we have explored of making a profit in mortgage investments. At the start, we know there are two primary ways of increasing yield when purchasing mortgages. The first is to buy the mortgage at a discount, and the second is to buy a mortgage that provides for an earlier pay back. In the last chapter, you were introduced to the concept of combining these two tactics by reinvesting interest and principal as it is received. This method is of such importance that we have developed its underlying techniques fully in Chapter 3, in the section on pyramiding.

There is yet another way of increasing profit in mortgage investing, and that is through selling. Here, we will explore not only the reasons why this is so but the mechanics of selling as well.

CHECKLIST OF REASONS FOR SELLING A MORTGAGE

Basically, a mortgage is sold because the mortgagee (lender) wishes to liquidate that asset. That wish may stem from any number of

149

sources, but it will primarily be the result of a wish to raise capital. Hopefully, it will be for the purpose of raising reinvestment capital. There are an infinite number of considerations, only a few of which are given in the following checklist:

1. to make a stronger and more secure investment
2. to make a larger return
3. to accumulate more mortgages
4. to broaden lists of accounts for buying and selling
5. to acquire capital to work with
6. to look for more leverage, faster returns, or larger profits
7. to structure a package deal
8. to utilize different types of discounts
9. to support other business ventures
10. to take advantage of unusual market conditions
11. to follow a primary source lead into another geographical area
12. to leave a geographical area that is not doing well
13. to cultivate new connections, partnerships, or syndications
14. to buy out partners
15. to enhance personal cash flow
16. to structure an exchange
17. to invest in properties with depreciation or maintenance management
18. to terminate an unpleasant relationship with mortgagor or partner
19. to limit or reduce exposure
20. to take advantage of new growth areas as they open up in your region

FOUR QUESTIONS MOST FREQUENTLY ASKED BY A BUYER

In considering your own purposes for selling, it is always a good idea to remember the reasons buyers are buying. The four most frequently asked questions by a buyer are:

1. Why is this mortgage being sold?
2. What will be my yield on this investment?

3. How much money will I need?

4. What are the risks involved?

THE MECHANICS OF SELLING MORTGAGES

There are three parameters involved in the sale of a mortgage: finding a purchaser, analyzing market conditions that will affect the sale, and computing the appropriate discount to offer. Let us turn now to an in-depth discussion of each of these variables.

Finding a Market

Mortgages can be marketed in a variety of ways. Basically, you can do this work yourself or pay a professional broker to assist you. Ideally, of course, you will work toward the goal of developing your own markets so that at some future point in time you can be in complete control of the purchase and sale of your investment properties. Until you feel completely confident, however, you may wish to rely upon the services of a broker.

How a Broker Can Assist You in a Mortgage Sale

Mortgage brokers are in the business of making and placing mortgages; as such, these professionals may be the primary market source for potential buyers. Brokers are involved on a day-to-day basis with realtors, banks, savings and loan associations, and other brokers. Obviously, they are an excellent resource to have available.

In addition to their wealth of contacts, qualified brokers typically have many other useful competencies. Brokers may serve, for example, as a consultant, a property manager, a mediator, or a liquidator. The broker will have a broad knowledge of the current real estate market and will probably be expert at creative financing techniques. He or she will also undoubtedly be very knowledgeable about the legal requirements for structuring mortgage transfers. In particular, brokers usually bring with them an expert ability to appraise real property in an ever-changing market. Many brokers, of course, offer advice to investors and borrowers, which is rendered all the more valuable by their professional detachment.

Unlike other investment professionals, loan brokers charge their commissions against the borrower—not the investor. Typically, the commission is simply deducted from gross loan proceeds and is then disbursed by the escrow holder at the conclusion of the transfer.

Brokers can be found by turning to your telephone directory. It's really that simple. Like finding a good doctor or attorney, however, it may take some investigating. One broker may specialize in only income properties, while another may have a personality or philosophy that clashes with your own. Some have more experience than others and correspondingly more contacts.

Developing Your Own Markets

Developing markets for the liquidation of your mortgages exactly parallels the steps outlined in Chapter 4 for developing markets for the acquisition of your mortgages. In fact, if you have gone through that process as outlined earlier, then you are already well on your way to having an established list of contacts for selling.

How to Cultivate Commercial Sources

Consider, for example, commercial banks and insurance companies with their trust departments and pension funds. Go straight to the top and meet the president. More importantly, it has been suggested, meet the *secretary* of the president. These are powerful people who can help you in many ways within a company. For example, a secretary who knows you personally and who knows you are on good terms with the boss will not hesitate to provide you with an introduction to the trust officer or pension fund director.

We would caution you at this point to remember to present yourself and your business in the most professional light possible. Cultivate these commercial sources carefully and leisurely—well in advance of any immediate need or problem.

How to Locate Private Investors

There are also private buyers, the most significant of which is the mortgagor. This is true because the mortgagor frequently has the most to gain by a purchase of the mortgage on the property. This party is also the most easily found (as no advertising is involved), and is generally the most overlooked source.

Additionally, as your experience grows you will develop and maintain your own private mailing list of buyers. Remember the contact cards you filled out when you first started to locate mortgages? These cards will now form the basis of your buyer's list. You can continue to add names and addresses to these files by directly contacting the people you see on a routine basis:

1. fellow workers
2. tradespeople (grocer, electrician, florist, and so on)
3. family, friends, neighbors
4. professionals (doctor, dentist, accountant, attorneys)

You may also want to advertise. The local newspaper is an excellent place to sell mortgages. We have found that a small, three-line advertisement in our local paper has brought outstanding results. Our newspaper experience has been so rewarding, in fact, that we have let it run for consecutive weeks at a time. For an appropriate ad format, simply refer to one of the larger daily papers where you will find several such ads.

HOW YOU CAN ENHANCE A SALE

Whether an investor is trying to sell a mortgage to a large commercial enterprise or to the original mortgagor or other private investor, there are several important techniques that will enhance such a sale. Primarily, these involve the gathering of factual information concerning the mortgage and the underlying real property and manipulating the data to fit the needs of the potential buyer. Let's take these one at a time.

In Chapter 9 you were shown how to set up a file on each of your investment properties. When you are contemplating a sale of a particular mortgage, you should take that file out and systematize the pertinent information for the potential buyer to peruse. The form that is used for this purpose, which is called our Mortgage Data Form, can be found in Appendix D.

In addition to the standard information called for on the Mortgage Data Form, you may also want to add any up-to-the-minute information you may have that might affect the value of the mortgage, such as a change in interest rates or zoning, or possibly legislative regulations. If the circumstances warrant, you may also wish to include a description of the demographics of the area including reference to nearby transportation, schools, shopping facilities, and churches. This description may be based upon maps and photographs as well.

Together, this information will comprise a business proposal that can be left with potential buyers to study. Because this proposal will also contain your name, address, and phone number, it can also serve as secondary advertising for your growing business.

HOW MARKET CONDITIONS AFFECT THE SALE OF MORTGAGES

Now that we have taken a close look at the mechanics of mortgage selling, it is important that we consider those factors that determine the price at which a mortgage should be offered for sale. Such a determination is a two-step analysis involving both market conditions and mathematical computations.

Assuming that we are working with experienced mortgage buyers and sellers, the amount of a discount will generally be what the market will bear. The easy answer is that the discount must be sufficient to sell the paper. The more complex answer is that investors will require a discount that produces a greater yield than the yield on the property that secures the paper. In general, there will be a direct relationship between the amount of the discount and the risk to the investor. In addition to the current discount market and risk factors, there are other variables that can influence discount. These may include the terms of the note or possibly the amount of any broker commission.

The seller's motivation is another relevant factor to be considered. If cash must be raised instantly in order to post bail in Mexico for a wayward child, then the seller will be placed in the unfortunate position of increasing the discount until the mortgage sells. On the other hand, if the seller is in a good investment position, the mortgage can be used as security for any needed loans. In that case, the yield offered by way of discount could be entirely offset by the interest paid on such a loan.

HOW TO COMPUTE THE APPROPRIATE DISCOUNT FOR SALE

Now that you are already well versed in the art of discount computation by virtue of your working through the previous chapter, you will find that the calculations involved in figuring the appropriate discount are relatively simple. In fact, you already know how these computations are made. You may recall from the previous chapter the example of John who had inherited a $100,000 first mortgage from his grandmother. During the course of that example, John was required to work through the calculations necessary to determine the amount of discount he must offer in order to sell his mortgage under its terms. If you have forgotten how John utilized the mortgage yield tables to arrive at his discount, this would be an appropriate time to review Chapter 11 on the subject of yields.

UNDERSTANDING WHAT IT MEANS TO SELL "WITH RECOURSE"

There are a few tricks of the trade that John could have used to enhance the sale of his $100,000 first mortgage. The simplest would have been to offer the mortgage for sale "with recourse." What does this mean? It's really quite simple. To transfer a mortgage "with recourse" means that you will *guarantee* that the mortgagor will pay the debt. For the buyer of such a note, the risk is greatly reduced and the discount would be reduced accordingly.

This is not an action to be taken lightly. However, where an investor has been closely involved with the mortgage purchase and management and is confident that the mortgagor will pay off the loan, it may not be a bad risk. Each case must obviously be evaluated on its own merits in this regard.

A WORD OF CAUTION: USURY

Individual states fix by law a maximum rate of interest; a lender who collects more than that fixed amount would be in violation of that law and the rate would be usurious. Depending upon the state, the lender may collect only the allowable rate of interest or may lose all of the interest earned on the loan or even the entire amount of the principal and interest.

The issue of usury has been raised in connection with the sale of discounted mortgages in one particular regard. Where a loan is discounted out of a new sales escrow or immediately thereafter, it may be argued that the borrower should have had a first option to purchase it. By doing so, the borrower would be able to save the amount of the discount. If the mortgage is sold without the borrower's knowledge, it may be construed that the borrower is paying an additional charge, which may be considered usury.

The obvious way to get around this possibility is to be certain that the borrower is allowed the chance to raise the money to pay off the loan. Of course, in most situations, this would amount to begging the question as most home buyers able to purchase the mortgage would not have made it in the first place. However, a word of caution to investors is in order. If there is any question whatsoever regarding the discount and its ultimate construction as a discount, fee, or commission, an investor should direct that question to legal counsel for clarification.

HOW THE IRS VIEWS INTEREST-FREE LOANS

One final consideration in the vein of caution concerns the case where too *little* interest may be charged. This situation occurs most frequently when family members "loan" money to one another interest-free or at low-interest. You should be aware that the IRS will *impute* interest, presently at the rate of 10 percent, under certain circumstances in order to counteract tax avoidance—whether intentional or not.

The IRS will treat such a loan as two transactions:

1. The borrower is assumed to pay interest to the lender. Thus, the borrower claims an interest deduction (if excess itemized deductions are relied upon), and the lender reports the imputed interest as income.

2. The lender is assumed to have given the borrower a taxable gift in the amount of the foregone interest.

There is an important exception to the imputed interest rule, and that exception relates to the use to which the loans are put. Interest will not be imputed to a lender if the aggregate amount loaned to that borrower does not exceed $100,000, *and* the borrower's net investment income does not exceed $1,000 for the year in which the loan is made. For example, a mother may give her child an interest-free loan of $100,000 or less in order to purchase a home, if that child's income from investments does not exceed $1,000 in that year.

TWENTY-ONE CONSIDERATIONS IN SELLING MORTGAGES

In conclusion, let us summarize all of those considerations that should be a part of an investor's decision to sell a mortgage:

1. You must plan ahead, know your market, be familiar with the going rate of discounts, and be acquainted with the sources to contact for a sale.

2. You should give yourself sufficient time to locate a buyer.

3. Start the process of locating buyers on the first day you purchase a mortgage; cultivate real estate brokers, bankers, and attorneys.

4. One of your best leads to sell a discounted mortgage is the mortgagor.

5. Know intimately the details of any mortgage you wish to sell; have available all of the information you can gather, including a credit report on the mortgagor, escrow papers, photographs of the property inside and outside, title report, and other relevant documents.

6. If you are in a position to guarantee the mortgage payments, you will be able to offer a much lower discount.

7. The better seasoned a mortgage is, the less discount you should offer.

8. Weigh carefully the advantages of utilizing a professional mortgage broker when selling your mortgages.

9. Generally, try to have the broker who handled the original sale of the property work with you on its sale; that person will be acquainted with the property as well as with the people involved.

10. Don't fall into the trap of marrying your investments; always see investments as simply means to better and better equity position.

11. Always take a slight discount if you can when it means you can gain a better equity position.

12. Remember, the lower your mortgages are on the recording ladder, the higher the discount you will be forced to give on a sale.

13. Be prepared to show potential buyers how the structure of the mortgage you are trying to sell can benefit the buyer.

14. Be ready to point out that the buyer can always use the mortgage as good collateral to obtain a preferred loan at a low interest rate while at the same time continue to receive income from the mortgage payments.

15. Relate to a potential buyer any tax savings or postponements that may accrue as a result of the sale.

16. Be prepared to teach potential buyers all you have learned regarding the time value of money and compounding to reinvest.

17. Point out to a buyer that each month additional security is earned on the mortgage investment.

18. Try to sell mortgages without guaranteeing mortgagor payments where the risk outweighs the benefit gained by a lower discount. On the other hand, it may be that the higher price is worth the risk.

19. Try to structure an exchange of your mortgage for equity in another property that frequently is done without discounting the face value of the note.

20. Where appropriate, emphasize that the mortgage is seasoned.

21. Remember: Liquidating a second mortgage or trading it for a new equity position is an essential step in building that fortune in real estate.

CONCLUSION

In this chapter you began to consider the subject of yield from the point of view of the *seller* of the mortgage. In particular, we investigated the mechanics of such a sale and then turned our attention to the ways in which a sale could be structured to bring a higher profit to the seller.

There are many reasons an investor may have for selling a mortgage. In the best case, a sale will be for the purpose of improving an investor's equity position one way or another.

Before selling, you should be clear about your own reasons for doing so. And you should also take a moment to reflect upon the questions a buyer might typically ask about your motivations for the sale.

The mechanics of a sale were discussed through two different avenues—by the investor's own efforts and by the utilization of a professional broker. You were shown how to develop your own markets, cultivate commercial sources, and locate private investors.

There are many things an investor can do to enhance the possibility of a sale and to analyze current market conditions in order to make the proposal as attractive to potential buyers as possible while retaining maximum yield for the investor.

Calculations that were given in the previous chapter were briefly reviewed to see how the variables can be manipulated to maximum advantage.

A word of caution goes to an investor considering a sale in several different regards. The first is where a sale "with recourse" is contemplated. A careful weighing of risk against the benefit of a higher yield that results from the discount reduction is in order. Usury is another area that the novice will want to watch out for and seek professional advice where questions arise as to the source of the discount. The last area of concern is the case where a lender desires to loan money interest-free. Investors should be aware that such a "gift" may have serious tax consequences that should be reviewed by a tax professional before such a loan is made.

Finally, twenty-one different considerations were summarized to keep in mind when contemplating a sale of one of your investment properties.

Afterward

THE PURPOSE OF THIS BOOK

Throughout this book, a case for investments in discounted mortgages as a relatively safe—but curiously unknown and therefore unexploited—means to attain substantial wealth has been presented. We are firmly committed to the belief that this is truly The #1 Real Estate Investment No One Talks About.

HOW THIS VOLUME CAN HELP YOU

Mastery of the terms and techniques described within this volume will place investors in an enviable position to take advantage of this curious fact. Furthermore, this particular path to wealth is available to lay investors without any prior expertise in real estate, law, or investing; however, those who want to succeed must be willing to devote the necessary ingredient of self-education. We have attempted to provide all of the information, material, and forms necessary for lay investors to commence that education. In particular, we have tried to flag areas of uncertainty or complexity where the novice may want to seek professional help.

THE ULTIMATE INVESTMENT DECISION

At the start of this volume we quoted Thoreau's observation that there is nothing wrong with having dreams—"castles in the air"—as long as you set about the business of building a structure to support those dreams. If you have shared the dream of countless others of financial independence and wealth, you *can* achieve that dream. You *can* do it!

The reality is that more and more people have a surplus of money available for investing. Of that number, most will appreciate the eroding effect of inflation and attempt in some fashion to offset that loss by placing that surplus in high-yield investments.

The ultimate decision of where an investor will choose to put such a surplus to work will be a combination of many factors: financial resources, willingness to risk, personality, temperament, time, knowledge, anxiety, tolerance, and finally, pleasure. It has been our experience that investments in discounted mortgages fit these parameters perfectly, providing us with what we believe is the ideal combination of safety and earnings. Our goal has been to provide a book with all of the information necessary to determine whether investing in discounted mortgages will fit *your* investment parameters. We hope it will prove to be useful and profitable to each of you.

Appendix A
Mortgage Documents and Clauses

Samples of standard forms frequently utilized in mortgage investment practice are included for your reference. These include, in order of appearance, the following:

Mortgage

Trust Deed (Oregon)

Promissory Note

Promissory Note (Installment)

Promissory Note (Straight)

Promissory Note Secured by Deed of Trust

Deed of Trust and Assignments of Rents and Request for Special Notice (Short Form—California)

Deed of Trust and Assignment of Rents (Long Form)

Assignment of Deed of Trust and Request for Special Notice

Assignment of Deed of Trust

Corporation Assignment of Deed of Trust

Accommodation Recording Order Form

Declaration of Default

Joint Tenancy Grant Deed

Quitclaim Deed

Individual Quitclaim Deed

Sale of Trust Deed (Informational Sheet)

Loan Summary Sheet

Escrow Accounting Sheet

Escrow Instructions (Buyer and Seller)

Full Release Covering All Claims

The mortgagor warrants that the proceeds of the loan represented by the above described note and this mortgage are:
(a)* primarily for mortgagor's personal, family, household or agricultural purposes (see Important Notice below),
(b) for an organization or (even if mortgagor is a natural person) are for business or commercial purposes other than
agricultural purposes.

Now, therefore, if said mortgagor shall keep and perform the covenants herein contained and shall pay said note according
to its terms, this conveyance shall be void, but otherwise shall remain in full force as a mortgage to secure the performance of
all of said covenants and the payment of said note; it being agreed that a failure to perform any covenant herein, or if a proceeding of any kind be taken to foreclose any lien on said premises or any part thereof, the mortgagee shall have the option to
declare the whole amount unpaid on said note or on this mortgage at once due and payable, and this mortgage may be foreclosed at any time thereafter. And if the mortgagor shall fail to pay any taxes or charges or any lien, encumbrance or insurance
premium as above provided for, the mortgagee may at his option do so, and any payment so made shall be added to and become
a part of the debt secured by this mortgage, and shall bear interest at the same rate as said note without waiver, however, of
any right arising to the mortgagee for breach of covenant. And this mortgage may be foreclosed for principal, interest and all sums
paid by the mortgagee at any time while the mortgagor neglects to repay any sums so paid by the mortgagee. In the event of any
suit or action being instituted to foreclose this mortgage, the mortgagor agrees to pay all reasonable costs incurred by the mortgagee for title reports and title search, all statutory costs and disbursements and such further sum as the trial court may adjudge
reasonable as plaintiff's attorney's fees in such suit or action, and if an appeal is taken from any judgment or decree entered
therein mortgagor further promises to pay such sum as the appellate court shall adjudge reasonable as plaintiff's attorney's fees
on such appeal, all sums to be secured by the lien of this mortgage and included in the decree of foreclosure.

Each and all of the covenants and agreements herein contained shall apply to and bind the heirs, executors, administrators
and assigns of said mortgagor and of said mortgagee respectively.

In case suit or action is commenced to foreclose this mortgage, the Court, may upon motion of the mortgagee, appoint a
receiver to collect the rents and profits arising out of said premises during the pendency of such foreclosure, and apply the same,
after first deducting all of said receiver's proper charges and expenses, to the payment of the amount due under this mortgage.

In construing this mortgage, it is understood that the mortgagor or mortgagee may be more than one person; that if the
context so requires, the singular pronoun shall be taken to mean and include the plural, the masculine, the feminine and the neuter,
and that generally all grammatical changes shall be made, assumed and implied to make the provisions hereof apply equally to
corporations and to individuals.

IN WITNESS WHEREOF, said mortgagor has hereunto set his hand the day and year first above
written.

....

....

*IMPORTANT NOTICE: Delete, by lining out, whichever warranty (a) or (b) is not ap-
plicable; if warranty (a) is applicable and if the mortgagee is a creditor, as such word
is defined in the Truth-in-Lending Act and Regulation Z, the mortgagee MUST comply
with the Act and Regulation by making required disclosures; for this purpose, if this
instrument is to be a FIRST lien to finance the purchase of a dwelling, use Stevens-Ness
Form No. 1305 or equivalent; if this instrument is NOT to be a first lien, use Stevens-
Ness Form No. 1306, or equivalent.

....

STATE OF OREGON,
}ss.
County of ....

............................, 19........

Personally appeared the above named ....

....

and acknowledged the foregoing instrument to be......................................voluntary act and deed.

Before me:

(OFFICIAL SEAL)   ....
                                          Notary Public for Oregon
                                          My commission expires: ....

MORTGAGE	STATE OF OREGON, }ss.
(FORM No. 105A)	County of ....
STEVENS-NESS LAW PUB. CO., PORTLAND, ORE.	I certify that the within instru-
	ment was received for record on the
....	............day of ...., 19.......,
....	at...............o'clock.....M., and recorded
TO	in book/reel/volume No...........................on
	page................or as document/fee/file/
....	instrument/microfilm No. ....,
....	Record of Mortgages of said County.
AFTER RECORDING RETURN TO	Witness my hand and seal of
	County affixed.

SPACE RESERVED
FOR
RECORDER'S USE

....
NAME   TITLE

By ....Deputy

FORM No. 105A—MORTGAGE—One Page Long Form.
TN

STEVENS-NESS LAW PUBLISHING CO., PORTLAND, OR. 97204

THIS MORTGAGE, Made this .... day of .... , 19 .... , by

....

....

Mortgagor, to ....

....

.... Mortgagee,

WITNESSETH, That said mortgagor, in consideration of ....

.... Dollars,
to him paid by said mortgagee, does hereby grant, bargain, sell and convey unto said mortgagee, his heirs, ex-
ecutors, administrators and assigns, that certain real property situated in .... County,
State of Oregon, bounded and described as follows, to-wit:

Together with all and singular the tenements, hereditaments and appurtenances thereunto belonging
or in anywise appertaining, and which may hereafter thereto belong or appertain, and the rents, issues and
profits therefrom, and any and all fixtures upon said premises at the time of the execution of this mortgage
or at any time during the term of this mortgage.

TO HAVE AND TO HOLD the said premises with the appurtenances unto the said mortgagee, his
heirs, executors, administrators and assigns forever.

This mortgage is intended to secure the payment of .... promissory note .... , of which the
following is a substantial copy:

The date of maturity of the debt secured by this mortgage is the date on which the last scheduled principal payment becomes due, to-wit: .... , 19 ....

And said mortgagor covenants to and with the mortgagee, his heirs, executors, administrators and assigns, that he is lawfully
seized in fee simple of said premises and has a valid, unencumbered title thereto

and will warrant and forever defend the same against all persons; that he will pay said note, principal and interest, according to
the terms thereof; that while any part of said note remains unpaid he will pay all taxes, assessments and other charges of every
nature which may be levied or assessed against said property, or this mortgage or the note above described, when due and payable and before the same may become delinquent; that he will promptly pay and satisfy any and all liens or encumbrances that
are or may become liens on the premises or any part thereof superior to the lien of this mortgage; that he will keep the buildings
now on or which hereafter may be erected on the said premises continuously insured against loss or damage by fire and such other
hazards as the mortgagee may from time to time require, in an amount not less than the original principal sum of the note or
obligation secured by this mortgage, in a company or companies acceptable to the mortgagee, with loss payable first to the mortgagee and then to the mortgagor as their respective interests may appear; all policies of insurance shall be delivered to the mortgagee as soon as insured. Now if the mortgagor shall fail for any reason to procure any such insurance and to deliver said policies
to the mortgagee at least fifteen days prior to the expiration of any policy of insurance now or hereafter placed on said buildings,
the mortgagee may procure the same at mortgagor's expense; that he will keep the buildings and improvements on said premises
in good repair and will not commit or suffer any waste of said premises. At the request of the mortgagee, the mortgagor shall
join with the mortgagee in executing one or more financing statements pursuant to the Uniform Commercial Code, in form satisfactory to the mortgagee, and will pay for filing the same in the proper public office or offices, as well as the cost of all lien
searches made by filing officers or searching agencies as may be deemed desirable by the mortgagee.

The grantor covenants and agrees to and with the beneficiary and those claiming under him, that he is law-fully seized in fee simple of said described real property and has a valid, unencumbered title thereto

and that he will warrant and forever defend the same against all persons whomsoever.

The grantor warrants that the proceeds of the loan represented by the above described note and this trust deed are:
(a)* primarily for grantor's personal, family or household purposes (see Important Notice below),
(b) for an organization, or (even if grantor is a natural person) are for business or commercial purposes.

This deed applies to, inures to the benefit of and binds all parties hereto, their heirs, legatees, devisees, administrators, executors, personal representatives, successors and assigns. The term beneficiary shall mean the holder and owner, including pledgee, of the contract secured hereby, whether or not named as a beneficiary herein. In construing this deed and whenever the context so requires, the masculine gender includes the feminine and the neuter, and the singular number includes the plural.

IN WITNESS WHEREOF, *said grantor has hereunto set his hand the day and year first above written.*

* IMPORTANT NOTICE: Delete, by lining out, whichever warranty (a) or (b) is not applicable; if warranty (a) is applicable and the beneficiary is a creditor as such word is defined in the Truth-in-Lending Act and Regulation Z, the beneficiary MUST comply with the Act and Regulation by making required disclosures; for this purpose use Stevens-Ness Form No. 1319, or equivalent. If compliance with the Act is not required, disregard this notice.

....

....

....

(If the signer of the above is a corporation, use the form of acknowledgement opposite.)

STATE OF OREGON,	) ss.	STATE OF OREGON,	) ss.
County of	)	County of	)

This instrument was acknowledged before me on ...., 19...., by ....

....

....

....

_____
Notary Public for Oregon
(SEAL)
My commission expires:

This instrument was acknowledged before me on ...., 19...., by ....
as ....
of ....

_____
Notary Public for Oregon
My commission expires: (SEAL)

REQUEST FOR FULL RECONVEYANCE
To be used only when obligations have been paid.

TO: ...., Trustee

The undersigned is the legal owner and holder of all indebtedness secured by the foregoing trust deed. All sums secured by said trust deed have been fully paid and satisfied. You hereby are directed, on payment to you of any sums owing to you under the terms of said trust deed or pursuant to statute, to cancel all evidences of indebtedness secured by said trust deed (which are delivered to you herewith together with said trust deed) and to reconvey, without warranty, to the parties designated by the terms of said trust deed the estate now held by you under the same. Mail reconveyance and documents to ....

DATED: ...., 19...... .

....
Beneficiary

Do not lose or destroy this Trust Deed OR THE NOTE which it secures. Both must be delivered to the trustee for cancellation before reconveyance will be made.

TRUST DEED

(FORM No. 881)
STEVENS-NESS LAW PUB. CO., PORTLAND, ORE.

....

....

Grantor

....

....

Beneficiary

AFTER RECORDING RETURN TO

SPACE RESERVED
FOR
RECORDER'S USE

STATE OF OREGON,	} ss.
County of	}

I certify that the within instrument was received for record on the .... day of ...., 19......, at .... o'clock ......M., and recorded in book/reel/volume No. .... on page .... or as fee/file/instru-ment/microfilm/reception No. ...., Record of Mortgages of said County.

Witness my hand and seal of County affixed.

....
NAME   TITLE

By .... , Deputy

FORM No. 881—Oregon Trust Deed Series—TRUST DEED.

OK

STEVENS-NESS LAW PUB. CO., PORTLAND, OR. 97204

TRUST DEED

THIS TRUST DEED, made this .... day of ...., 19........., between

....,

as Grantor, ..., as Trustee, and

....,

as Beneficiary,

WITNESSETH:

Grantor irrevocably grants, bargains, sells and conveys to trustee in trust, with power of sale, the property
in ....County, Oregon, described as:

together with all and singular the tenements, hereditaments and appurtenances and all other rights thereunto belonging or in anywise
now or hereafter appertaining, and the rents, issues and profits thereof and all fixtures now or hereafter attached to or used in connection with said real estate.

FOR THE PURPOSE OF SECURING PERFORMANCE of each agreement of grantor herein contained and payment of the
sum of ....

....Dollars, with interest thereon according to the terms of a promissory
note of even date herewith, payable to beneficiary or order and made by grantor, the final payment of principal and interest hereof, if
not sooner paid, to be due and payable ...., 19 ....

The date of maturity of the debt secured by this instrument is the date, stated above, on which the final installment of said note
becomes due and payable. In the event the within described property, or any part thereof, or any interest therein is sold, agreed to be
sold, conveyed, assigned or alienated by the grantor without first having obtained the written consent or approval of the beneficiary,
then, at the beneficiary's option, all obligations secured by this instrument, irrespective of the maturity dates expressed therein, or
herein, shall become immediately due and payable.

The above described real property is not currently used for agricultural, timber or grazing purposes.

To protect the security of this trust deed, grantor agrees:
1. To protect, preserve and maintain said property in good condition
and repair; not to remove or demolish any building or improvement thereon;
not to commit or permit any waste of said property.
2. To complete or restore promptly and in good and workmanlike
manner any building or improvement which may be constructed, damaged or
destroyed thereon, and pay when due all costs incurred therefor.
3. To comply with all laws, ordinances, regulations, covenants, conditions and restrictions affecting said property; if the beneficiary so requests, to
join in executing such financing statements pursuant to the Uniform Commercial Code as the beneficiary may require and to pay for filing same in the
proper public office or offices, as well as the cost of all lien searches made
by filing officers or searching agencies as may be deemed desirable by the
beneficiary.
4. To provide and continuously maintain insurance on the buildings
now or hereafter erected on the said premises against loss or damage by fire
and such other hazards as the beneficiary may from time to time require, in
an amount not less than $ ...., written in
companies acceptable to the beneficiary, with loss payable to the latter; all
policies of insurance shall be delivered to the beneficiary as soon as insured;
if the grantor shall fail for any reason to procure any such insurance and to
deliver said policies to the beneficiary at least fifteen days prior to the expiration of any policy of insurance now or hereafter placed on said buildings,
the beneficiary may procure the same at grantor's expense. The amount
collected under any fire or other insurance policy may be applied by beneficiary upon any indebtedness secured hereby and in such order as beneficiary
may determine, or at option of beneficiary the entire amount so collected, or
any part thereof, may be released to grantor. Such application or release shall
not cure or waive any default or notice of default hereunder or invalidate any
act done pursuant to such notice.
5. To keep said premises free from construction liens and to pay all
taxes, assessments and other charges that may be levied or assessed upon or
against said property before any part of such taxes, assessments and other
charges become past due or delinquent and promptly deliver receipts therefor
to beneficiary; should the grantor fail to make payment of any taxes, assessments, insurance premiums, liens or other charges payable by grantor, either
by direct payment or by providing beneficiary with funds with which to
make such payment, beneficiary may, at its option, make payment thereof,
and the amount so paid, with interest at the rate set forth in the note secured
hereby, together with the obligations described in paragraphs 6 and 7 of this
trust deed, shall be added to and become a part of the debt secured by this
trust deed, without waiver of any rights arising from breach of any of the
covenants hereof and for such payments, with interest as aforesaid, the property hereinbefore described, as well as the grantor, shall be bound to the
same extent that they are bound for the payment of the obligation herein
described, and all such payments shall be immediately due and payable without notice, and the nonpayment thereof shall, at the option of the beneficiary,
render all sums secured by this trust deed immediately due and payable and
constitute a breach of this trust deed.
6. To pay all costs, fees and expenses of this trust including the cost
of title search as well as the other costs and expenses of the trustee incurred
in connection with or in enforcing this obligation and trustee's and attorney's
fees actually incurred.
7. To appear in and defend any action or proceeding purporting to
affect the security rights or powers of beneficiary or trustee; and in any suit,
action or proceeding in which the beneficiary or trustee may appear, including
any suit for the foreclosure of this deed, to pay all costs and expenses, including evidence of title and the beneficiary's or trustee's attorney's fees; the
amount of attorney's fees mentioned in this paragraph 7 in all cases shall be
fixed by the trial court and in the event of an appeal from any judgment or
decree of the trial court, grantor further agrees to pay such sum as the appellate court shall adjudge reasonable as the beneficiary's or trustee's attorney's fees on such appeal.
It is mutually agreed that:
8. In the event that any portion or all of said property shall be taken
under the right of eminent domain or condemnation, beneficiary shall have the
right, if it so elects, to require that all or any portion of the monies payable
as compensation for such taking, which are in excess of the amount required
to pay all reasonable costs, expenses and attorney's fees necessarily paid or
incurred by grantor in such proceedings, shall be paid to beneficiary and
applied by it first upon any reasonable costs and expenses and attorney's fees,
both in the trial and appellate courts, necessarily paid or incurred by beneficiary in such proceedings, and the balance applied upon the indebtedness
secured hereby; and grantor agrees, at its own expense, to take such actions
and execute such instruments as shall be necessary in obtaining such compensation, promptly upon beneficiary's request.
9. At any time and from time to time upon written request of beneficiary, payment of its fees and presentation of this deed and the note for
endorsement (in case of full reconveyances, for cancellation), without affecting
the liability of any person for the payment of the indebtedness, trustee may

(a) consent to the making of any map or plat of said property; (b) join in
granting any easement or creating any restriction thereon; (c) join in any
subordination or other agreement affecting this deed or the lien or charge
thereof; (d) reconvey, without warranty, all or any part of the property. The
grantee in any reconveyance may be described as the "person or persons
legally entitled thereto," and the recitals therein of any matters or facts shall
be conclusive proof of the truthfulness thereof. Trustee's fees for any of the
services mentioned in this paragraph shall be not less than $5.
10. Upon any default by grantor hereunder, beneficiary may at any
time without notice, either in person, by agent or by a receiver to be appointed by a court, and without regard to the adequacy of any security for
the indebtedness hereby secured, enter upon and take possession of said property or any part thereof, in its own name sue or otherwise collect the rents,
issues and profits, including those past due and unpaid, and apply the same,
less costs and expenses of operation and collection, including reasonable attorney's fees upon any indebtedness secured hereby, and in such order as beneficiary may determine.
11. The entering upon and taking possession of said property, the
collection of such rents, issues and profits, or the proceeds of fire and other
insurance policies or compensation or awards for any taking or damage of the
property, and the application or release thereof as aforesaid, shall not cure or
waive any default or notice of default hereunder or invalidate any act done
pursuant to such notice.
12. Upon default by grantor in payment of any indebtedness secured
hereby or in his performance of any agreement hereunder, the beneficiary may
declare all sums secured hereby immediately due and payable. In such an
event the beneficiary at his election may proceed to foreclose this trust deed
in equity as a mortgage or direct the trustee to foreclose this trust deed by
advertisement and sale. In the latter event the beneficiary or the trustee shall
execute and cause to be recorded his written notice of default and his election
to sell the said described real property to satisfy the obligation secured
hereby whereupon the trustee shall fix the time and place of sale, give notice
thereof as then required by law and proceed to foreclose this trust deed in
the manner provided in ORS 86.735 to 86.795.
13. After the trustee has commenced foreclosure by advertisement and
sale, and at any time prior to 5 days before the date the trustee conducts the
sale, the grantor or any other person so privileged by ORS 86.753, may cure
the default or defaults. If the default consists of a failure to pay, when due,
sums secured by the trust deed, the default may be cured by paying the
entire amount due at the time of the cure other than such portion as would
not then be due had no default occurred. Any other default that is capable of
being cured may be cured by tendering the performance required under the
obligation or trust deed. In any case, in addition to curing the default or
defaults, the person effecting the cure shall pay to the beneficiary all costs
and expenses actually incurred in enforcing the obligation of the trust deed
together with trustee's and attorney's fees not exceeding the amounts provided
by law.
14. Otherwise, the sale shall be held on the date and at the time and
place designated in the notice of sale or the time to which said sale may
be postponed as provided by law. The trustee may sell said property either
in one parcel or in separate parcels and shall sell the parcel or parcels at
auction to the highest bidder for cash, payable at the time of sale. Trustee
shall deliver to the purchaser its deed in form as required by law conveying
the property so sold, but without any covenant or warranty, express or implied. The recitals in the deed of any matters of fact shall be conclusive proof
of the truthfulness thereof. Any person, excluding the trustee, but including
the grantor and beneficiary, may purchase at the sale.
15. When trustee sells pursuant to the powers provided herein, trustee
shall apply the proceeds of sale to payment of (1) the expenses of sale, including the compensation of the trustee and a reasonable charge by trustee's
attorney, (2) to the obligation secured by the trust deed, (3) to all persons
having recorded liens subsequent to the interest of the trustee in the trust
deed as their interests may appear in the order of their priority and (4) the
surplus, if any, to the grantor or to his successor in interest entitled to such
surplus.
16. Beneficiary may from time to time appoint a successor or successors to any trustee named herein or to any successor trustee appointed hereunder. Upon such appointment, and without conveyance to the successor
trustee, the latter shall be vested with all title, powers and duties conferred
upon any trustee herein named or appointed hereunder. Each such appointment
and substitution shall be made by written instrument executed by beneficiary,
which, when recorded in the mortgage records of the county or counties in
which the property is situated, shall be conclusive proof of proper appointment
of the successor trustee.
17. Trustee accepts this trust when this deed, duly executed and
acknowledged is made a public record as provided by law. Trustee is not
obligated to notify any party hereto of pending sale under any other deed of
trust or of any action or proceeding in which grantor, beneficiary or trustee
shall be a party unless such action or proceeding is brought by trustee.

NOTE: The Trust Deed Act provides that the trustee hereunder must be either an attorney, who is an active member of the Oregon State Bar, a bank, trust company
or savings and loan association authorized to do business under the laws of Oregon or the United States, a title insurance company authorized to insure title to real
property of this state, its subsidiaries, affiliates, agents or branches, the United States or any agency thereof, or an escrow agent licensed under ORS 696.505 to 696.585.

$ ...., ... , 19 ......

....after date, I (or if more than one maker) we jointly and

severally promise to pay to the order of ....

....at...

.... DOLLARS,

with interest thereon at the rate of ....% per annum from...until paid; interest to be paid
....and if not so paid, all principal and interest, at the option of the holder of this note, to become immediately due and collectible. Any part hereof may be paid at any time. If this note is placed in the hands of an attorney for collection, I/we
promise and agree to pay holder's reasonable attorney's fees and collection costs, even though no suit or action is filed hereon; if a suit or
an action is filed, the amount of such reasonable attorney's fees shall be fixed by the court or courts in which the suit or action, including any
appeal therein, is tried, heard or decided.

FORM No. 216—PROMISSORY NOTE.   TB   STEVENS-NESS LAW PUB. CO., PORTLAND, ORE.

DISCLOSURES   (Installment Notes)

(NOTICE: If this is a consumer credit transaction as defined by the Truth-in-Lending Act and Regulation Z, federal law requires that the creditor, lender or payee MUST make disclosures to the borrower or maker, for which purpose the following or equivalent must be used; if this is not a consumer credit transaction, a note form similar to that below, but without printed disclosures, is available.)

1. Proceeds . . . . $_____   4. **FINANCE CHARGE;** interest $_____
2. _____ $_____   Other _____ $_____ total $_____
   _____   5. Number of payments_____; Total of payments 3 + 4 $_____
   Other charges not part of line 4—itemize
3. Amount financed (1 + 2) . . $_____   6. **ANNUAL PERCENTAGE RATE**_____%

If note is prepaid, no part of **FINANCE CHARGE** will be refunded, but pre-computed interest, then unearned, will be abated; (if, in the note below, interest is payable **in addition** to regular equal principal payments, make the following additional disclosures); each payment on principal, $_____; amount of **FINANCE CHARGE** in first scheduled payment, $_____, and in last scheduled payment, $_____.

I/We acknowledge receipt of a copy of the (1) note below and (2) above disclosures before signing the note.

_____   _____
              Maker-Borrower   Maker-Borrower

$ ...., ..., 19.......

    I (or if more than one maker) we, jointly and severally, promise to pay to the order of ....

....*at*..

.... *DOLLARS,*

with interest thereon at the rate of ....*percent per annum from* .... *until paid, payable in*

.............................*installments of not less than $* ....*in any one payment; interest shall be paid* ....*and*

° *in addition to*
* *is included in*   *the minimum payments above required; the first payment to be made on the* ....*day of* ....,

19   , *and a like payment on the* ....*day of* ....*thereafter, until the whole sum, principal and interest has been paid; if any of said installments is not so paid, all principal and interest to become immediately due and collectible at the option of the holder of this note. If this note is placed in the hands of an attorney for collection, I/we promise and agree to pay holder's reasonable attorney's fees and collection costs, even though no suit or action is filed hereon; however, if a suit or an action is filed, the amount of such reasonable attorney's fees shall be fixed by the court, or courts in which the suit or action, including any appeal therein, is tried, heard or decided.*

* *Strike words not applicable.*

....

....

(If this note, without disclosures, is required for any purpose, such a form is available.)

FORM No. 1317—Truth-in-Lending Series—INSTALLMENT NOTE.   TB   Stevens-Ness Law Publishing Co., Portland, Ore.

NOTE-STRAIGHT

$_____ _____, California, _____, 19___

_____ after date, for value received, _____ promise to pay to

_____

_____, or order,

at_____

the sum of_____DOLLARS,

with interest from_____until paid, at the rate of

_____ per cent per annum, payable _____

    Should interest not be so paid it shall thereafter bear like interest as the principal. Should default be made in payment of interest when due the whole sum of principal and interest shall become immediately due at the option of the holder of this note. Principal and interest payable in lawful money of the United States. If action be instituted on this note _____ promise to pay such sum as the Court may fix as attorney's fees.

_____   _____

_____   _____

NOTE—STRAIGHT—ATTORNEY'S FEES—WOLCOTTS FORM 1449

Form 3 E

𝔑ote 𝔖ecured by 𝔇eed of 𝔗rust

INSTALLMENT NOTE — INTEREST INCLUDED

$_____, California, _____, 19___

In installments as herein stated, for value received, I promise to pay to_____

_____, or order,

at_____

the sum of_____DOLLARS,

with interest from_____on unpaid principal at the

rate of_____per cent per annum; principal and interest payable in installments of

_____Dollars

each on the_____day of each_____month, beginning

on the_____day of_____19_____. _____

_____

_____

_____

_____

Each payment shall be credited first on interest then due and the remainder on principal; and interest shall thereupon cease upon the principal so credited. I promise to pay to the holder hereof a "late" charge of five cents for each one dollar of each installment more than ten days in arrears, but no "late" charge on any one such installment in arrears may be accrued in excess of five dollars. Upon default in payment of any installment then, the balance of this obligation shall become due immediately at the option of the holder hereof. Principal and interest payable in any coin or currency which at the time of payment is legal tender in the United States for public and private debts.

If this note is not paid when due I promise to pay in addition all costs of collection and reasonable attorneys' fees incurred by the holder hereof on account of such collection, whether or not suit is filed hereon. Each maker consents to renewals, replacements and extensions of time for payment hereof before, at or after maturity, consents to the acceptance of security for this note and waives demand and protest.

Privilege is reserved to pay the within note in full at any time by paying principal, accrued interest and 180 days unearned interest as consideration for the right to make such prepayment. This note is secured by a Deed of Trust to Los Angeles Title and Abstract Corporation, a California corporation.

_____   _____

_____   _____

RECORDING REQUESTED BY

AND WHEN RECORDED MAIL TO

Name

Street
Address

City &
State

──── SPACE ABOVE THIS LINE FOR RECORDER'S USE ────

TO 499—1 C　　**SHORT FORM DEED OF TRUST AND ASSIGNMENT OF RENTS AND REQUEST FOR SPECIAL NOTICE**

This Deed of Trust, made this　　　　　　　　　　day of　　　　　　　　　　　　　　　　　　　　, between

, herein called TRUSTOR,

whose address is

　　　　　　　　　　(number and street)　　　　　　(city)　　　　　(zone)　　　　(state)

and

, herein called BENEFICIARY,

whose address is

　　　　　　　　　　(number and street)　　　　　　(city)　　　　　(zone)　　　　(state)

and **TITLE INSURANCE AND TRUST COMPANY,** a California corporation, herein called TRUSTEE,
Witnesseth: That Trustor IRREVOCABLY GRANTS, TRANSFERS AND ASSIGNS to TRUSTEE IN TRUST, WITH POWER OF SALE,
that property in　　　　　　　　　　　　　　　　　County, California, described as:

TOGETHER WITH the rents, issues and profits thereof, SUBJECT, HOWEVER, to the right, power and authority given to and conferred
upon Beneficiary by paragraph (10) of the provisions incorporated herein by reference to collect and apply such rents, issues and profits.
For the Purpose of Securing: 1. Performance of each agreement of Trustor incorporated by reference or contained herein. 2. Payment of
the indebtedness evidenced by one promissory note of even date herewith, and any extension or renewal thereof, in the principal sum of
$_____ executed by Trustor in favor of Beneficiary or order.
To Protect the Security of This Deed of Trust, Trustor Agrees: By the execution and delivery of this Deed of Trust and the note
secured hereby, that provisions (1) to (14), inclusive, of the fictitious deed of trust recorded in Santa Barbara County and Sonoma County
October 18, 1961, and in all other counties October 23, 1961, in the book and at the page of Official Records in the office of the county recorder
of the county where said property is located, noted below opposite the name of such county, viz.:

COUNTY	BOOK	PAGE	COUNTY	BOOK	PAGE	COUNTY	BOOK	PAGE	COUNTY	BOOK	PAGE	COUNTY	BOOK	PAGE
Alameda	435	684	Kings	792	833	Placer	895	301	Sierra	29	335			
Alpine	1	250	Lake	362	39	Plumas	151	5	Siskiyou	468	181			
Amador	104	348	Lassen	171	471	Riverside	3005	523	Solano	1105	182			
Butte	1145	1	Los Angeles	T2055	899	Sacramento	4331	62	Sonoma	1851	689			
Calaveras	145	152	Madera	810	170	San Benito	271	383	Stanislaus	1715	456			
Colusa	296	617	Marin	1508	339	San Bernardino	5567	61	Sutter	572	297			
Contra Costa	3978	47	Mariposa	77	292	San Francisco	A332	905	Tehama	401	289			
Del Norte	78	414	Mendocino	579	530	San Joaquin	2470	311	Trinity	93	366			
El Dorado	568	456	Merced	1547	538	San Luis Obispo	1151	12	Tulare	2294	275			
Fresno	4626	572	Modoc	184	851	San Mateo	4078	420	Tuolumne	135	47			
Glenn	422	184	Mono	52	429	Santa Barbara	1878	860	Ventura	2062	386			
Humboldt	657	527	Monterey	2194	538	Santa Clara	5336	341	Yolo	653	245			
Imperial	1091	501	Napa	639	86	Santa Cruz	1431	494	Yuba	334	486			
Inyo	147	598	Nevada	305	320	Shasta	684	528						
Kern	3427	60	Orange	5889	611	San Diego	Series 2 Book 1961, Page 183887								

(which provisions, identical in all counties, are printed on the reverse hereof) hereby are adopted and incorporated herein and made a part
hereof as fully as though set forth herein at length; that he will observe and perform said provisions; and that the references to property,
obligations, and parties in said provisions shall be construed to refer to the property, obligations, and parties set forth in this Deed of Trust.
The undersigned Trustor requests that a copy of any Notice of Default and of any Notice of Sale hereunder be mailed to him at his address
hereinbefore set forth.

In accordance with Section 2924b, Civil Code, request is hereby made by the undersigned TRUSTOR that a copy of
any Notice of Default and a copy of any Notice of Sale under Deed of Trust recorded_____
in Book_____, Page_____, Official Records of_____County, California, as
affecting above described property, executed by_____
as Trustor in which_____
is named as Beneficiary, and_____as Trustee,
be mailed to_____
whose address is_____
　　　　　　　　(Number and Street)　　　　　　(City)　　　　　(Zone)　　　　(State)

Signature of Trustor　　　　　　　　　　　　　　　　　*Signature of Trustor*

_____　　　　　　　　　　　　　　　　_____

STATE OF CALIFORNIA,
COUNTY OF_____ } ss.
On_____, before me, the undersigned, a Notary Public in and for said State, personally
appeared_____

known to me to be the person____whose name____subscribed to the within instrument and acknowledged that____
executed the same.
WITNESS my hand and official seal.
Signature_____

_____
Name (Typed or Printed)

(This area for official notarial seal)

—— DO NOT RECORD ——

The following is a copy of provisions (1) to (14), inclusive, of the fictitious deed of trust, recorded in each county in California, as stated in the foregoing Deed of Trust and incorporated by reference in said Deed of Trust as being a part thereof as if set forth at length therein.

To Protect the Security of This Deed of Trust, Trustor Agrees:

(1) To keep said property in good condition and repair; not to remove or demolish any building thereon; to complete or restore promptly and in good and workmanlike manner any building which may be constructed, damaged or destroyed thereon and to pay when due all claims for labor performed and materials furnished therefor; to comply with all laws affecting said property or requiring any alterations or improvements to be made thereon; not to commit or permit waste thereof; not to commit, suffer or permit any act upon said property in violation of law; to cultivate, irrigate, fertilize, fumigate, prune and do all other acts which from the character or use of said property may be reasonably necessary, the specific enumerations herein not excluding the general.

(2) To provide, maintain and deliver to Beneficiary fire insurance satisfactory to and with loss payable to Beneficiary. The amount collected under any fire or other insurance policy may be applied by Beneficiary upon any indebtedness secured hereby and in such order as Beneficiary may determine, or at option of Beneficiary the entire amount so collected or any part thereof may be released to Trustor. Such application or release shall not cure or waive any default or notice of default hereunder or invalidate any act done pursuant to such notice.

(3) To appear in and defend any action or proceeding purporting to affect the security hereof or the rights or powers of Beneficiary or Trustee; and to pay all costs and expenses, including cost of evidence of title and attorney's fees in a reasonable sum, in any such action or proceeding in which Beneficiary or Trustee may appear, and in any suit brought by Beneficiary to foreclose this Deed.

(4) To pay: at least ten days before delinquency all taxes and assessments affecting said property, including assessments on appurtenant water stock; when due, all incumbrances, charges and liens, with interest, on said property or any part thereof, which appear to be prior or superior hereto; all costs, fees and expenses of this Trust.

Should Trustor fail to make any payment or to do any act as herein provided, then Beneficiary or Trustee, but without obligation so to do and without notice to or demand upon Trustor and without releasing Trustor from any obligation hereof, may: make or do the same in such manner and to such extent as either may deem necessary to protect the security hereof, Beneficiary or Trustee being authorized to enter upon said property for such purposes; appear in and defend any action or proceeding purporting to affect the security hereof or the rights or powers of Beneficiary or Trustee; pay, purchase, contest or compromise any incumbrance, charge or lien which in the judgment of either appears to be prior or superior hereto; and, in exercising any such powers, pay necessary expenses, employ counsel and pay his reasonable fees.

(5) To pay immediately and without demand all sums so expended by Beneficiary or Trustee, with interest from date of expenditure at the amount allowed by law in effect at the date hereof, and to pay for any statement provided for by law in effect at the date hereof regarding the obligation secured hereby any amount demanded by the Beneficiary not to exceed the maximum allowed by law at the time when said statement is demanded.

(6) That any award of damages in connection with any condemnation for public use of or injury to said property or any part thereof is hereby assigned and shall be paid to Beneficiary who may apply or release such moneys received by him in the same manner and with the same effect as above provided for disposition of proceeds of fire or other insurance.

(7) That by accepting payment of any sum secured hereby after its due date, Beneficiary does not waive his right either to require prompt payment when due of all other sums so secured or to declare default for failure so to pay.

(8) That at any time or from time to time, without liability therefor and without notice, upon written request of Beneficiary and presentation of this Deed and said note for endorsement, and without affecting the personal liability of any person for payment of the indebtedness secured hereby, Trustee may: reconvey any part of said property; consent to the making of any map or plat thereof; join in granting any easement thereon; or join in any extension agreement or any agreement subordinating the lien or charge hereof.

(9) That upon written request of Beneficiary stating that all sums secured hereby have been paid, and upon surrender of this Deed and said note to Trustee for cancellation and retention and upon payment of its fees, Trustee shall reconvey, without warranty, the property then held hereunder. The recitals in such reconveyance of any matters or facts shall be conclusive proof of the truthfulness thereof. The grantee in such reconveyance may be described as "the person or persons legally entitled thereto." Five years after issuance of such full reconveyance, Trustee may destroy said note and this Deed (unless directed in such request to retain them).

(10) That as additional security, Trustor hereby gives to and confers upon Beneficiary the right, power and authority, during the continuance of these Trusts, to collect the rents, issues and profits of said property, reserving unto Trustor the right, prior to any default by Trustor in payment of any indebtedness secured hereby or in performance of any agreement hereunder, to collect and retain such rents, issues and profits as they become due and payable. Upon any such default, Beneficiary may at any time without notice, either in person, by agent, or by a receiver to be appointed by a court, and without regard to the adequacy of any security for the indebtedness hereby secured, enter upon and take possession of said property or any part thereof, in his own name sue for or otherwise collect such rents, issues and profits, including those past due and unpaid, and apply the same, less costs and expenses of operation and collection, including reasonable attorney's fees, upon any indebtedness secured hereby, and in such order as Beneficiary may determine. The entering upon and taking possession of said property, the collection of such rents, issues and profits and the application thereof as aforesaid, shall not cure or waive any default or notice of default hereunder or invalidate any act done pursuant to such notice.

(11) That upon default by Trustor in payment of any indebtedness secured hereby or in performance of any agreement hereunder, Beneficiary may declare all sums secured hereby immediately due and payable by delivery to Trustee of written declaration of default and demand for sale and of written notice of default and of election to cause to be sold said property, which notice Trustee shall cause to be filed for record. Beneficiary also shall deposit with Trustee this Deed, said note and all documents evidencing expenditures secured hereby.

After the lapse of such time as may then be required by law following the recordation of said notice of default, and notice of sale having been given as then required by law, Trustee, without demand on Trustor, shall sell said property at the time and place fixed by it in said notice of sale, either as a whole or in separate parcels, and in such order as it may determine, at public auction to the highest bidder for cash in lawful money of the United States, payable at time of sale. Trustee may postpone sale of all or any portion of said property by public announcement at such time and place of sale, and from time to time thereafter may postpone such sale by public announcement at the time fixed by the preceding postponement. Trustee shall deliver to such purchaser its deed conveying the property so sold, but without any covenant or warranty, express or implied. The recitals in such deed of any matters or facts shall be conclusive proof of the truthfulness thereof. Any person, including Trustor, Trustee, or Beneficiary as hereinafter defined, may purchase at such sale.

After deducting all costs, fees and expenses of Trustee and of this Trust, including cost of evidence of title in connection with sale, Trustee shall apply the proceeds of sale to payment of: all sums expended under the terms hereof, not then repaid, with accrued interest at the amount allowed by law in effect at the date hereof; all other sums then secured hereby; and the remainder, if any, to the person or persons legally entitled thereto.

(12) Beneficiary, or any successor in ownership of any indebtedness secured hereby, may from time to time, by instrument in writing, substitute a successor or successors to any Trustee named herein or acting hereunder, which instrument, executed by the Beneficiary and duly acknowledged and recorded in the office of the recorder of the county or counties where said property is situated, shall be conclusive proof of proper substitution of such successor Trustee or Trustees, who shall, without conveyance from the Trustee predecessor, succeed to all its title, estate, rights, powers and duties. Said instrument must contain the name of the original Trustor, Trustee and Beneficiary hereunder, the book and page where this Deed is recorded and the name and address of the new Trustee.

(13) That this Deed applies to, inures to the benefit of, and binds all parties hereto, their heirs, legatees, devisees, administrators, executors, successors and assigns. The term Beneficiary shall mean the owner and holder, including pledgees, of the note secured hereby, whether or not named as Beneficiary herein. In this Deed, whenever the context so requires, the masculine gender includes the feminine and/or neuter, and the singular number includes the plural.

(14) That Trustee accepts this Trust when this Deed, duly executed and acknowledged, is made a public record as provided by law. Trustee is not obligated to notify any party hereto of pending sale under any other Deed of Trust or of any action or proceeding in which Trustor, Beneficiary or Trustee shall be a party unless brought by Trustee.

—— DO NOT RECORD ——

REQUEST FOR FULL RECONVEYANCE
To be used only when note has been paid.

To TITLE INSURANCE AND TRUST COMPANY, Trustee: Dated_____

The undersigned is the legal owner and holder of all indebtedness secured by the within Deed of Trust. All sums secured by said Deed of Trust have been fully paid and satisfied; and you are hereby requested and directed, on payment to you of any sums owing to you under the terms of said Deed of Trust, to cancel all evidences of indebtedness, secured by said Deed of Trust, delivered to you herewith together with said Deed of Trust, and to reconvey, without warranty, to the parties designated by the terms of said Deed of Trust, the estate now held by you under the same.

MAIL RECONVEYANCE TO: _____

_____

_____

_____

Do not lose or destroy this Deed of Trust OR THE NOTE which it secures. Both must be delivered to the Trustee for cancellation before reconveyance will be made.

DEED OF TRUST
WITH POWER OF SALE
(SHORT FORM)
ASSIGNMENT OF RENTS AND
REQUEST FOR SPECIAL NOTICE

Title Insurance
and
Trust Company
AS TRUSTEE

Title Insurance
and
Trust Company

COMPLETE STATEWIDE TITLE SERVICE
WITH ONE LOCAL CALL

——————————————— SPACE ABOVE THIS LINE FOR RECORDER'S USE ———————————————

Deed of Trust and Assignment of Rents (Long Form)

498 7-55

This Deed of Trust, Made this   day of   , between

, herein called TRUSTOR,

whose address is

     (Number and Street)   (City)   (Zone)   (State)

TITLE INSURANCE AND TRUST COMPANY, a California corporation, herein called TRUSTEE, and

, herein called BENEFICIARY,

Witnesseth: That Trustor IRREVOCABLY GRANTS, TRANSFERS AND ASSIGNS to TRUSTEE IN TRUST, WITH POWER OF SALE,

that property in   County, California, described as:

TOGETHER WITH the rent, issues and profits thereof, SUBJECT, HOWEVER, to the right, power and authority hereinafter given to and conferred upon Beneficiary to collect and apply such rents, issues and profits.

For the Purpose of Securing:
   1. Performance of each agreement of Trustor herein contained. 2. Payment of the indebtedness evidenced by one promissory note of even date herewith, and any extension or renewal thereof, in the principal sum of $..............................executed by Trustor in favor of Beneficiary or order.

To Protect the Security of This Deed of Trust, Trustor Agrees:
   (1) To keep said property in good condition and repair; not to remove or demolish any building thereon; to complete or restore promptly and in good and workmanlike manner any building which may be constructed, damaged or destroyed thereon and to pay when due all claims for labor performed and materials furnished therefor; to comply with all laws affecting said property or requiring any alterations or improvements to be made thereon; not to commit or permit waste thereof; not to commit, suffer or permit any act upon said property in violation of law; to cultivate, irrigate, fertilize, fumigate, prune and do all other acts which from the character or use of said property may be reasonably necessary, the specific enumerations herein not excluding the general.
   (2) To provide, maintain and deliver to Beneficiary fire insurance satisfactory to and with loss payable to Beneficiary. The amount collected under any fire or other insurance policy may be applied by Beneficiary upon any indebtedness secured hereby and in such order as Beneficiary may determine, or at option of Beneficiary the entire amount so collected or any part thereof may be released to Trustor. Such application or release shall not cure or waive any default or notice of default hereunder or invalidate any act done pursuant to such notice.
   (3) To appear in and defend any action or proceeding purporting to affect the security hereof or the rights or powers of Beneficiary or Trustee; and to pay all costs and expenses, including cost of evidence of title and attorney's fees in a reasonable sum, in any such action or proceeding in which Beneficiary or Trustee may appear, and in any suit brought by Beneficiary to foreclose this Deed.
   (4) To pay: at least ten days before delinquency all taxes and assessments affecting said property, including assessments on appurtenant water stock; when due, all incumbrances, charges and liens, with interest, on said property or any part thereof, which appear to be prior or superior hereto; all costs, fees and expenses of this Trust.
   Should Trustor fail to make any payment or to do any act as herein provided, then Beneficiary or Trustee, but without obligation so to do and without notice to or demand upon Trustor and without releasing Trustor from any obligation hereof, may: make or do the same in such manner and to such extent as either may deem necessary to protect the security hereof, Beneficiary or Trustee being authorized to enter upon said property for such purposes; appear in and defend any action or proceeding purporting to affect the security hereof or the rights or powers of Beneficiary or Trustee; pay, purchase, contest or compromise any incumbrance, charge or lien which in the judgment of either appears to be prior or superior hereto; and, in exercising any such powers, pay necessary expenses, employ counsel and pay his reasonable fees.
   (5) To pay immediately and without demand all sums so expended by Beneficiary or Trustee, with interest from date of expenditure at seven per cent per annum.
   (6) That any award of damages in connection with any condemnation for public use of or injury to said property or any part thereof is hereby assigned and shall be paid to Beneficiary who may apply or release such moneys received by him in the same manner and with the same effect as above provided for disposition of proceeds of fire or other insurance.
   (7) That by accepting payment of any sum secured hereby after its due date, Beneficiary does not waive his right either to require prompt payment when due of all other sums so secured or to declare default for failure so to pay.
   (8) That at any time or from time to time, without liability therefor and without notice, upon written request of Beneficiary and presentation of this Deed and said note for endorsement, and without affecting the personal liability of any person for payment of the indebtedness secured hereby, Trustee may: reconvey any part of said property; consent to the making of any map or plat thereof; join in granting any easement thereon; or join in any extension agreement or any agreement subordinating the lien or charge hereof.
   (9) That upon written request of Beneficiary stating that all sums secured hereby have been paid, and upon surrender of this Deed and said note to Trustee for cancellation and retention and upon payment of its fees, Trustee shall reconvey, without warranty, the property then held hereunder. The recitals in such reconveyance of any matters or facts shall be conclusive proof of the truthfulness thereof. The grantee in such reconveyance may be described as "the person or persons legally entitled thereto." Five years after issuance of such full reconveyance, Trustee may destroy said note and this Deed (unless directed in such request to retain them).
   (10) That as additional security, Trustor hereby gives to and confers upon Beneficiary the right, power and authority, during the continuance of these Trusts, to collect the rents, issues and profits of said property, reserving unto Trustor the right, prior to any default by Trustor in payment of any indebtedness secured hereby or in performance of any agreement hereunder, to collect and retain such rents, issues and profits as they become due and

SPACE ABOVE THIS LINE FOR RECORDER'S USE

payable. Upon any such default, Beneficiary may at any time without notice, either in person, by agent, or by a receiver to be appointed by a court, and without regard to the adequacy of any security for the indebtedness hereby secured, enter upon and take possession of said property or any part thereof, in his own name sue for or otherwise collect such rents, issues, and profits, including those past due and unpaid, and apply the same, less costs and expenses of operation and collection, including reasonable attorney's fees, upon any indebtedness secured hereby, and in such order as Beneficiary may determine. The entering upon and taking possession of said property, the collection of such rents, issues and profits and the application thereof as aforesaid, shall not cure or waive any default or notice of default hereunder or invalidate any act done pursuant to such notice.

(11) That upon default by Trustor in payment of any indebtedness secured hereby or in performance of any agreement hereunder, Beneficiary may declare all sums secured hereby immediately due and payable by delivery to Trustee of written declaration of default and demand for sale and of written notice of default and of election to cause to be sold said property, which notice Trustee shall cause to be filed for record. Beneficiary also shall deposit with Trustee this Deed, said note and all documents evidencing expenditures secured hereby.

After the lapse of such time as may then be required by law following the recordation of said notice of default, and notice of sale having been given as then required by law, Trustee, without demand on Trustor, shall sell said property at the time and place fixed by it in said notice of sale, either as a whole or in separate parcels, and in such order as it may determine, at public auction to the highest bidder for cash in lawful money of the United States, payable at time of sale. Trustee may postpone sale of all or any portion of said property by public announcement at such time and place of sale, and from time to time thereafter may postpone such sale by public announcement at the time fixed by the preceding postponement. Trustee shall deliver to such purchaser its deed conveying the property so sold, but without any covenant or warranty, express or implied. The recitals in such deed of any matters or facts shall be conclusive proof of the truthfulness thereof. Any person, including Trustor, Trustee, or Beneficiary as hereinafter defined, may purchase at such sale.

After deducting all costs, fees and expenses of Trustee and of this Deed, including cost of evidence of title in connection with sale, Trustee shall apply the proceeds of sale to payment of: all sums expended under the terms hereof, not then repaid, with accrued interest at seven per cent per annum; all other sums then secured hereby; and the remainder, if any, to the person or persons legally entitled thereto.

(12) That Trustor, or if said property shall have been transferred, then record owner, together with Beneficiary, may from time to time, by instrument in writing, substitute a successor or successors to any Trustee named herein or acting hereunder, which instrument, executed and acknowledged by each and recorded in the office of the recorder of the county or counties where said property is situated, shall be conclusive proof of proper substitution of such successor Trustee or Trustees, who shall, without conveyance from the Trustee predecessor, succeed to all its title, estate, rights, powers and duties. Said instrument must contain the name of the original Trustor, Trustee and Beneficiary hereunder, the book and page where this Deed is recorded, and the name and address of the new Trustee. If notice of default shall have been recorded, this power of substitution cannot be exercised until after the costs, fees and expenses of the then acting Trustee shall have been paid to such Trustee, who shall endorse receipt thereof upon such instrument of substitution. The procedure herein provided for substitution of Trustees shall be exclusive of all other provisions for substitution, statutory or otherwise.

(13) That this Deed applies to, inures to the benefit of, and binds all parties hereto, their heirs, legatees, devisees, administrators, executors, successors and assigns. The term Beneficiary shall mean the owner and holder, including pledgees, of the note secured hereby, whether or not named as Beneficiary herein. In this Deed, whenever the context so requires, the masculine gender includes the feminine and/or neuter, and the singular number includes the plural.

(14) That Trustee accepts this Trust when this Deed, duly executed and acknowledged, is made a public record as provided by law. Trustee is not obligated to notify any party hereto of pending sale under any other Deed of Trust or of any action or proceeding in which Trustor, Beneficiary or Trustee shall be a party unless brought by Trustee.

The undersigned Trustor requests that a copy of any Notice of Default and of any Notice of Sale hereunder be mailed to him at his address hereinbefore set forth.

STATE OF CALIFORNIA
COUNTY OF ⎫ SS.

Signature of Trustor

....

On .... ,
before me, the undersigned, a Notary Public in
and for said County and State, personally appeared

....

....

....

....

known to me to be the person...... whose name........................
subscribed to the within instrument and acknowledged that
.................................executed the same.

WITNESS my hand and official seal.

(Seal)
        Notary Public in and for said County and State.

*If executed by a Corporation the Corporation Form of
Acknowledgment must be used.*

SPACE BELOW FOR RECORDER'S USE ONLY
Index as Trust Deed and Assignment of Rent.

WHEN RECORDED MAIL TO

....

....

....

Title Order No..

Escrow or Loan No..

Deed of Trust
WITH POWER OF SALE
(LONG FORM)
TITLE INSURANCE
AND
TRUST COMPANY
as TRUSTEE

Home Office:
433 SO. SPRING ST. • LOS ANGELES 54, CALIFORNIA
Other Offices in:
BAKERSFIELD • FRESNO • INDEPENDENCE • RIVERSIDE
SANTA ANA • SANTA BARBARA • SAN DIEGO
SAN LUIS OBISPO • VENTURA • VISALIA

DO NOT RECORD

REQUEST FOR FULL RECONVEYANCE
To be used only when note has been paid.

Dated..............................

To TITLE INSURANCE AND TRUST COMPANY, TRUSTEE:

The undersigned is the legal owner and holder of all indebtedness secured by the within Deed of Trust. All sums secured by said Deed of Trust have been fully paid and satisfied; and you are hereby requested and directed, on payment to you of any sums owing to you under the terms of said Deed of Trust, to cancel all evidences of indebtedness, secured by said Deed of Trust, delivered to you herewith together with the said Deed of Trust, and to reconvey, without warranty, to the parties designated by the terms of said Deed of Trust, the estate now held by you under the same.

MAIL RECONVEYANCE TO:

Do not lose or destroy this Deed of Trust OR THE NOTE which it secures.
Both must be delivered to the Trustee for cancellation before reconveyance will be made.

RECORDING REQUESTED BY

AND WHEN RECORDED MAIL TO

NAME

ADDRESS

CITY &
STATE

Title Order No._____ Escrow No._____

INDEX AS ASSIGNMENT OF DEED OF TRUST AND AS REQUEST FOR SPECIAL NOTICE.

SPACE ABOVE THIS LINE FOR RECORDER'S USE

Assignment of Deed of Trust and Request For Special Notice

L-62-A

FOR VALUE RECEIVED, the undersigned hereby grants, assigns and transfers to

all beneficial interest under that certain Deed of Trust dated
executed by

, Trustor ,

to   , Trustee.

and recorded as Instrument No.   on   in book   ,

page   , of Official Records in the County Recorder's office of   County.

California, describing land therein as:

TOGETHER with the note or notes therein described or referred to, the money due and to become due thereon with
interest, and all rights accrued or to accrue under said Deed of Trust.

Dated

In accordance with Section 2924b, Civil Code, request is hereby made by the undersigned assignor that a copy
of any Notice of Default and a copy of any Notice of Sale under Deed of Trust recorded_____
in Book_____, Page_____, Official Records of_____County, California,
as affecting above described property, executed by_____
as Trustor in which_____
is named as Beneficiary, and_____ as Trustee.
be mailed to_____ .
whose address is_____
(Number and Street)   (City)   (Zone)   (State)

STATE OF CALIFORNIA
COUNTY OF_____ } SS.
On_____before me, the under-
signed, a Notary Public in and for said County and State, personally
appeared_____

_____

_____, known to me
to be the person_____whose name_____subscribed to the within
instrument and acknowledged that_____executed the same.

FOR NOTARY SEAL OR STAMP

_____

Name (Typed or Printed)
Notary Public in and for said County and State
*If Assignor is a corporation, then the corporation form of ack-
nowledgment, as to it, must be used.*

L-62-A (G.S.) Rev. 12-63 **(8 pt.)**

RECORDING REQUESTED BY

AND WHEN RECORDED MAIL TO

Name

Street
Address

City &
State

——————————— SPACE ABOVE THIS LINE FOR RECORDER'S USE ———————————

Assignment of Deed of Trust

ADT 874 HC   THIS FORM FURNISHED BY TRUSTORS SECURITY SERVICE   181619

For Value Received, the undersigned hereby grants. assigns and transfers to_____

_____

all beneficial interest under that certain Deed of Trust dated_____,

executed by_____

_____, Trustor   ,

to_____, Trustee,

and recorded as Instrument No. _____on_____in book_____,

page_____, of Official Records in the County Recorder's office of___ _____ _____County,

describing land therein as:

Together with the note or notes therein described or referred to, the money due and to become due thereon with interest, and all rights accrued or to accrue under said Deed of Trust.

Dated _____

State of

County of _____

On this the _____ day of _____ 19___ ,

before me, _____

the undersigned Notary Public, personally appeared

☐ personally known to me

☐ proved to me on the basis of satisfactory evidence

to be the person(s) whose name(s)_____ subscribed to the

within instrument, and acknowledged that _____ executed it.

WITNESS my hand and official seal.

Notary's Signature _____

(This area for official notarial seal)

Title Order No. _____   **Escrow, Loan or Attorney File No.** _____

——— SPACE ABOVE THIS LINE FOR RECORDER'S USE ———

Corporation Assignment of Deed of Trust

160A 11-55   THIS FORM FURNISHED BY TITLE INSURANCE AND TRUST COMPANY

For Value Received, the undersigned hereby grants, assigns and transfers to...

all beneficial interest under that certain Deed of Trust dated..,

executed by..

...., Trustor......,

to ....

...., Trustee......, and recorded as Instrument No.......................

on ...., in book......................................, page.............................

of Official Records in the office of the county recorder of..

County, California, describing land therein as:

Together with the note or notes therein described or referred to, the money due and to become due thereon with interest, and all rights accrued or to accrue under said Deed of Trust.

Dated...

STATE OF CALIFORNIA
COUNTY OF   } ss.

By...

....   *President*

By...

....   *Secretary*

On..,

before me, the undersigned, a Notary Public in and for

said County and State, personally appeared..................

....,

known to me to be the.......................President, and

known to me to be the.......................Secretary of
the Corporation that executed the within Instrument, known
to me to be the persons who executed the within Instrument
on behalf of the Corporation therein named, and acknowledged to me that such Corporation executed the within Instrument pursuant to its by-laws or a resolution of its board
of directors.

WITNESS my hand and official seal.

(Seal)...
          Notary Public in and for said County and State.

SPACE BELOW FOR RECORDER'S USE ONLY

WHEN RECORDED MAIL TO

....

....

....

Title Order No...

Escrow or Loan No..

TO 39 CA 19.1 (12 - 68)

ACCOMMODATION RECORDING

Order Form

Title Insurance and Trust Company
433 SOUTH SPRING STREET · P.O. BOX 2586
LOS ANGELES, CALIFORNIA 90054

Attn: Accommodation Recording Dept., Title Service Div.

DATE _____

FOR TITLE COMPANY USE ONLY
NO. _____
SUB. NO. _____
DATE _____
CHECK REC'D _____ BILL _____

We hand you the following instruments which you will record as an accommodation and without liability on the part of your company. We are also enclosing check in the amount of $ _____ payable to Title Insurance and Trust Company to cover recording fees and DTT as shown hereon.

DOCUMENT	1ST PARTY	2ND PARTY	DTT	RECORDING FEE
1.				
2.				
3.				
4.				
5.				
6.				
		TOTAL		

NOTE: Compute County Recorder's Fees, per 1957 Code, as follows:
$2.00 Minimum for each document (includes first page)
PLUS $ .80 for each additional page or portion thereof.

We understand that said instruments will not be filed for record until after 9:00 A.M. on the day they are presented to the County Recorder.

Customers Name _____

Address _____

City _____

Phone Document No. [ ]   By _____

PHONE NO. _____   Escrow or Loan No. _____

Declaration of Default

TRUST ORDER NO.

YOU ARE HEREBY NOTIFIED: That you are Trustee under a deed of trust dated.. executed by.......................................
....as Trustor,
to secure certain obligations in favor of...
....as Beneficiary, recorded ...., in
Book........................., Page..........................., of Official Records in the office of the Recorder of.......................
....County, California, describing land therein as:

said obligations including...............note.........for the...sum of $.............................;

That a breach of, and default in, the obligations for which such deed is security has occurred in that payment has not been made of:

That by reason thereof, the undersigned hereby declares all sums secured by said deed immediately due and payable;
That there is now due, owing and unpaid upon said note (s) the...................................principal sum of $..................., with interest thereon from..., as in said note (s) provided...................................., and all sums properly advanced or expended under the terms of said deed, with interest as therein provided. Therefore you are hereby requested and directed to sell the property now covered thereby to satisfy the obligations so secured. Said deed, note (s) and receipts for sums advanced are herewith handed you, and you are instructed to record the accompanying Notice of Default and Election to Sell. The undersigned will deliver to you receipts for all sums, if any, hereafter properly advanced or expended under the terms of said deed, immediately upon payment thereof. If, prior to sale, payment in full be made to you of all sums herein declared to be due, as well as any advances hereafter properly made, of which you have been advised, together with your fees and expenses, you shall cancel said note or notes and reconvey said property, as provided in said deed, but without expense to the undersigned. The undersigned hereby guarantees payment of all fees and expenses of said Trusts and of the Trustee pertaining to said sale, and hands you herewith the sum

of $... on account thereof.

DATED..   ....

PROPERTY SITUATED AT   ....

....   Address..
          NUMBER AND STREET

....   Phone..
  CITY   ZONE   STATE

PLEASE FURNISH INFORMATION REQUESTED ON REVERSE SIDE HEREOF

GIVE NAMES AND ADDRESSES OF ALL PARTIES HAVING AN INTEREST IN THE PROPERTY

(OVER)

FORM NO. 18   ESCROW PUBLICATIONS

RECORDING REQUESTED BY

AND WHEN RECORDED MAIL TO

Name
Street Address
City & State

MAIL TAX STATEMENTS TO

Name
Street Address
City & State

——— SPACE ABOVE THIS LINE FOR RECORDER'S USE ———

TO 404 CA (9-68)

Joint Tenancy Grant Deed   D.T.T.$_____

THIS FORM FURNISHED BY TITLE INSURANCE AND TRUST COMPANY

FOR A VALUABLE CONSIDERATION, receipt of which is hereby acknowledged,

hereby GRANT(S) to

, AS JOINT TENANTS,

the real property in the
County of

State of California, described as:

Dated:_____

STATE OF CALIFORNIA
COUNTY OF_____ }SS.
On_____before me, the under-
signed, a Notary Public in and for said State, personally appeared

_____, known to me
to be the person____whose name____subscribed to the within
instrument and acknowledged that____executed the same.
WITNESS my hand and official seal.

Signature_____

____Name (Typed or Printed)

(This area for official notarial seal)

Title Order No._____   Escrow or Loan No._____

MAIL TAX STATEMENTS AS DIRECTED ABOVE

RECORDING REQUESTED BY

AND WHEN RECORDED MAIL TO

Name

Street
Address

City &
State

———————— SPACE ABOVE THIS LINE FOR RECORDER'S USE ————————

MAIL TAX STATEMENTS TO

Name

Street
Address

City &
State

TO 402 CA (12-68)

D.T.T. $_____

Quitclaim Deed

THIS FORM FURNISHED BY TITLE INSURANCE AND TRUST COMPANY

FOR A VALUABLE CONSIDERATION, receipt of which is hereby acknowledged,

hereby REMISE(S), RELEASE(S) AND FOREVER QUITCLAIM(S) to

the following described real property in the   county of
state of California:

Dated _____

STATE OF CALIFORNIA
COUNTY OF_____ }SS.
On _____ before me, the under-
signed, a Notary Public in and for said State, personally appeared

_____
_____
_____, known to me
to be the person____whose name____ subscribed to the within
instrument and acknowledged that_____executed the same.
WITNESS my hand and official seal.

Signature _____

_____
Name (Typed or Printed)
*If executed by a Corporation the Corporation Form
of Acknowledgment must be used.*

(This area for official notarial seal)

Title Order No._____   Escrow or Loan No._____

MAIL TAX STATEMENTS AS DIRECTED ABOVE

RECORDING REQUESTED BY

AND WHEN RECORDED MAIL TO

Name

Street
Address

City &
State

MAIL TAX STATEMENTS TO

Name

Street
Address

City &
State

———— SPACE ABOVE THIS LINE FOR RECORDER'S USE ————

Individual Quitclaim Deed

THIS FORM FURNISHED BY TICOR TITLE INSURERS

TO 1922 CA (1.75)   A.P.N.

The undersigned grantor(s) declare(s):
Documentary transfer tax is $_____ .
( ) computed on full value of property conveyed, or
( ) computed on full value less value of liens and encumbrances remaining at time of sale.
( ) Unincorporated area: ( ) City of_____ , and

FOR A VALUABLE CONSIDERATION, receipt of which is hereby acknowledged,

hereby REMISE(S), RELEASE(S) AND FOREVER QUITCLAIM(S) to

the following described real property in the   County of
State of California:

Dated _____

STATE OF CALIFORNIA
COUNTY OF_____ } SS.
On _____ before me, the under-
signed, a Notary Public in and for said State, personally appeared

_____ , known to me
to be the person____whose name_____ subscribed to the within
instrument and acknowledged that_____executed the same.
WITNESS my hand and official seal.

Signature _____

(This area for official notarial seal)

Title Order No._____   Escrow or Loan No._____

MAIL TAX STATEMENTS AS DIRECTED ABOVE

SALE OF TRUST DEED

PROPERTY ADDRESS_____CITY_____

DESCRIPTION_____

TERMS OF SALE:

DOWN PAYMENT $_____   LENDER   PAYT   INT   YRS

2nd TRUST DEED   _____   _____ $_____   __%____

1st TRUST DEED   _____   _____   _____   ____ ____

    TOTAL $_____ $_____

ESCROW NO._____OPENED_____CLOSED_____

TRUSTOR:

NAME_____,_____AGE_____ _____AGE____
      (Last)   (First)   (Wife)

Employer_____   Employer_____

Address _____   Adress _____

Position_____   Position_____

How Long _____   How Long_____

Income (Wk)_____(Mo)_____   Income-Wk_____Mo._____

PREVIOUS:

Employer_____   EMployer_____

Address _____   Address _____

Yrs _____Income_____   Yrs_____ Income_____

ASSETTS: LIABILITIES:

Cash on Hand $_____   Installment Accts $_____

Personal Prop._____   Notes or Accts Pay _____

Deposit In Escrow $_____   Mortgages, R.E.   _____

Other   _____   Other   _____

Other Real Prop _____   Net Worth   _____

    Total $_____   Total $_____

LOAN SUMMARY SHEET

BORROWER_____

AFFILIATION OF PRINCIPALS_____

PURPOSE OF LOAN_____

CREDIT STATUS

Average Balance	$_____ $_____	Current Ratio	_____
Date of Statement	_____ _____	Net Income	$_____ $_____
Net Worth	$_____ $_____	Customer Since	_____ _____
Other Bank Credit	$_____ $_____	Commercial Officer	_____ _____

Remarks_____

PROPERTY

Location_____ Type_____

☐ In Escrow
IF PURCHASE $_____ ☐ Open Escrow UB   APPRAISAL — Land $_____
       PRICE   Imps. $_____
IF CONSTRUCTION   Other $_____
                                                     TOTAL $_____

Name — Address — Telephone No.

☐ Contractor_____
☐ Supervisor_____
☐ Take-Out Lender_____
☐ Bond and/or Control_____
COSTS — Land $_____   SOURCE OF FUNDS_____
      Buildings $_____
      Other $_____
      TOTAL $_____   (   ) % of Loan to Appraisal Value

LOAN RECOMMENDATION

$_____   ☐ Yrs. $_____
  AMOUNT   INT. RATE   ☐ Mos.   INT. ONLY   MO P I PMTS.
                         TERM
Prepayment Privilege_____

Fees _____ $_____ $_____
  UB LOAN FEE   UB COMMIT. FEE   UB CONTINGENT FEE   COMPLETION DATE

LOAN DOCUMENTATION

☐ UB Form of Financial Statement
☐ Credit Report ☐ RCA ☐ D & B ☐ BMCDA   ☐ Note Co-signed by_____
☐ Partnership Agreement
☐ Title Policy ☐ LP-10 ☐ ATA ☐ _____   ☐ Note Guaranteed by_____
☐ Cash Collateral — Amount $_____
  ☐ Cash ☐ Coml. Note ☐ _____   ☐ Continuing Guarantee from_____
                                        Amt. $_____
☐ Bond ☐ Record and Have Contract Filed   ☐ Indemnity Agent ☐ On File ☐ T/Co.
      ☐ Do Not Record   ☐ Foundation Endorsement
☐ Completion Agreement by_____   ☐ Type of Disbursement Schedule_____
☐ Subordination Agreement
☐ Lease ☐ Record ☐ Before ☐ After   ☐ Chattel Mortgage
☐ Lease Assignment   ☐ Future Chattel Mortgage Agreement
☐ Future Lease Agreement   ☐
☐ _____   ☐ _____

REMARKS_____
_____
_____
_____
_____
_____
_____
_____

DISBURSE LOAN PROCEEDS TO_____   CHARGES ☐ Bill Direct ☐ Charge Account
                                           CHARGES ☐ Deduct ☐ _____
INVESTOR SALE ☐ Yes ☐ No EXPLANATION_____

LOAN APPROVED BY_____ BY_____   ☐ Loan Committee _____
            R. E. LENDING OFFICER (S)   DATE

APPLICATION TO REAL ESTATE LOAN PROCESSING_____
                          DATE   LOAN ESCROW SECRETARY

REL-254 5M 1-63 23348

Title Insurance
Escrows

MC **Mid-Columbia Title Company**

114 CASCADE AVENUE / HOOD RIVER, OREGON 97031 / (503) 386-5300

ESCROW DEPARTMENT
STATEMENT

ESCROW NO._____

_____

_____   _____, 19____

DESCRIPTION		DEBITS		CREDITS	
		$		$	
Deposit					
Demand					
Title Insurance Policy					
Broker's Commission					
Escrow Fee					
Taxes					
RECORDING					
Deed	to				
	to				
Trust Deed	to				
Mortgage	to				
Release of	to				
Taxes Prorated					
Insurance Prorated					
Fuel Prorated					
Rents Prorated					
Balance Due					
Balance—Our Check Herewith					
TOTAL					

TI 44   **This covers money settlement only. Any papers to which you are entitled will follow later.**

Mid-Columbia Title Company

BY_____

ESCROW INSTRUCTIONS

(BUYER AND SELLER)

_____, 19___
(Name of Bank)   (City)   (State)

I _____ hand you herewith check for $_____ drawn on_____

_____and will within _____ days

from this date hand you $_____ additional. I _____ also deliver to you
any instruments which this escrow requires shall be executed by me, all of which you are instructed to

use, provided within _____ days from date the necessary instruments are delivered

to you to enable you to have a _____

_____

_____ on the following described property:

_____

_____

_____

_____

showing title vested in _____

_____

_____

free of incumbrance except _____ taxes for fiscal year_____
Subject to conditions, restrictions and reservations of record_____
Record regardless of any judgments that may be of record against any one of my name or a similar name.

_____

Mortgage
Trust Deed   executed by_____
in favor of_____securing note for $_____

dated_____due (payable on or before)_____

years after date, payable in installments of $_____on the_____

day of every_____

_____beginning_____until the whole amount has been paid

with interest at _____ per cent per annum, payable_____

at_____

_____

Insurance?_____

Interest?_____

_____

It is understood that the_____made under above instructions shall
be subject to all the conditions contained in the regular form of_____

_____, which does not include an examination of the city records of any city

except_____
When this transaction has been completed you will instruct the County Recorder to mail to my address

all documents recorded for me. I agree to pay escrow fee $_____ and $_____

for showing title in me in addition to the fee for recording_____

In the event that the conditions of this escrow have not been complied with at the expiration of the time
provided for herein, you are instructed to complete the same at the earliest possible date thereafter, unless
I have made written demand upon you for the return of all instruments deposited by me.

Signature_____

Phone_____   Address_____

ESCROW INSTRUCTIONS
WOLCOTTS FORM 602   This standard form covers most usual problems in the field indicated. Before you sign, read it, fill in all blanks,
and make changes proper to your transaction. Consult a lawyer if you doubt the form's fitness for your purpose.

_____ , 19____
(Name of Bank)   (City)   (State)

The conditions as above are hereby approved and I_____hand you herewith

a deed executed by_____

_____

to_____

conveying property above described, which you are authorized to deliver upon payment to you for my

account of the sum of $_____within the time as above provided.

Pay: Charges for_____

Revenue on Deed $_____

Escrow Fee $_____

_____your check for balance_____

All of the demands of the purchaser of the property as set forth above are hereby agreed to and the provision
for extension of time within which escrow may be closed applies equally to me.

Signature_____

Phone_____   Address_____

———•—•———

ESCROW AGREEMENT

It is agreed by the undersigned that so far as the rights and liabilities of the_____

_____

(Name of Bank or Escrow Company)

are involved, this transaction is an escrow, and not any other legal relation, and the_____

_____is an escrow holder only, on the following terms:

No recission of this escrow or modification of its terms or any notice or demand shall be of any effect

without joint consent in writing subscribed by the undersigned and assented to by the_____

_____

Bankruptcy, insolvency, absence, death or disability of any of the parties hereto shall not affect or pre-

vent performance by the escrow holder of its instructions. The _____ shall
be under no obligation to institute, defend or participate in any litigation representing its own interest
or the interest of the other parties hereto. The undersigned, however, jointly and severally undertake

and agree to indemnify and protect said_____from and against any and all losses,
demands, judgments, expenses including attorney's fees, and other liabilities which it may sustain or incur
should it institute or become involved in any such litigation, or which it may otherwise sustain or incur in
good faith as holder of this escrow.

Negotiable or non-negotiable instruments received in this escrow may be transmitted by the_____

_____for collection either directly or to the drawee or other persons
obligated, or otherwise through collecting agents, in the usual course of business; and the_____

_____shall not be responsible for default of any such
drawee or obligator, or any such collecting agent; and credit given for any such items is understood to be
conditional on the proceeds in actual cash being received.

As security for the prompt and faithful performance by the undersigned of this agreement said_____

_____shall have, and it is hereby given, a first and prior lien on the rights, titles and
interests of the undersigned and each of them in the documents, moneys and other property which may
be held or received in this escrow.

Dated_____ , 19____
(City)   (State)

_____

_____

_____

_____

𝕱𝖚𝖑𝖑 𝕽𝖊𝖑𝖊𝖆𝖘𝖊 𝕮𝖔𝖛𝖊𝖗𝖎𝖓𝖌 𝕬𝖑𝖑 𝕮𝖑𝖆𝖎𝖒𝖘

OR RIGHTS OF ACTION OF EVERY DESCRIPTION, PAST, PRESENT OR FUTURE

KNOW ALL MEN BY THESE PRESENTS, That

in consideration of

Dollars to   in hand paid by

do   hereby for   heirs, executors, administrators and assigns, fully and forever release and discharge the said

of and from all claims, demands, damages, rights of action and causes of action, on account of either known or unknown, concealed or hidden, external or internal, personal, physical or mental or nervous injuries or disease, or damage to any portion of   bod   or anat-omy, or damage to personal property of whatsoever description resulting, or which could or may result from an accident or anything which occurred to   on or about the

            day of   , 19

............understand that Section 1542 of the Civil Code of California reads as follows: "1542. (Certain claims not affected by general release.) A general release does not extend to claims which the creditor does not know or suspect to exist in his favor at the time of executing the release, which if known by him must have materially affected his settlement with the debtor."

............hereby waive the provisions of this Section No. 1542.

It is further understood and agreed that this full and final release is intended to cover and does cover all and any future injuries not known to either party hereto, or which may later develop, or be discovered, including the effects or consequences thereof and including all causes of action therefor.

............understand that this is a compromise settlement without any admission of liability on the part of

Executed at ....this..................day of.., 19..........

....

....

STATE OF.. }
                                                         } ss.
COUNTY OF.................................... }

On _____
before me, the undersigned, a Notary Public in and for said County and State, personally appeared

_____

_____

_____

known to me to be the person____ whose name_____
subscribed to the within instrument and acknowledged
that _____ executed the same.
WITNESS my hand and official seal.

(Seal)_____
Notary Public in and for said County and State.

SPACE BELOW FOR RECORDER'S USE ONLY

Appendix B
Sample Amortization Payback Schedule

The following sample amortization table illustrates the principal, interest, and declining balance on a $10,000, two-year note, at 12 percent interest, with monthly payments of $470.74. These figures are for informational purposes only; specific loan arrangements should be obtained directly from the lender with whom you are working.

Payment Number	Principal	Interest	Balance
1	370.74	100.00	9628.26
2	375.48	95.29	9252.78
3	378.21	92.53	8874.57
4	381.99	88.75	8492.58
5	385.81	84.93	8106.77
6	389.67	81.07	7717.10
7	393.57	77.17	7323.53
8	397.50	73.24	6926.03
9	401.48	69.26	6524.55
10	405.49	65.25	6119.06
11	409.55	61.19	5709.51
12	413.64	57.10	5295.87
13	417.78	52.96	4878.09
14	421.96	48.78	4456.13
15	426.18	44.56	4029.95
16	430.44	40.30	3599.51
17	434.74	36.00	3164.77
18	439.09	31.65	2725.68
19	443.48	27.26	2282.20
20	447.92	22.82	1834.28
21	452.40	18.34	1381.88
22	456.92	13.82	924.96
23	461.49	9.25	463.47
24	458.84	4.63	0

Appendix C
Sample Mortgage Management Form Letters and Assignments

FORM 1: NOTIFICATION OF MORTGAGE TRANSFER (TO SENIOR MORTGAGE HOLDERS)

[LETTERHEAD]

Date:
Our Loan Number:
Property Address:
Re: Transfer of Mortgage

Dear_____:

The purpose of this letter is to notify you that on the _____ day of _____, 19____, we purchased a second mortgage on the following described real property on which our records reflect that you are a senior mortgage holder, where _____ is the grantor and _____ is the grantee, dated the _____ day of _____, 19____:

[Provide legal or street description of property.]

A copy of the trust deed involved is enclosed for your reference.

We look forward to working with you and the mortgagor in insuring the continued growth of this investment. Please feel free to call us at the number above should you have any questions regarding this transfer.

Yours very truly,

_____

Enc.

FORM 2: NOTIFICATION OF MORTGAGE TRANSFER (TO MORTGAGOR)

[LETTERHEAD]

Date:
Our Loan Number:
Property Address:
Re: Transfer of Mortgage

Dear_____:

The purpose of this letter is to notify you of our recent purchase of the Deed of Trust on premises located at:

[Provide legal or street description of real property.]

where _____ is the grantor and _____ is the grantee, dated the _____ day of _____, 19____. A copy of the Trust Deed is enclosed for your reference.

Please find enclosed a new payment book that shows the balance due and the due date on this note. Payments should be mailed to us at the letterhead address. We like to advise borrowers that a late charge will be imposed if payment is not made within five (5) days of the due date. A stamped, self-addressed envelope is enclosed for your convenience in this regard.

As co-investors in this property, we want you to know that we stand ready to assist you in any way we can to insure the continued growth and safety of this investment. Please feel free to call us at the number above should you have any questions or concerns regarding this transfer.

Yours very truly,

_____

Enc.

FORM 3: OVERDUE PAYMENT (FIRST NOTICE)

[LETTERHEAD]

Date:
Our Loan Number:
Property Address:
Re: Overdue Payment

Dear _____:

Our records reflect that your monthly payment in the amount of $_____ was due and payable on the _____ day of _____, 19____. As of the date of this letter, we have failed to receive this payment. Pursuant to the terms of the note and mortgage instrument, a penalty of _____ is charged against each late payment.

To date, you have enjoyed an excellent payment record, and we trust that this is a simple oversight. If not, we invite you to contact us at your earliest convenience in order to discuss this matter.

Yours very truly,

_____

FORM 4: OVERDUE PAYMENT (SECOND NOTICE)

[LETTERHEAD]

Date:
Our Loan Number:
Property Address:
Re: Overdue Payment

Dear _____:

On the _____ day of _____, 19____, we wrote to you regarding the status of your overdue payment on the above-noted loan. This payment is now over fifteen (15) days past due, and we have received neither payment nor response to our earlier inquiry.

Please understand that it is our wish to cooperate with mortgagors in any way possible when payment problems arise. Won't you please take a moment to call us and explain your present circumstances?

If there has been no response to this inquiry within ten (10) days of the date hereof, we will be forced to protect our interests.

Yours very truly,

_____

FORM 5: OVERDUE PAYMENT (FINAL NOTICE)

[LETTERHEAD]

Date:
Our Loan Number:
Property Address:
Re: Overdue Payment
Certified Number:

Dear _____:

Payment on the above-described loan is now twenty-five (25) days overdue, and there has been no response to our inquiries regarding the payment.

The purpose of this letter is to place you on notice that a formal Notice of Default has been prepared in this matter and will be filed if no payment is received within five days of the date hereof. In that event, you will be liable for all our costs and fees incurred, as provided in the promissory note.

Yours very truly,

_____

FORM 6: NOTICE OF DEFAULT

[LETTERHEAD]

Date:
Our Loan Number:
Property Address:
Re: Notice of Default
Certified Number:

Dear _____:

You are hereby advised that a Notice of Default was filed by the Trustee relative to the above-noted loan on the _____ day of _____, 19____.

The laws of this state provide a reinstatement period of _____ days within which you may cure this default before the Notice of Sale is advertised. Your loan may be reinstated during the reinstatement period by payment of all delinquent installments, in addition to the costs and trustee's fees amounting to $_____.

After the expiration of the reinstatement period, the loan can only be reinstated by payment of the above-noted costs and fees, *and the entire unpaid balance of the note.*

By giving this matter your immediate attention, you may save not only your valuable investment but your credit record as well.

Yours very truly,

_____

FORM 7: COMBINATION

[LETTERHEAD]

Date:

Our Loan Number:

Re: ___ Failure to Pay

___ Late Charge

___ Late on Tax Payment(s)

___ No Copy of Insurance Coverage

___ Failure to Pay Senior Mortgage or Lien Holder

___ Failure to Keep Premises in Good Repair

___ Failure to Lift Mechanic's Lien

___ Other

Explanation:

FORM 8: DISCOUNT OPTION (FIRST LETTER)

[LETTERHEAD]

Date:
Our Loan Number:
Property Address:
Re: Discount Options

Dear _____:

As you know, we are the holders of the note and mortgage on the above-described property.

To assist you in reducing this debt and simultaneously saving considerable sums of money, we would be happy to discuss granting a generous discount for all payments made over and above your monthly payment. This discount would not only save you money but would also operate to reduce substantially the term of the loan.

If you are interested in this substantial saving, please let us hear from you at your earliest convenience.

Yours very truly,

_____

FORM 9: ASSIGNMENT (GENERAL FORM)

ASSIGNMENT

For the sum of $_____ [or for value received], I/we hereby assign, sell, and transfer to _____ all right, title, and interest in that certain Agreement dated the _____ day of _____, 19____, by and between _____ and _____, subject to all of the terms and conditions therein contained, and I/we hereby remise, release, assign, transfer, and Quit Claim to _____ all right, title, and interest in and to said Agreement.

_____

(Signature)

_____

(Date)

FORM 10: ASSIGNMENT (WITH DOCUMENT ANNEXED)

ASSIGNMENT

For good and valuable consideration I hereby assign, transfer, and convey all of my right, title, and interest in the attached instrument marked exhibit "A" and by this reference incorporated herein to _____.

In witness whereof, I have set my hand and seal this _____ day of _____, 19____, in the City of _____, County of _____, State of _____.

_____
(Signature)

FORM 11: ASSIGNMENT (WITH GUARANTEE)

ASSIGNMENT WITH GUARANTEE

For value received I hereby assign, transfer, and convey all of my right, title, and interest in and to that certain _____, dated the _____ day of _____, 19____, by and between _____ and _____ with recourse and guarantee the full performance of the terms and conditions of the said _____.

In witness whereof, I have set my hand and seal this _____ day of _____, 19____, in the City of _____, County of _____, State of _____.

_____
(Signature of Guarantor)

Appendix D
Mortgage Data Form

[LETTERHEAD]

Name of Mortgagor: _____

Street Address of Property: _____

_____

Legal Description of Property: _____

_____

_____

_____

Lot Size: _____

Description of Improvements: _____

_____

_____

_____

Area Demographics: _____

_____

_____

_____

_____

_____

_____

Credit Data on Mortgagor: _____

_____

_____

_____

Terms of Mortgage: _____

    Loan Date: _____

    Term: _____

    Original Balance: _____

    Monthly Payments: _____

    Interest Rate: _____

    Outstanding Balance: _____

Recourse Status: _____

Reason for Selling: _____

_____

_____

Attachments:
___ Payment History of Mortgagor
___ Photographs
___ Maps
___ Relevant Zoning Regulations
___ Other Legislative Data
___ Title Report
___ Appraisals
___ Escrow Documents
___ Other

Appendix E
Mathematical Equations for Yield Calculations

Despite its limitations the internal rate of return (IRR)* is a useful and widely accepted measure of yield on investment capital. It is used to determine the impact on yield of alternative investment assumptions. Its generalized formula representation may be given by:

$$P = p_1/(1 + r)^1 + \ldots + p_i/(1 + r)^i + \ldots + p_n/(1 + r)^n \tag{1}$$

Where P is the initial investment or the price one would pay for a mortgage,

the p_i, $i = 1, 2, \ldots, n$ for n periods, are the payments or cash flows received over n periods,

where pn includes the return of capital or balloon payment as well as the final cash flow.

It is not possible to prepare a single table to compute the discount or price one must pay for nonlevel payment mortgages. However, many relatively inexpensive hand-held calculators are available on the market today that can be used to compute the internal rate of return for a series of nonequal payments.

For mortgages that have periodic level payments, you can con-

---

*For mortgage yield computations the IRR is normally unique and is a good measure of yield. For some investments that have both positive and negative cash flows, equation (1) reduces to a polynomial with both positive and negative signs and consequently may have multiple real as well as complex roots. In such cases the IRR may be misleading. Furthermore, if there are both negative and positive cash flows, it may not make sense to treat them mathematically the same from a tax or financial management standpoint as positive cash flows may have to be reinvested at a more conservative rate to cover anticipated negative flows. Another assumption made with the IRR is that regardless of its size, the cash flow may be reinvested at the same IRR. Certainly the size of the investment can influence the return, as one may not readily invest small cash flows in as high a return as larger ones.

205

struct a set of tables or graphs using a specialized internal rate of return formula. These can give us a comparison of different mortgages as investment alternatives at a glance.

Since a great number of mortgage yield applications are based on periodic level payment loans that have either a balloon payment or are retired through a normal amortization sequence, they lend themselves to a geometric series form of (1) above. Equation (1) in turn reduces to a specialized form of the IRR. Using various algebraic techniques taught in a good high school algebra class, we find the internal rate of return for a periodic set of equal payments reduces to the mortgage yield equation:

$$P = \{F(1 + i)^n - p[(1 + i)^n - 1]/i + p[(1 + r)^n - 1]/r\}/ \\ (1 + r)^n, \qquad\qquad (2)$$

where P is the price one pays for a note with a face value F bearing a rate of i per period, with a payment p per period.

The value r is the internal rate of return or mortgage yield after n periods with a balloon payment (remaining balance)

$$\mathbf{RB} = F(1 + i)^n - p[(1 + i)^n - 1]/i, \qquad\qquad (3)$$

and an annuity of payments, p, each collected at a rate r and given by

$$\mathbf{AN} = p[(1 + r)^n - 1]/r \qquad\qquad (4)$$

Of course the discount, d, off the face value F expressed as a percent is given by

$$d = [(F - P)/F] \times 100\%$$

For those so inclined, we illustrate how one computes the discount using (2) above. Suppose we desire to find the discount on the note George created in Chapter 11. You recall the note was restructured at a 12 percent per annum rate, a face value of $25,743.71, with a 1.5 percent pay-back rate per month, for a total of 36 monthly periods, where George desired an 18 percent yield. The price one must pay for the note is found by calculating the remaining balance, RB, from (3) above by

$$\mathbf{RB} = 25,743.71 \times (1 + .01)^{36} - 386.16 \times [(1 + .01)^{36} - 1]/.01$$
$$\mathbf{RB} = 25,743.71 \times 1.430768 - 386.16 \times .430768/.01$$
$$\mathbf{RB} = 36833.29 - 16634.35$$
$$\mathbf{RB} = 20198.94$$

We compute the annuity AN one collects at the desired 18 percent yield by using (4) after reducing the 18 percent to a monthly decimal rate of 0.015:

$$AN = 386.16 \times [(1 + .015)^{36} - 1]/.015$$
$$AN = 386.16 \times (1.70914 - 1)/.015$$
$$AN = 386.16 \times .70914/.015$$
$$AN = 18256.10$$

We then combine the remaining balance with the annuity and discount this amount by the rate r for the 36-month period to arrive at the price:

$$P = (RB + AN)/(1.015)36$$
$$P = (20198.94 + 18256.10)/1.70914$$
$$P = 22499.64$$

The price one must pay for George's $25,743.71 note to achieve a yield of 18 percent per annum, that is, 1.5 percent per month was found to be $22,499.64. To obtain the discount as a percent of the face value we use (5) as follows:

$$d = [(25743.71 - 22499.64)/25743.71] \times 100\%, \text{ or } d$$
$$= 12.601\%$$

which is the value we arrived at in Chapter 11 by using the tables.

Appendix F
Utilizing Mortgage Yield Graphs

In order to facilitate your understanding of at least one alternative method of computing yield, you may wish to work through the hypothetical yield calculation problem set out in the text at pages 138–143 in Chapter 11.

John could just as easily have used a yield graph to arrive at the 36 percent discount. Although graphs do not lend themselves to as much precision as do the tables, you may find it easier to interpolate with them. The 10 percent yield graph given below for a fully amortized loan has been reproduced for your convenience.

To use it to solve John's problem set out in Chapter 11, find 18 percent on the yield line, then go vertically up the line until it intersects the 1 percent monthly pay-back curve. At the point of intersection, trace a line to your left until it intersects the discount line. You can see that this line intersects the discount line a little above 36 percent.

If you want to find the discount for an 18½ percent yield, you would first locate the point halfway between 18 and 19 percent. Next, trace a vertical line until it intersects the 1 percent pay-back line, and find the horizontal intersection on the discount line at approximately 37½ percent.

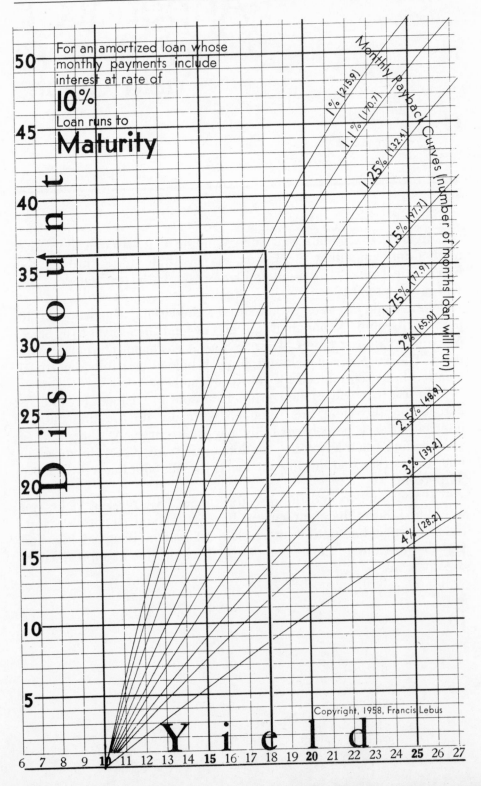

For an amortized loan whose monthly payments include interest at rate of

10%

Loan runs to

Maturity

Monthly Payback Curves (number of months loan will run)

1% (215.9)
1.1% (170.7)
1.25% (132.4)
1.5% (97.7)
1.75% (77.9)
2% (65.9)
2.5% (48.9)
3% (39.2)
4% (28.2)

Discount

Yield

50 45 40 35 30 25 20 15 10 5

6 7 8 9 10 11 12 13 14 15 16 17 18 19 20 21 22 23 24 25 26 27

Copyright, 1958, Francis Lebus

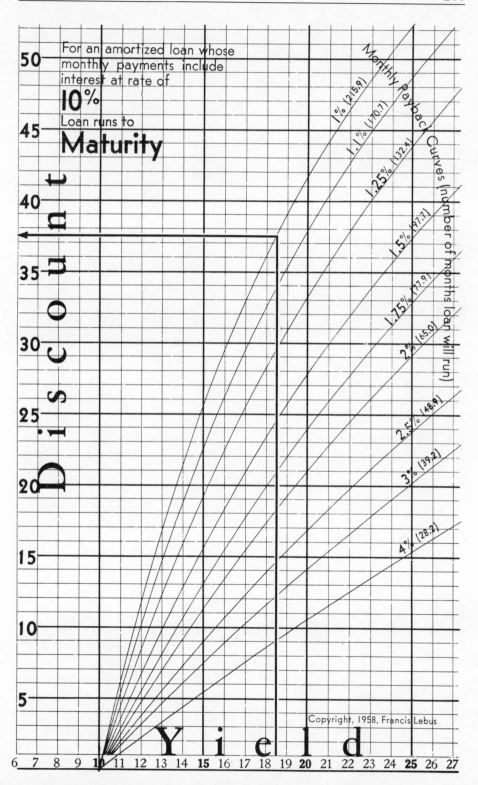

For an amortized loan whose monthly payments include interest at rate of
10%
Loan runs to
Maturity

Discount

Monthly Payback Curves (number of months loan will run)

1% (215.9)
1.1% (170.7)
1.25% (132.4)
1.5% (97.7)
1.75% (77.9)
2% (65.0)
2.5% (48.9)
3% (39.2)
4% (28.2)

Yield

6 7 8 9 10 11 12 13 14 15 16 17 18 19 20 21 22 23 24 25 26 27

Glossary

AAA Tenant–One who pays a *pro rata* share of expenses, taxes, and insurance.

Abstract of Title–A short history of ownership, encumbrances, liens of record, transfers, conveyances, and legal proceedings of record that may impair title.

Accelerated Depreciation–To depreciate property at a faster rate.

Acceleration Clause–A clause stipulating that the entire debt is due upon a single default or duty of the borrower relative to the terms of the mortgage.

Acceptance–Consent to the terms of an offer, which consent establishes a meeting of the minds.

Accounts Payable–Computation of monies owing.

Accounts Receivable–Credits or rights to claim monies.

Accretion–The gradual addition of something to property.

Accrued Appreciation–To accumulate value.

Accrued Depreciation–The difference between cost of replacement and present appraised value.

Acknowledgment–Recognize publicly a fact, like a notorized statement.

Acquisition–Act of acquiring or procuring property.

Acquittance–A written document that releases a person from a debt or contractual obligation.

Administrator–A person appointed to settle the estate of an intestate decedent. He or she holds the legal title for the benefit of the equitable owners.

Ad Valorem–Latin for "according to value" in real estate.

Advance Fee–To supply money beforehand.

Adverse Possession–Actual holding of land under claim of right for statutory period, which is opposed to or inconsistent with another's claims.

Affidavit–A written statement sworn before a proper officer to administer oath.

Affirmation–A solemn declaration confirming or ratifying a fact.

Agency–Relationship where one acts for or in place of another.

Agent–One who acts for and with authority from another who is called the principal.

Aging–To become or make old; to season like an aged mortgage.

Agreement of Sale–A written contract between buyer and seller wherein a full agreement is reached.

Alienate–The absolute transfer of title and possession of real property from one person to another.

All-Inclusive–A mortgage that encompasses or wraps around other mortgages.

Alluvium–Soil or land formed by deposits of sand or earth.

Amalgamation–To unite or combine.

Amenities–A beneficial influence from improvements not measured by monetary considerations.

Amortization–Reduction of a debt by paying off in equal or nearly equal installments.

Annualized–Happening once a year.

Appraisal–An estimate and opinion of the value of property. A statement of value defined by the appraiser such as the market value; loan value of a definite property as of a certain date.

Appraisal Report–An estimate of value. An appraisal report sets forth the values, experiences, and conclusion of the writer.

Appreciation–To raise the value or worth. It comes from inflation or special supply and demand.

Appurtenances–Rights which go with the land although not within the boundary of property covered by the description.

Assemblage–A collection of individuals or particular things.

Assessed Value–The valuation of property as calculated by a government agency for taxation purposes.

Assessment–A charge made by the government agency against property.

Assessor–One appointed to assess property for taxation.

Assign–Transfer.

Assignee–The party who is given interest or rights by a trustee or individual.

Assignment–Written transfer of claims and rights or benefits.

Assignments of Rents–A provision in a trust deed or mortgage under which beneficiary may, upon default by payor, take possession and collect rent and apply it to debt.

Assignor–One who makes an assignment or transfers property to another.

Assumed–To undertake an obligation.

Assumption Agreement–An agreement or contract by deed or otherwise where buyer assumes the obligation of a mortgage or trust deed.

Assumption Fee–Charge for buyer to assume (take over) the seller's existing loan.

Assumption of Mortgage–A contract where buyer assumes the obligation of the mortgage or becomes co-guarantor.

ATLA Title Policy–A title insurance policy that expands the risks normally insured against.

Attachment–A procedure in law by which property is seized to pay a judgment.

Attorney in Fact–One authorized to act for another by a writing, designated as Power of Attorney.

Avulsion–Separation of land by violent action of waters.

Bad Title–A title that is not marketable.

Bailee–An agent who holds goods in trust for another.

Bailor–One who places or delivers goods in trust to a bailee.

Balance Sheet–Designation of the financial condition as of one moment in time.

Balloon Payment–An installment payment that is greater than twice the amount of the smallest installment payment on a note that evidences the loan.

Bankrupt–A person who has suffered some act to be done which causes creditors to proceed against the entire property.

Bankruptcy–The state of one who is bankrupt.

Bargain and Sale–A deed or contract that conveys property without a guarantee of title.

Base and Meridian–Lines (imaginary) used by surveyors to describe property. Meridians run north to south; base lines run east to west.

Basis Point–One point is 1 percent of the loan amount that is paid to lenders so that they can adjust their effective interest rate to the prevailing market rate.

Beneficiary–A person who has the right to principal and income from a deed or mortgage.

Bequeath–To give personal property to another by will.

Bequest–Personal property given by will.

Bill of Sale–A written instrument evidencing the transfer of personal property.

Blanket Encumbrance–Where more than one lot in a subdivision is made for the security for payment of mortgage note or other lien or encumbrance.

Blanket Mortgage–One mortgage that covers more than one parcel of real estate.

Blighted Area–An area where there is decay or cessation of growth.

Bond–Written instrument guaranteeing an obligation.

Book Value–Method of property valuation reached by deducting accumulated depreciation from original cost plus capital additions.

Borrower–One who receives money and expresses intention of returning it.

Breach–The violation of an obligation or the breaking of a law.

Brokerage Agreement–Agreement between a seller and an agent who arranges sales.

Builder–One whose occupation is building.

Building Code–Regulation of construction established by code, ordinance, or law.

Building Line–The legal boundary of permitted building.

Building Restrictions–Zoning regulations or a provision in a deed limiting use and size of a building.

Building Zoning–The types of structures permitted in a particular location.

Business–A commercial or industrial enterprise.

Capital Gains–Profit realized on resale of capital items.

Capitalization–Value of property based on a consideration of net income to return on investment.

Cash-on-Cash Return–A property's projected cash flow, calculated on net operating and cash investment required.

Cash Flow–Net income generated by a property before depreciation and other noncash expenses.

Cash Payback–The amount of cash paid back by an investment after all expenses and mortgages are paid.

Caveat Emptor–A rule of law that the buyer purchases at his or her own risk. (Let the buyer beware.)

C.C. and R.–Covenants, conditions, and restrictions; the basic rules establishing the rights and obligations of owners within a tract of land.

Chain of Title–A complete history of conveyances and encumbrances that affect the ownership covering the entire recorded history of the property.

Chattel Mortgage–A mortgage on personal property, as distinguished from one on real property.

Chattel Real–An estate relating to real estate, such as a lease on property.

Chattels–Personal property; any estate less than a freehold.

Closing Statement–An accounting of funds made to buyer and seller separately at completion of transaction.

Cloud on Title–A defect in the chain of title that obstructs or prevents a good delivery.

Collateral–Property or security pledged as security for payment of a debt.

Collateral Security–A secondary security to be available if the chief security fails.

Collusion–Secret agreement and cooperation for fraud.

Color of Title–Apparent title; a *prima facie* title that is, in fact, invalid.

Commercial Acre–That portion of a full acre that remains in a new subdivision after allowance for dedication of roads and alleys.

Commission–Monies paid for performance of specific duties in real estate.

Commitment–Promise to perform a certain act.

Common Law–English law that developed over the years and is now used in the United States.

Community Property–Property (both real and personal) accumulated after marriage by a husband and wife who hold it as co-owners.

Compound Interest–Interest due on the original principal plus the added interest on accrued interest.

Condemnation–An act declaring structure not fit for use; the taking of private property for public use by a government agency.

Conditional Sales Contract–A contract where title remains vested in the seller until conditions of the contract have been fulfilled.

Condo–Short for condominium.

Condominium–Unit in a multifamily building owned in fee and combined with joint ownership of common areas.

Consideration–Anything used to induce a person to enter into a contract.

Constant Annual Payment Percentage–An annual percentage rate that remains unchanged, fixed, and invariable.

Constant Rate–Rate that remains fixed.

Construction Cost–Cost of permits, plans, materials, and labor in building.

Construction Loan–A loan to cover the cost of building covering the construction period only.

Constructive Notice–Notice given by public records.

Consumer Price Index–A group of indexes published by the Bureau of Labor Statistics of the United States Department of Labor.

Contiguous–Touching or adjoining parcels of land.

Contingent Commission–Monies based on future payments required of a buyer of real property.

Contingent Liability–A fortuitous event that occurs without design or expectation.

Conversion–Change from one character or use to another.

Conveyance–The transferring of an instrument of title to land from one person to another.

Cooperative Apartments–The investor is a part owner in the property evidenced by stock participation in a corporation. The investor has a right to lease a particular apartment, but does not own that apartment.

Corporation–An association of shareholders acting as an entity or person to engage in business.

Correlation and Final Value Conclusion–The process of interpretation of data derived from the three approaches to value (cost, market, and income).

Cost–That which is paid in money, goods, or services.

Cost of Living Index–An index published by the Bureau of Labor Statistics that is an average of other indexes of the United States Department of Labor.

Creative Financing–A modern concept of property financing.

Cubic Number–A number reached by multiplying a number by itself twice.

Cul de Sac–A dead-end street.

Curtail Schedule–A listing of the amounts by which the principal sum of an obligation is to be reduced by partial payments and of the dates when each payment will become payable.

Dedication–The giving and acceptance of land by authorized officials on behalf of the public.

Deed–A written instrument that, when properly executed and delivered, conveys title to real property.

Deed Restrictions–Limitations in the deed dictating certain uses that may or may not be made of the property.

Deed of Trust–See *Trust Deed.*

Default–Failure to perform any act in a written instrument that has been agreed upon; nonpayment of a legal obligation.

Deferred Maintenance–Existing but unfulfilled requirements for repairs and rehabilitation; delayed maintenance.

Deferred Payment Option–The privilege of deferring income payments to take advantage of statutes affording tax benefits.

Deficiency Judgment–A judgment obtained upon default when the pledged security does not satisfy the debt.

Demand Mortgage–A mortgage that is payable on demand on the part of the holder of the evidence of the debt.

Demise–To transfer the title or lease of an estate.

Deposit Receipt–The written offer to purchase real property upon stated terms and conditions, accompanied by a deposit toward the purchase price, which becomes the contract for the sale of the property upon acceptance by the owner.

Depreciation–Loss of property value due to age, deterioration, or obsolescense. The term is also used in accounting to identify the amount of the decrease in value of an asset that is allowed in computing the value of the property for tax purposes.

Devise–Real property gifted in last will and testament.

Devisee–A person who receives real property by a will.

Devisor–One who gives real property by a will.

Directional Growth–The location or direction toward which the residential sections of a city are destined to grow.

Discharge–The termination of the legal duty of one party.

Discount–To sell a promissory note before maturity at a price less than the outstanding principal balance of the note at the time of sale. Also an amount deducted in advance by the lender from the nominal principal of a loan as part of the cost to the borrower of obtaining the loan.

Discount Points–Each point is one percent per hundred dollars of the loan amount, which is part of the charge for granting.

Double Depreciation–A method of accelerated depreciation allowed by the IRS in certain circumstances and computed by using double the rate used for straight-line depreciation.

Due-on-Sale Clause–An acceleration clause granting the lender the right to demand full payment of the mortgage upon the sale of the property.

Duress–Unlawfully forcing someone to do an act against his or her will.

Dwelling Unit–A place of residence; the living quarters of one household.

Easement–An acquired use and enjoyment, falling short of actual ownership, which an owner or possessor of land may have in land of another.

Economic Life–Time when a property will yield a return on investment above the rent for the ground.

Economic Obsolescense–Loss in value arising from lack of demand.

Economic Rent–The reasonable rental expectancy if the property were available for renting at the time of its evaluation.

Eminent Domain–Right of a government agency to take private property for public use by condemnation.

Encroachment–A trespass or building on property of another.

Encumbrance–Anything affecting or limiting the title to or value of property, for example, mortgages or easements.

Endorse–See *Indorsement*.

Equity–The interest or value an owner has over and above the liens.

Equity of Redemption–The right to redeem property before or after the foreclosure period.

Erosion–The gradual loss of soil by water, wind, or glacial ice.

Escalator Clause–The right reserved by the lender to increase the amount of payments and/or interest upon the happening of an event.

Escheat–The reverting of property to the State when heirs capable of inheriting are lacking.

Escrow–The deposit of instruments, instructions, and/or funds with a third neutral party to carry out the provisions of an agreement or contract.

Estate–The interest a person owns in real property.

Estate of Inheritance–An estate that may descend to heirs.

Estate for Life–See *Life Estate*.

Estimate–A preliminary opinion of value.

Estoppel–A legal theory under which a person is barred from asserting or denying a fact because of previous acts or words.

Exchange–A means of trading equities in two or more real properties, treated as a single transaction through a single escrow.

Exclusive Agency Listing–A listing agreement employing a broker as the sole agent for the seller of real property for which the broker is entitled to a commission unless the sale is arranged by the owner.

Exclusive Right to Sell Listing–A listing agreement where the broker is entitled to a commission if the property is sold by anyone during the listing.

Execute–To follow out to the end; signed, sealed, and delivered.

Executed Contract–A completed contract.

Executor/Executrix–A person appointed in a will to carry out its provisions as to the disposition of the estate of a deceased person.

Executor's Deed–A deed to real property granted by an executor of an estate.

Executory Contract–A contract in which something remains to be done.

Extension Agreement–An agreement that extends a contract longer than the term that was originally contemplated.

Fair Market Value–This is the amount of money that would be paid for a property offered on the open market for a reasonable period of time with neither party under pressure to buy or sell.

Fannie Mae–An acronymic nickname for Federal National Mortgage Association (FNMA).

Federal Home Loan Bank (FHLB)–A district bank of the Federal Home Loan Bank System that lends only to member savings and loans.

Federal National Mortgage Association (FNMA)–A quasi-public agency converted into a private corporation whose primary function is to buy and sell FHA and VA mortgages in the secondary market.

Fee–An estate in real property.

Fee Simple–The greatest interest that one can have in real property consisting of indefinite duration, and absolutely transferable.

FHA–Federal Housing Administration.

Fiduciary–A person in a position of trust and confidence.

First Mortgage–A lien against real property that has priority over all other claims against the property except taxes and bonded indebtedness.

Fixtures–Improvements to real property that are considered permanent and, as such, cannot be removed without agreement.

Foreclosure–Procedure whereby property pledged as security for a debt is sold to pay the debt when there has been a default in payments or terms.

Forfeiture–Loss of money or anything of value resulting from a failure to perform.

Fraud–Deception; deceit; trickery.

Freehold Estate–An interest in property of indeterminable duration; a fee simple or life estate.

Front Foot–Property measurement for valuation purposes consisting of the measure of the property along its street line.

Functional Obsolescense–A loss of value due to adverse factors from within a structure.

General Lien–A charge against all the property of a debtor.

Graduated Lease–Lease that provides for a variable rental rate.

Graduated Payment Mortgage–A mortgage that provides for partially deferred payments of principal at start of loan.

Grant–A legal term that bestows an interest in real property on another.

Grantee–A person to whom a grant is made.

Grantor–A person who transfers interest in property to another by grant.

Gross Income–Total income from property before any expenses are deducted.

Gross Rental Multiplier–A number which, multiplied by the gross income of a property, produces an estimate of the value of the property.

Ground Lease–An agreement for the use of the land only.

Ground Rent–Earnings of improved property credited to earnings of the ground itself after allowance is made for earnings of improvements.

Guarantee–To undertake to answer for the debt, default, or miscarriage of another.

Guarantee of Title–Title company assurance of the extent of ownership in a specified piece of real property.

Hard Money Mortgage–A mortgage made other than a purchase money mortgage.

Heir–One who is entitled to inherit property.

Holder in Due Course–One who takes a note, check, or bill of exchange before it is due, in good faith, and for value, without any notice of defects.

Homestead–A statutory benefit afforded to homeowners for property used as a residence and protected from certain creditors and judgments to a specified amount.

HUD–Housing and Urban Development agency.

Hypothecate–Pledging of a matter as security without giving up possession.

Impound–A trust account established by agreement for accumulation of funds from borrower to meet taxes and other contingencies and expenses.

Income Property–A property that produces a money income.

Incompetent–One who is by reason of old age, disease, weakness of mind, or other causes unable without assistance to properly manage or take care of self or property.

Increment–An increase.

Indorsement–Signing one's name on back of negotiable instrument or agreement.

Inflated–Exaggerated; undue expansion of value.

Injunction–A writ or order issued by court restraining parties to suit from doing certain acts or compelling performance of certain acts.

Installment Note–A note that calls for a series of periodic payments until paid.

Institutional Lenders–A financial intermediary or depository such as a bank, savings and loan, life insurance company, or finance company.

Instrument–A legal document that has been written down.

Interest–The rent paid for the use of money or an asset.

Interim Loan–A short-term, temporary loan placed on property until permanent financing is arranged.

Involuntary Lien–A lien placed against property without consent of owner.

Irrevocable–Incapable of being recalled or revoked; unchangeable.

Joint Note–A note signed by two or more persons having equal liability for its payment.

Joint and Several Note–A note signed by two or more persons, the makers of which may be sued jointly or individually for the amount of money due.

Joint Tenancy–An undivided and equal ownership of a property interest with a right of survivorship.

Joint Venture–Two or more parties, or firms, or entities joining together on a project as partners.

Judgment–A determination on matters duly before the court.

Judgment Lien–A legal claim against property rendered by a court that enables a creditor to proceed against the property for the award.

Junior Mortgage or Encumbrance–A mortgage or lien recorded subsequent to another mortgage on same property, or made subordinate by agreement to a later-recorded mortgage.

Jurisdiction–The authority by which a judicial officer or court takes cognizance of and decides causes.

Laches–Delay or negligence in asserting one's legal rights.

Land–The solid material of the earth and anything affixed to it.

Land Contract–A contract used in the sale of real property wherein the seller retains title until all or a prescribed part of the purchase price has been paid. It is also known as an installment sales contract, conditional sales agreement, and real property sales contract.

Landlord–One who rents property or property rights to another.

Lease–An agreement between owner and tenant stating conditions under which the tenant may use and occupy premises and terms of the occupancy. Under certain circumstances a lease may be oral.

Leasehold Estate–A tenant's right to occupy and have possession of real estate during term of a lease.

Legal Description–A land description as set out by law; a description by which property can be definitely located referring to governmental surveys.

Lending Agent–One who acts for lenders.

Lending Fees–Fees or points charged by lenders.

Lending Institutions–An entity engaged in lending money or arranging loans.

Lessee–One who rents, occupies, and uses property under a lease agreement.

Lessor–An owner or one having a right to rent who enters into lease agreement with a tenant.

Level Payment Mortgage–Real estate loan paid off in series of equal regular payments.

Leverage–Use of debt financing to maximize the return per dollar of equity invested.

Levy–An extraction of payments or services to the State.

Lien–An encumbrance identifying specific property as security for the debt or discharge of an obligation.

Life Estate–A possessory freehold estate in land held by a person only for the duration of his or her life or the life of another.

Limitations, Statute of–A statute set out by code that requires a legal action be commenced within a prescribed period of time after the accrual of the right to seek relief.

Limited Partnership–A partnership consisting of a general partner or partners who manage and control the business affairs and limited partners who have no control and whose liability is limited to the amount or initial investment.

Liquidity–Ability to convert assets into cash or its equivalent.

Lis Pendens–A recorded claim giving notice to all parties that the title or right of possession of certain real property is in litigation.

Listing–An employment contract between principal and agent authorizing the agent to perform services for the principal involving the principal's property.

Loan–That which one lends or borrows.

Loan Application–A source of information provided to the lender on which he or she bases a decision to make the loan; it gives pertinent information as to assets and liability of borrower as well as the amount requested and conditions of payment.

Loan Commitment–Lender's contractual commitment to make a loan based on the appraisal and underwriting.

Loan-to-Value Ratio–Where total loan is based upon a percentage of real property value.

Market Comparison–See *Market Data Approach*.

Market Data Approach–One of the three methods used in the appraisal process; a means of comparing similar types of properties recently sold.

Market Price–The price a piece of property brings in a given market.

Market Value–The highest amount of money a property will bring in a competitive and open market and conditions required for a fair sale.

Marketability/Marketable Title–A title that a purchaser who has been advised of all pertinent facts and legal meanings and acting with reasonable care, would be willing, and ought, to accept; a title free and clear of objectionable items such as liens, defects, or encumbrances.

Mechanic's Lien–A lien on real property created by law in favor of parties who perform work or furnish materials for the improvement of real estate.

Metes and Bounds–A term used in describing the boundary lines of land setting forth their terminal points and angles; length is measured in meter, boundaries by bounds.

Minors–In most jurisdictions, persons under 18 years of age.

Mobile Home–A structure transportable in one or more sections designed and equipped to contain not more than two dwelling units with or without a foundation system.

Monument–An object or point established by surveyors to fix land location.

Moratorium–A temporary extension granted by a person or by statute to delay payments of money due.

Mortgage–A written instrument pledging property to secure the payment of a debt or an obligation.

Mortgage Banker–A person whose principal business is concerned with all aspects of mortgage financing.

Mortgage Guarantee Insurance–Insurance against financial losses available to mortgage lenders and obtained from private mortgage insurance companies.

Mortgage Investment Company–A group of investors, a firm, or other entity that deals in mortgages, usually for investment purposes.

Mortgage Loan Disclosure Statement–Statement on approved form required by law to be furnished by loan broker to prospective borrower before loan is approved.

Mortgagee–Lender; one who receives a mortgage from mortgagor to secure a loan or performance of an obligation.

Mortgagor–Borrower; one who gives a mortgage on property to secure a loan or assure a performance of an obligation.

Multiple Listing Service–An association of real estate brokers wherein all members have the right to find a buyer, giving owner of property expanded market exposure.

Negotiable–Capable of being negotiated; transferable.

Net Income–Value remaining after deducting all expenses.

Net Lease–See *NNN Lease*.

Net Listing–An agreement that provides that an agent's compensation for services is to be all sums received over set price.

Net Worth–The value of an entity or an individual that is remaining after deducting the liabilities from the assets.

NNN Lease–A lease requiring a lessee to pay charges against the property such as taxes, insurance, and maintenance costs in addition to rental payments. (Also known as a Triple A or AAA lease.)

Notary Public–An official authorized by law to attest to or witness the signature of another.

Note–A signed, written acknowledgment of a debt and promising payment according to its terms and conditions.

Notice of Default–A notice setting out a failure to fulfill a duty or promise or to discharge an obligation; notice of omission or failure to perform an act.

Notice of Nonresponsibility–A notice provided by law designated to relieve property owners from responsibility for work done, or materials ordered, by another without authorization.

Novation–The substitution of a new obligation or contract for an old one by all parties' mutual consent.

Null and Void–A condition of no legal validity or effect.

Obsolescence–Value loss incidental to reduced desirability and usefulness.

Offer–Proposal made to an owner of property by potential buyer to purchase, lease, or obtain property under specific terms.

Offer and Acceptance–A completed contract between buyer and seller wherein there is a meeting of the minds.

Offset Statement–A statement made by an owner of property, lessee or owner of lien that sets out the present status of liens or obligations against property.

Open-End Mortgage–A mortgage or trust deed providing that balance due can be increased to advance additional funds to the original maker.

Open Listing–An agreement between owner and broker or agent, wherein the broker or agent is granted a non-exclusive right to obtain a buyer for owner's property.

Option–An agreement wherein for consideration a right is given for a specified period of time to purchase, lease, or obtain a property upon specific terms.

Oral Contract–An agreement between the parties that is not reduced to writing.

Ownership–The right of one or more persons to possess or use a property to the exclusion of all others.

Package Mortgage–A type of mortgage used in home financing covering real property, improvements, and movable equipment.

Partial Conveyance–A part conveyance.

Partial Release–Release of a part of the mortgage.

Participation–Sharing of an interest in property by a lender (also called equity or revenue sharing).

Participation Loan–See *Participation*.

Partnership–A legal relationship between two or more persons who unite property, labor, or skill in pursuit of lawful business.

Party Wall–A structured wall erected on the boundary line between two adjoining properties.

Patent–A written conveyance of land title to government-owned property.

Penalty–An extra charge or payment required of borrower for noncompliance with original loan agreement.

Percentage Lease–The rental of leased property that provides additional sums determined by amount of business done by the lessee.

Performance–A thing done, discharged, or achieved.

Permanent Loan–A loan taken out after construction is finished, which is not of a temporary nature.

Personal Property–Any property that is considered not to be real property.

Physical Deterioration–Impairment of condition, a loss in value due to wear and tear, disintegration, abuse, and actions of elements.

Plat–A map or plan concerning a particular parcel of land.

Pledge–Depositing of personal property by debtor with creditor as, and for, a security for a debt.

Points–A sum paid to lenders as prepaid interest or service charges, or other fees for making a loan.

Police Power–The right of a government agency to enact laws and enforce them for the order, safety, health, morals, and general welfare of the public.

Power of Attorney–A written instrument wherein the principal gives authority to an agent to act within the authority given.

Power of Sale–The power of a mortgagee or trustee where instrument so provides, to sell the secured property without judicial proceedings if a borrower defaults in payment of the promissory note or otherwise breaches the terms of the trust deed or mortgage.

Prepayment Penalty–A charge payable to a lender by a borrower under the terms of a loan agreement when the balance on a loan is paid prior to maturity.

Prescription–Obtaining title to property through adverse possession.

Principal–The employer of an agent; the amount of money borrowed.

Prior Lien–A lien superior to others. See *Priority of Lien.*

Priority of Lien–The order in which liens are given legal precedence or preference.

Property–Everything capable of being owned lawfully.

Property Rights–The interest one possesses in the land and the improvements thereto.

Proration–Adjustments of interest, taxes, or insurance, on a *pro rata* basis as of a closing or agreed date.

Proration of Taxes—To divide or prorate the taxes equally or proportionately to time of use.

Public Records—Notice given by public records such as recording.

Purchase Money Mortgage or Trust Deed—Mortgage given to a seller as part or all of the purchase consideration for real property.

Quiet Title—Legal action for the purpose of establishing title and to remove a cloud on the title.

Quit Claim Deed—A deed by which grantor relinquishes all interest in property without any guarantee or warranty of interest.

Range—A strip or column of land six miles wide running in a north-south direction, parallel to a meridian.

Ready, Willing, and Able Buyer—One who is fully prepared to enter into the contract, really wants to buy, and unquestionably meets the financing requirements of purchase.

Real Estate—A tangible thing that includes both land and improvements.

Real Estate Board—An organization whose members consist primarily of real estate brokers and sales persons.

Real Estate Trust (R.E.I.T).—A special arrangement under federal and state law whereby investors may pool funds for investment in real estate and mortgages, and yet escape corporation taxes, by passing profits to individual investors.

Real Property—Land and appurtenances affixed to the land.

Realtor—A real estate broker holding active membership in a real estate board affiliated with the National Association of Realtors.

Reconveyance—The transfer of the title of land from one person to the immediate preceding owner. This instrument of transfer is common, and is used to transfer the legal title from the trustee to the trustor (borrower) after a deed debt has been paid in full.

Recording—The process of placing a document on file usually with a County Recorder; priority is given on the basis of earliest time recorded.

Redemption—Buying back one's property after a judicial sale.

Release Clause—A stipulation that upon the payment of a specific sum to the holder of a deed, one lien in a parcel shall be removed from the blanket lien on the entire parcel.

Renegotiable Rate Mortgage (RRM)—A "long-term" mortgage of any term not exceeding 30 years, securing a series of short-term loans.

The loans are automatically renewable every period and the interest rate and payments remain fixed in each period.

Request for Notice–Mortgage clause requiring senior mortgagees to give advance notice to junior mortgagees notice of pending default, thereby allowing junior holders to cure the default.

Rescission–The cancellation of a contract and restoration of the parties to the same position they held before the contract was entered into.

Reservation–A right retained by a grantor in conveying property.

Restriction–A limitation on the use of real property.

Return on Investment–Profit from an investment; the yield.

Reverse Annuity Mortgage (RAM)–The lender pays the borrower (usually elderly homeowners) a fixed annuity, based on a percentage of the value of the property for a fixed period of time.

Reversion–The right to future possession or enjoyment by a person or a person's heirs.

Right of Way–A privilege operating as an easement upon land (such as roads or electric lines) whereby the owner agrees to allow another the right to pass over owner's land.

Riparian Rights–The right of a landowner to use and enjoy water that is adjacent to or flows over the owner's land, provided such use does not injure other riparian rights.

Roll-Over Mortgage–A loan wherein the interest rate is renegotiated at specific periods of time. A roll-over mortgage is called a renewable mortgage with a fixed rate and balloon payment; the monthly payments remain constant over the period and outstanding principal balance becomes due at the end of each period.

Sales Contract–A contract by which buyer and seller agree on terms of a sale.

Satisfaction of Lien–A recorded discharge of a mortgage, trust deed, or lien upon payment of the debt.

Seal–An impression made to attest the execution of an instrument.

Season–See *Aging*.

Secondary Financing–A loan secured by a mortgage or trust deed on real property that is junior to a prior mortgage; can be second, third, fourth, fifth, sixth, *ad infinitum*.

Security Agreement–Agreement between the secured party and the debtor placing security as a pledge for the performance of an obligation which creates the security interest.

Seizin–Possession of real estate by one entitled thereto.

Separate Property–Property owned by a married person in his or her own right outside of community interest including property acquired by the spouse before marriage, by gift or inheritance, or from rents and profits on separate property.

Service Charge or Costs–Charges for collecting and keeping records of payments.

Servicing Loans–Supervising and administering a loan after it is made; collecting and keeping records and foreclosure of defaulted loans, etc.

Setback Ordinance–An ordinance requiring improvements built on property to be a specified distance from the property line, street, or curb.

Severalty Ownership–Owned by one person only.

Shared Appreciation Mortgage (SAM)–The lender has an agreed percentage of the appreciation in the market value of the property that is security for the loan, in exchange for which the loan is extended at, perhaps, below-market interest rate.

Sheriff's Deed–Deed given by Court Order in connection with sale of property to satisfy a judgment.

Simple Interest–Interest computed on the principal amount of a loan.

Sinking Fund–Fund set aside from income property that, with accrued interest, will eventually pay for replacement of improvements.

Special Assessment–Legal charge against real estate by a public authority to pay cost of public improvements such as street lights, sidewalks, and street improvements.

Special Power of Attorney–A written instrument whereby a principal confers limited authority upon an agent to perform certain prescribed acts on behalf of the principal.

Special Warranty Deed–A deed in which the grantor guarantees the title only against defects arising during grantor's ownership of the property and not against defects existing before the time of grantor's ownership.

Specific Performance–An action to compel performance of an agreement, *e.g.*, sale of land as an alternative to damages or rescission.

S.R.A.–Society of Real Estate Appraisers.

Standby Commitment–The mortgage banker frequently protects a builder by a "standby" agreement, under which banker agrees to make mortgage loans at an agreed price in the future.

Statute of Frauds–A law requiring certain contracts to be in writing and signed before they will be enforceable at law.

Statutory Warranty Deed–A deed that warrants that the seller has the sole right to convey the property and will defend the title against all claims.

Straight-Line Depreciation–A method of depreciation under which improvements are depreciated at a constant rate throughout the estimated useful life of the improvements.

Subject to Mortgage–When a grantee takes title to real property subject to a mortgage, grantee is not responsible to the holder of a promissory note for the payment of any portion of the amount due. The most that the grantee can lose in the event of a foreclosure is grantee's equity in the property. No liability is assumed more than the grantee's equity in the property.

Subordination Clause–An agreement by the holder of an encumbrance against real property to permit the claim to take an inferior position to other encumbrances.

Subrogation–Replacing one person with another in regard to a legal right or obligation; where one person agrees to stand surety for a contract of another person.

Surety–One who guarantees the performance of another; guarantor.

Survey–The process by which a parcel of land is measured and its area is ascertained.

Takeout Loan–The permanent financing of real property.

Title–The right of ownership.

Tort–A wrongful act for which a civil remedy may lie.

Transfer Fee–A charge made by a lender of real estate to reflect a different ownership.

Trust Account–A separate account required by law to deposit funds collected for clients.

Trust Deed–A promise to repay a loan that is secured by real property involving three parties: lender (beneficiary), borrower (trustor), and a neutral third party (trustee). The trustee can sell the property and transfer the money obtained at the sale to lender as payment of the debt.

Trustee–One who holds property in trust for another to secure the performance of an obligation; the third party under a deed of trust.

Trustor–One who borrows money under a trust deed. Lender then deeds the real property securing the loan to a trustee to be held as security until trustor has performed the obligation to the lender under terms of the deed of trust.

Truth in Lending–The name given to federal statutes and regulations designed to insure that prospective borrowers and purchasers on credit receive credit cost information before entering into a transaction.

Underwriting–Insuring something against loss; guaranteeing financially.

Unit in Place (Cost Method)–Cost of erecting a building by estimating the cost of each component part.

Usury–Collecting interest on a loan greater than permitted by law.

Valid–Legally sufficient.

V.A. Loan–A loan insured or guaranteed by the Veterans Administration made to veterans for housing or business.

Value–The relationship between a thing desired and a potential purchaser. It is the ratio of exchange of one commodity for another.

Variable Rate Mortgage (VRM)–A mortgage loan that provides for adjustments of interest rate as market interest rates change. Also called adjustable, fluctuating, or floating rate mortgage. All Federal savings and loans are authorized to issue VRMs.

Vendee–A purchaser or buyer.

Vendor's Lien–A lien put on property by a seller.

Vested–Owned or secured by someone.

Warranty Deed–A deed used to convey real property that contains warranties of title and quiet possession, and the grantor thus agrees to defend the premises against lawful claims of a third person.

Waste–The destruction, or material alteration of, or injury to premises by a tenant.

Wraparound–A mortgage that encompasses or wraps around other mortgages.

Yield–Profit stated in terms of percentage invested; the return on an investment. In real estate, yield is the *effective* amount of annual income being accrued on investments. As such, it is the *ratio* of annual (net) income from an investment to the cost or market value of the property.

Zoning–The rules of a city or county specifying the uses to which land may be put.

Index